THE VOW

Descending to five hundred feet in a "Huey," with eight Green Berets on board, I slowly flew over the Montagnard village where we saw everything had been burned down. In the central open area, there was a large circle of dead Ruff Puff soldiers and village men. Inside the circle was a pile of bloody, naked, obviously dead women who had been raped, disemboweled, and grotesquely mutilated. Several of the women were pregnant, and their babies had been cut out of their bellies. A group of twenty to thirty small children was tied together and had been burned alive with gasoline.

Apparently, the village men were forced to watch as their wives, children and families were abused, butchered, and set aflame by the Viet Cong and NVA soldiers. I was horrified and sickened by what I saw and can only describe the scene as Satan's playground: *straight out of hell!*

Unleashing the raging anger I felt, every part of my being screamed this solemn vow. ***"I will seek revenge for these atrocities!"*** Over the next sixteen months, with grim determination and merciless efficiency, I fulfilled my vow — again and again and again!

VIET NAM SAGA

KHE SANH

SAGA

ACKNOWLEDGMENTS:
Design Services: Melinda Martin - Martin Publishing Services.
PUBLISHING INFORMATION:
ICB - Scripture taken from the International Children's Bible®. Copyright © 1986, 1988, 1999 by Thomas Nelson All rights reserved.
NLT - New Living Translation, copyright © 1996, 2004, 2015 by Tyndale House Foundation. Carol Stream, Illinois 60188.
NKJV - Scripture taken from the New King James Version®. Copyright © 1982 by Thomas Nelson. All rights reserved.
NIV - Scripture quotations marked (NIV) are taken from the Holy Bible, New International Version®, NIV®. Copyright © 1973, 1978, 1984, 2011 by Biblica, Inc.™ Used by permission of Zondervan. All rights reserved worldwide. The "NIV" and "New International Version" are trademarks registered in the United States Patent and Trademark Office by Biblica, Inc.™

ISBN: 978-0-9989222-3-2 (paperback), 978-0-9989222-4-9 (epub),
978-0-9989222-5-6 (hardback)

PUBLISHED BY: Southwestern Legacy Press
                  8901 Tehama Ridge Parkway
                  Suite 127-115
                  Fort Worth, TX 76177
                  www.swlegacypress.com

LIBRARY CATALOGING:
Names: Corvin, Stanley E. (Stanley E. Corvin, Jr.)
Vietnam Saga/Stan Corvin, Jr.
325 pages 23cm × 15cm (9in. × 6 in.)
Description: Vietnam Saga is the very personal story of Stan Corvin's often-perilous times in the U.S. Army as a two-tour helicopter pilot in Vietnam. It is a true-life story of a pilot who fought for freedom and often his very life. Vietnams Saga is also a story about the meaning of life. Standing back from his war experience, Stan reflects on his ever-present faith and how it carried him through this challenging period of his life. Originally written as a legacy to Stan Corvin's family-something that will be passed down for many generations-Vietnam Saga is now an opportunity for you to share in the legacy and the personal recollections, memories, thoughts, fears and shed tears of a decorated and dedicated American military pilot. The book also contains numerous photos.
Key Words: Aviation, Helicopters, Combat, Flying, Vietnam War

KHE SANH

VIET NAM SAGA

EXPLOITS OF A
COMBAT HELICOPTER PILOT

STAN CORVIN, JR.

SOUTHWESTERN
LEGACY PRESS

*We have shared the incommunicable experience of war.
In our youth, our hearts were touched with fire.*[1]

– Oliver Wendell Holmes, 1884

DEDICATION

This book is dedicated to my loving wife, Peggy, whose gentle encouragement and sweet spiritual nature helped me through the "dark times" when I wrote about certain traumatic wartime events.

Stan Corvin

CONTENTS

INTRODUCTION

"Not all those that wander are Lost."

J.R.R. Tolkien
Lord of the Rings [2]

I've written this book to share my military flying experiences only with my family and a few select friends and individuals! I have written in essay style with each chapter more or less standing on its own. The story all revolves around the central theme of the perilous times I spent in the U.S. Army as a combat helicopter pilot. The time period covers my first deployment to Vietnam in 1968, my subsequent transfer to Schweinfurt, Germany, in 1970, my voluntary second deployment back to Vietnam in 1971, and finally, my separation from the U.S. Army in 1973.

This has been an intensely personal endeavor for me and one that I never intend to repeat. I have chosen to tell you most of the truth about my military experiences, but not everything. Some events were too horrifying; others were too highly classified. In war, people kill people, and I was a ruthless and merciless killer of North Vietnamese soldiers and combatants. Given the opportunity, they would have instantly done the same to me. Many tried, but all failed.

Regarding what I've not told you, *You can't handle the*

truth! as Jack Nicholson said in the movie *A Few Good Men.* Sorry about that, everyone!

In order to write this book, I had to go back in time forty-nine years and deliberately descend into a hell of death, destruction, and depravity. I knowingly unearthed feelings of rage and revulsion that I had purposefully suppressed and buried long ago. Writing about certain events frequently caused my heart to race (up to 120 bpm), my blood pressure to spike (up to 180/115), and my adrenaline to surge. Thankfully, all were of short term duration. Obviously, my feelings about the Vietnam War, and my role while flying there, are still buried deep within my psyche and probably will never entirely disappear.

While I have always been asymptomatic for Post-Traumatic Stress Disorder (PTSD), I do occasionally exhibit some of its *signs*; i.e., I jump at loud, unexpected noises. The "wop, wop, wop" of a helicopter flying overhead causes my heart to beat faster. In a public place, I try to never to sit with my back to an open door, and always stay aware of my immediate surroundings.

The U.S. Army 5th Special Forces in Vietnam had a saying. *You've never lived until you've almost died; for those that have fought for it, life has a meaning the sheltered will never know.* I whole heartedly agree with them.

I needed many years and numerous life experiences, both good and bad, to see the meaning in my life. The meaning is very clear to me now that I'm seventy two years of age. I am to love the Lord with all my heart and to love my wife and family unconditionally—I absolutely do! And usually I don't sweat the small stuff, because it's all very small stuff.

What you are about to read are my personal recollections, memories, thoughts, fears, and shed tears from that period in my life. Minor parts of this work, mostly personal dialog with individuals, came from my fertile, albeit twisted, imagination. The dialog is not verbatim for any particular conversation, but gives emotional context, insight, and understanding to the specific event being described. I've told some funny stories, although not many, because that was not a funny era in American history.

Some of the names contained within are the actual names of people with whom I served. Many of the names have been changed to protect the guilty; for, in the end, none of us were innocent.

While en route to Vietnam, I wrote several poems. When I arrived at the "Warlords," I began to keep a journal and wrote more poetry, prose, and stream of consciousness meanderings. In three years, living in Vietnam, I wrote almost eleven hundred pages of material in six large spiral-bound notebooks. I envisaged myself a "Warrior Poet."

Writing helped me to stay somewhat sane in what ultimately became a very insane environment. (Although never as insane as the movie *Apocalypse Now* portrayed that war!) I destroyed all of the notebooks in 2006, after I moved to Franklin, Tennessee, ending the final vestige of the Vietnam War for me.

Following is the first poem I wrote while flying on a TWA airline on my initial deployment to Vietnam. Near the end of this book is the last poem I wrote on April 28, 1972—the night before I was shot down and severely wounded trying to save an American fighter pilot who had also been shot down near the DMZ. I've never written again, until now.

EAGLES OF THE REALM

Hurtling through the purple sky,
we approach our waiting war.
Apprehensive, nervous, uneasy, we fear the unknown.
Building our own private hell,
we try not to think of what's behind or ahead.
Each of us with glued-on smile,
presenting a stoic face of manly detachment from fear.
Unknowingly, we die a little more
with each passing mile.
Is that a tear I see in a young soldier's eye?
No, certainly not, for only women and children
are allowed that exquisite luxury.
So, we press on silently,
never realizing that our rapidly beating heart is
as fragile as new-formed ice
and will soon stop forever.

– Stan Corvin,
En route to Vietnam, 1968

I've heard Lt. Col. Oliver North publicly speak several times and have read two of his books about the soldiers and Marines deployed to Iraq and Afghanistan. He says that before they left their bases, they would get together and pray for the success of their mission and the well-being of each other.

In the three years I served as a pilot in Vietnam, I never witnessed anybody pray before or after a mission or at any other time. In the Warlords officers' club at Christmas, 1968, an Army chaplain spoke the only prayer I can recall. Although I was a *born again* Christian (baptized at twelve years old and again at nineteen), I never prayed before or after I flew missions.

Notwithstanding my lack of prayers, my faith was always present with me and evident in my unwavering determination to avenge unspeakable moral injustices and to right heinous wrongs. I deeply believed the ultimate power of my faith was not to conquer evil, which is impossible, but to survive it! And indeed I did!

I sincerely hope you enjoy what I've written and will have a better understanding of the fearless young pilot I was then and the extraordinarily dangerous times in which I lived. I also want to make it very clear that the aggressive, militarily hardcore young man I was no longer exists, but the kinder and gentler old man I have become, does. *Just ask Nana!*

This book is my written legacy to my family and hopefully will be passed down to future generations.

With Love and Affection for *Almost* All of You
– Stan, Papa, Pop, Capt. Corvin (The Avenger!)

Finally, under **NO** circumstances will I approve of anyone arranging a reunion or "get together" with the still living people about whom I have written in this book. Reestablishing old relationships, after nearly fifty years, will tear open the scars of my long-healed wounds, and I'm no longer willing to experience that type of pain!

Listen up everyone!
That's a direct order from Captain Corvin!

NOTICE

I have purposely altered some classified, covert, and clandestine events in which I participated, because I signed a strict non-disclosure agreement, lasting "in perpetuity,", before leaving the U.S. Army. I also have censored the language in this book to protect the delicate sensibilities of some readers.

Stan Corvin, Jr.

CHAPTER 1

ARRIVAL IN COUNTRY

And the Lord said
"Whom shall I send and who will go for us?"
Then I said "Here am I. Send me."

Isaiah 6:8 NKJV

As I got off the Trans World Airline (TWA) Boeing 707 airplane at Cam Ranh Bay, Vietnam, at 10:00 a.m., a blast of hot and humid air hit me in the face. The weather was similar to Houston, Texas, but on major steroids. I wondered as I descended the stairs to the tarmac if I could survive the heat, especially at night. When I departed for Vietnam, from Seattle Tacoma International Airport, twenty-three hours earlier, the weather was cold and rainy. In those days, U.S. Army regulations required all officers traveling to a new permanent change of station (PCS) assignment, to wear their class "A" uniforms, which included a coat and tie. That was what I was wearing when I arrived in Vietnam. I would not wear a dress uniform again until I was transferred out of country eighteen months later.

The month before I had graduated from Army Aviation Helicopter Flight School at Hunter Army Airfield in Savannah, Georgia, as a Warrant Officer. Because I had attended four years of college, I applied for a direct commission before leaving Hunter and was told the application would take some time to be processed and possibly approved (or not). My deployment orders were to report to the 22nd Replacement Center in Cam Rahn Bay, Vietnam. Cam Rahn Bay was a deep water Naval port and Army facility located on the South China Sea from where military personnel were sent to their operational units. I walked into the airport terminal and waited for my B-4 bag and duffel bag full of clothing to be unloaded from the aircraft. The terminal had no air conditioning, so the temperature inside the metal building was in the 110° range. *Man, I'm not going to be able to function, let alone fly, in this heat,* I thought.

Once my bags were unloaded from the plane, I went to the transportation sergeant in the terminal and arranged a ride to the Replacement Center. The sergeant told me that I needed to convert all of my American dollars into military payment certificates (MPC). MPCs were military currency paper money issued to prevent the enemy from obtaining American dollars. They were issued in denominations of 5, 10, 25, and 50 cents. The dollar denominations were in $1s, $5s, $10s, and $20s. I had approximately $800 in cash that I converted into MPCs at the terminal's American Express office.

I ended up with a huge wad of strange looking paper bills that looked like Monopoly money and was about the same size. I still have $30 or $40 worth of MPCs of various denominations in a memorabilia box at my home.

At the Replacement Company area, I was assigned a bunk in the officers' barracks, which thankfully were air-conditioned, and given directions to the officers' club down the street. I changed into khakis and walked to the "O" club. Lots of other guys were there who were new in country like me. The club was air-conditioned, dark, and well-furnished. Many very pretty Vietnamese waitresses were walking around the bar area. All of them wore long white dresses called Ao Dais which were split up both sides with matching pants. They had long black hair, lots of makeup, and looked like Oriental dolls. And yes, for the most part, they all looked alike.

At the bar, I struck up a conversation with a couple of guys who were wearing pilot's wings and learned they had been there for two days waiting to be transported to their new units. They asked me if I would like to go waterskiing with them later that afternoon. "Yes!" I said, and we spent the rest of the morning drinking beer (at $.10 per can). After we had lunch, we went to the barracks, changed into swimsuits, caught a ride to the bayside R&R beach, and signed up to go skiing. We walked to a nearby thatched roof pavilion on the beach and drank more beer until our number was called, which meant we had a boat and driver assigned to pull us skiing. We spent the next two hours waterskiing in the bay, and I had a blast! No one had told me about this perk while in a combat zone, and I was amazed! *Maybe combat flying is not going to be as bad as I thought.* But I was wrong!

After returning to the barracks, we changed into civvies and went to the officers' club for dinner and to watch the entertainment. At 8:00 p.m., a floor show began that had a Filipino "Elvis Presley" impersonator who was really good. He was accompanied by a full band and about six go-go dancers and backup singers dressed in sheer white blouses and pink miniskirts with long white go-go boots. The show lasted for about two hours and was a rousing success.

Late that evening, my new friends and I returned to our quarters and went to bed. I was anxious to get my new orders and hoped they would come quickly. I was ready to get into a helicopter and fly combat missions!

One evening, shortly before my flight school graduation, my Dad called me in Savannah, Georgia, and told me that he had just received orders for Vietnam as an F-4 Phantom squadron commander in Danang. He was a Lieutenant Colonel in the United States Air Force, who had served in World War II and Korea as a fighter pilot. When he called, I had already received my orders for a permanent change of station (PCS) deployment to Vietnam as a helicopter pilot. Dad and I discussed his assignment that included flying F-4 Phantoms into North Vietnam knocking out SA-2 SAM (surface to air missile) sites.

When he first received his new orders, my mother was adamantly opposed to him flying in another war. Before I left the States on my overseas deployment, she and I had a discussion about how difficult it was for her to know that I was going into a combat zone in such a dangerous capacity as a helicopter pilot.

She told me how frightened she had been when my dad was in WWII and Korea and how she cried herself to sleep many nights worrying about him. Now, she told me she was sad and upset to be going through the same thing while I was in Vietnam.

Heart-wrenching as it was to hear her talk about the anguish, fear, and worry she had gone through with my dad, and was now going to go through with me, I knew that going was still something that I wanted and needed to do. (Writing about that conversation with her just now choked me up and brought me to tears after all these years! I loved my mother. She was a kind and gentle soul.)

I told my dad that I wanted to go to Vietnam and that I didn't think he should. He had spent almost thirty years of flying as a fighter pilot and was eligible to retire. Since I already had orders to deploy (and assured him that I wanted to go), he told me that he was going to put in for retirement. I knew that my mother would be relieved he wasn't going overseas to a third war.

As it turned out, the unit to which he was going to be assigned in Danang, (the 366th Tactical Fighter Wing, known as the "Gunslingers" and the 602nd SAR Squadron) would later play a major role in keeping me alive.

CHAPTER 2

ASSIGNED TO 71ST AHC

The morning after we had gone waterskiing, my orders came in assigning me to my new unit. I was to report to the 71st assault helicopter company, "The Rattlers," headquartered at Chu Lai in I Corp. Vietnam was divided into four military regions called Corps. I Corp was located in the north from the demilitarized zone (DMZ) with North Vietnam down approximately one hundred fifty miles to a city on the South China Sea called Quang Ngai. The other three Corps were spread out all the way to the southern border of Vietnam in the Mekong River delta.

That afternoon I went to the Cam Rahn Bay airfield and caught a ride north on an Air Force C-130 to Danang. From there, I hitched a ride south in a UH–1D (Huey) to Ky Ha heliport in Chu Lai, which was to be my home base for the next eighteen months. I reported to my company commander at headquarters (HQ) that evening when I arrived. We talked for a while and then he turned me over to an orderly who assigned me to an empty bed in a hooch with five other pilots. The orderly took me to the hooch, where I dropped off my bags, and then took me to the officers' club.

There I met several pilots who were playing cards and drinking. The officers club served as a club and mess hall, and basically was the center of all activity when the pilots were not flying or sleeping.

I met the operations officer who told me that I would be assigned as a "peter pilot" on a "slick" in a couple of days. That meant that I would be flying in the right seat, with a senior aircraft commander sitting in the left seat, on a UH-1D Huey until I had a total of 200-300 hours flying time. At that time, I would be considered for an aircraft commander position (if I hadn't screwed up or died).

The missions I flew primarily were for the delivery of personnel, food, ammunition, and mail for troops living on fire support bases located in the mountains west of Chu Lai. They were near the Ho Chi Minh Trail and the border with Laos. Three of the fire support bases (Ba Tho, Mihn Long and Gia Vuc) had a contingent of 5th Special Forces, *Green Berets* living there. They were in charge of the indigenous populations of Montagnard and Mung personnel who also lived in the compounds and fought alongside US forces against the North Vietnamese Army (NVA) and Vietcong (VC).

All of the areas of operations (AOs) west of the three Special Forces bases were designated as "free-fire zones." That meant that anyone, or anything, that "walked, crawled, or breathed" in those AOs was to be killed without seeking any higher command authority or permission.

In advanced helicopter flight school in Savannah, we usually flew no more than one to one and a half hours per day while we were in training. A couple of days after arriving at my new unit, the Rattlers, I was assigned a mission to fly what was called "ass and trash" to the fire support bases. I'd met the aircraft commander (AC) with whom I was to fly at the officers' club the night before. He was a twenty-one-year-old chief warrant officer from Michigan who had been in country for ten months.

At 0600 hours the next morning, after I'd had a long and sleepless night, we met at the aircraft and pre-flighted the helicopter. The crew chief and door gunner were already there with canteens full of water and a case of "C" rations. I had gotten up earlier that morning at 0400 hours and had gone to the supply room where I was issued an SPH-4 ballistic flight helmet, a .45-ACP caliber pistol, an M-16 rifle, ammo for both, and a "chicken plate."

The "chicken plates" were bulletproof vests made out of a large ceramic plate that were worn by the pilots and crew. The plate was in a cloth vest-like structure that had Velcro tabs and was worn all the time that you were flying. The vest weighed approximately thirty pounds and was very hot while strapped on, but it would stop a bullet up to 7.62mm. However, the chicken plate would not stop a .51-caliber machine-gun bullet that the NVA and VC frequently used to fire at high-flying helicopters.

I was excited to get to fly finally, and a little anxious to find out if I had what it took to be a combat helicopter pilot. I thought I did but wasn't sure. We took off about 0630 hours flying to a loading point to pick up our payload that would be distributed to various fire support bases.

We started making the rounds distributing the payload and then returning to the loading point to pick up another one. Every three hours, we refueled the helicopter without shutting the engine down which was called a "hot refueling." Everything outside the perimeter of our base, and all the fire support bases, was considered enemy territory. As a result, our only opportunity to go to the bathroom was when we came back to the staging area to pick up another payload.

I had been told not to eat much before flying because the two daily malaria medications we had to take at breakfast (Dapsone and Cloraquin Prima Quin) caused serious stomach cramps and diarrhea if we had much food in our stomachs.

We continued to pick up payloads and deliver them to fire support bases all day and into the night. Finally, we finished our last delivery around 2330 hours which meant that I'd flown continuously for seventeen hours on my first day!

The only meal and bathroom breaks that we took were when we refueled the aircraft. After we finally shut down the aircraft on the flight line, the aircraft commander (AC) and I went to the operations building to see if we were going to fly the next day.

Fortunately, we were not scheduled to fly for two days. I carried my gear back to my hooch that was only about a hundred yards away from the flight line and collapsed on the bed fully-clothed. I didn't wake up until the next morning about 0800 hours when the hooch maid came in to pick up all of our dirty jungle fatigues to wash.

That's when I met Hoa, the young Vietnamese girl who cleaned our hooch and washed our clothes each day. The five other pilots who were my hooch mates and I each pitched in $25 for her monthly pay of $150. She wore black pajamas and a straw coolie hat every day. She didn't look quite like the oriental-doll waitresses that were at the Cam Rahn Bay officers' club, but she was friendly and spoke good English.

When I got out of bed, my butt still hurt from sitting so many hours in the helicopter the day before. I thought that if I had to fly seventeen hours on every mission, I wasn't sure I could make it as a pilot. Later that day, I learned that usually the pilots only flew six to seven hours per day and that I had been tested to see how I reacted to extended, exhaustive, and harsh flying.

A few days later, after I'd flown a couple of normal daily missions, my commanding officer (CO) told me to come to the officers' club that evening dressed in a T-shirt, flip-flops, and Army OD (olive drab) green skivvies. He joked that I had passed the test and was to be officially welcomed/initiated into the Rattler brotherhood of pilots.

When I arrived at the club, there were two other new pilots waiting to be initiated as well. We were told to chug four beers, one after the other; then we were drenched from head to toe in liquid dish soap and water. After lying down on our stomachs, four pilots grabbed our arms and legs and swung us back and forth and let go, so that we slid down the length of the club (about forty feet) into the stacked empty beer can "bowling pins." I had never been initiated into anything, so it was a fun experience that made me feel like I was part of the group. I definitely was a "happy camper." Two days later, I began to fly typical "ass and trash" missions every day.

One of the first missions that I flew *(which was not typical)* included picking up the bodies of nine American soldiers that had been killed by the NVA and VC in ground combat. Once the fighting and shooting ceased, we quickly flew into an improvised landing zone (LZ) and the poncho-wrapped bodies were loaded into the cargo bay of the helicopter. They were badly mangled, decomposing, and had been lying on the ground in the heat for two days. The smell was horrific!

Soon the helicopter bay floor was covered in congealed blood, slime, maggots, and body fluids. The stench made everybody on board gag and throw up. When we took off, the rotor wash from the blades created huge wind vortices that blew all the disgusting mess on me, the other pilot, and crew members as well as coating the inside of the helicopter.

We flew the bodies back to Chu Lai and took them to their appropriate units for offloading. After going back to our flight line, we shut the aircraft down, got out, stripped naked, and burned our filthy clothes and boots in a nearby 55-gallon oil drum. Then we walked to the showers and vigorously scrubbed with soap to try and get the smell off our skin. *(It didn't entirely go away for a couple of days.)*

The aircraft wasn't used again until it had been completely hosed down, disinfected, and dried out for about a week. That definitely was not something I cared to do; however, someone had to do it, and those assigned that mission gutted up and pressed on.

CHAPTER 3

HUNTER/KILLER TEAMS

Frequently, as I was flying to the Special Forces compounds, I saw a group of six helicopters flying west into the free-fire zones. Leading the group was a small four-place OH–6 Hughes turbine-powered helicopter known as a "Loach" due to the acronym of LOH (light observation helicopter). The Loach flew slowly at very low altitudes, normally no more than two feet above the ground or trees, looking for the enemy. Accompanying the Loach were two AH1-G Cobra gunships flying slightly behind and above, about fifteen hundred feet over the Loach. Above and behind the Cobras, at about a thousand feet, were three UH-1D's Huey's, each containing seven to nine fully-equipped infantry soldiers.

On several occasions as I was flying ass and trash missions, I saw this grouping with the Loach flying slowly along the ground. One evening while playing cards with some pilots at the officers' club, I asked, "What are those guys doing?" They explained the group was called a Hunter/Killer team, and the Loach was looking for NVA soldiers, VC insurgents, machine-gun emplacements, and hidden enemy camps on the ground.

When the Loach found something, the pilot would either engage the enemy with his minigun or drop smoke grenades for the Cobras to make gun runs on the target with their rockets. The guys explained that some of the rockets contained twenty-pound high explosives warheads. Other rockets contained *flechettes* that were metallic darts approximately three-inches-long with little fins on the back. The flechettes were designed to kill personnel on the ground, and each rocket contained twenty-five hundred of them. All the pilots agreed Loach-flying was *the most dangerous type of flying in Vietnam.* I remember sitting at the table and deciding that I definitely wanted to transfer to that unit and fly Loaches.

When I first arrived at the Rattlers, I was surprised to find a friend of mine with whom I had gone to flight school. His name was Al Britt. He and his wife were from Long Beach, California, and Al had been drafted into the U.S. Army out of college as I had been. While in basic training, he had applied for helicopter flight school as I had also done. He didn't live in the same hooch at the Rattlers officers' compound as I did, but he was only a short distance away with his pilot roommates. About a month later, he and I were sent to Saigon in a helicopter to pick up much-needed mechanical parts for the maintenance platoon.

Our CO said that we could stay two days but had to return on the third day. As we were flying down to Saigon, Al told me that his mother-in-law and father-in-law lived in Saigon and had been there for nearly three years. His father-in-law was Emery J. Porter, the director of the U.S. Agency for International Development (USAID).

When we landed at Tan Son Nhut International Airport in Saigon, we contacted the maintenance division that had the critical parts we needed and arranged to have them loaded the next day. Securing the aircraft, we caught a taxi to Tu Do Street to find a hotel. We stayed at the Continental Hotel—an old French hotel built in the late 1890s, when Saigon was called the

"Paris of the East." Once in our rooms, Al called his in-laws, and they invited us over for dinner that evening. We had no civvies or khaki uniforms with us, so we went in our rather aromatic gray flight suits. We spent the evening with the Porters then took a taxi back to the hotel.

Before we left their apartment, Mr. Porter invited us to a cocktail luncheon the next morning at 11:00 a.m. Al and I both tried to decline the invitation because the only clothes we had to wear were our smelly flight suits. Mrs. Porter said that if we came early the next morning, she would have the maids wash them. They both were insistent, so we agreed.

The next morning we went to their apartment, which took up the entire top floor of a ten-story building near the U.S. Embassy in Saigon. It was beautifully appointed with many exotic furnishings they had acquired from living all around the world for many years. We ate breakfast in our T-shirts and Army OD green skivvies (that were clean) while our flight suits were being washed.

At 1100 hours people, all dressed up, started arriving for the brunch. The women wore brightly colored sundresses with large hats, and the men wore white sports coats with bow ties and black slacks. The party looked like a scene straight out of the 1940s Humphrey Bogart and Ingrid Bergman movie, *Casablanca*. Both Al and I felt really out of place and embarrassed by our non-formal clothing. The Porters insisted that it was okay and proceeded to introduce us to everyone. They explained that we had just come in the day before and had to leave the next morning to fly back to our base at Chu Lai.

Everyone we met was extremely cordial and supportive of us being in the military. Mr. Porter said he wanted to introduce us to a friend of his. He then took Al and me over to a tall, distinguished-looking, gray-haired gentleman who looked vaguely familiar.

At first I thought he was a Hollywood actor, then it dawned on me that he was General William C. Westmoreland, the commander of all forces in Vietnam. He was very friendly and somewhat amused at our discomfort in meeting him wearing flight suits at a semi-formal party. He showed a genuine interest in how we came to be in Saigon and told us that he too had gone through helicopter flight training a few years earlier and loved to fly. *(His training was done in Vietnam while he was a three-star lieutenant general and done one on one with a flight instructor and a ground school teacher.)* After talking with us for a while, he wished us well and then left the party.

He was a great officer, a real gentleman, and a true American patriot. Years later, in 1986, I met him again in Washington, D.C., when I attended the dedication of the three-man statues located near the Vietnam Veterans Wall. He remembered meeting Al and me at the Porters luncheon in Saigon.

We talked for a few minutes and then he left with President Reagan's entourage. Everywhere he went that day, he was approached by Vietnam vets who would respectfully come up to him to shake his hand. He was a great American!

Al and I took off from Ton Son Nhut air base and flew back to Chu Lai and began once more to fly our normal missions. A few days after returning, Al's aircraft was struck by machine-gun fire and a rocket-propelled grenade (RPG) causing it to crash after taking off from a fire support base.

During the crash, Al was struck in the face by the twenty-pound electric motor that operated the windshield wipers. The motor broke his nose and cheekbone and blackened both eyes, but he survived the crash. He and the other crew members were medevac'd back to our base Mobile Army Surgical Hospital (MASH) on China Beach where he was treated and then sent back to the Rattler compound the next day.

A few days later, Al went to see our commanding officer and informed him that he refused to fly helicopters anymore. The CO told him to think about it for a few days and that they would talk later. Al told him he didn't need to think anymore, that he wanted to turn in his flight wings immediately, and he would never get in another helicopter as a pilot again. The CO reluctantly accepted Al's resignation as a pilot and had the paperwork processed that day to remove him from flight status and terminate his flight pay. All pilots that fly do so voluntarily and cannot be required to fly against their wishes.

Later that afternoon, the operations officer (a captain and a pilot) came to Al's hooch and ordered him to pack up all of his things and move into the back storeroom of the supply building. He was instructed not to utilize the officers' club except for meals and not to have anything to do with the pilots in the unit. I helped him move his things into the store room. It was an emotional and gut-wrenching situation for him and me too because we were close friends.

After that day, I rarely saw him. He was stripped of his flight wings and was made the supply officer. He stayed in country for the remainder of his ten-month tour and then returned to the U.S. Later I learned that Al had resigned from the Army and moved back to California where he finished school and became a college professor.

CHAPTER 4

TRANSFER TO THE WARLORDS

I decided that I definitely wanted to transfer to "B" Company, 123rd Aviation Battalion, American Division ("Warlords"), and fly Loaches. So at the first opportunity, on a day off from flying for the Rattlers, I went to see the "B" Company commanding officer, Major Maher. He was very friendly, but couldn't understand why I was interested in flying as a Loach pilot when I had a relatively safe job flying slicks.

I explained to him that I wanted to take a more active role in fighting the NVA and VC. He told me that two of his Loach pilots had been shot down and killed within the last nine months, and he only had one pilot left who was qualified to continuously fly the Hunter/Killer missions. He admitted that he was shorthanded and could use the help. I asked him to give me a chance and promised not to let him down. He was quiet for a few minutes. "Okay, I'll call your CO at the Rattlers tomorrow and ask that you be transferred to my command," he said.

He told me to go back to my unit and immediately talk to my commander and explain that I wanted to transfer. After thanking him, and saluting smartly, I went back to my unit headquarters and talked to my CO. He was surprised that I wanted to fly

Loaches and tried to convince me how dangerous and difficult the missions were.

But I had made up my mind and told him so and asked him to approve my transfer to the Warlords. He finally agreed and said that he would talk to Major Maher the next day. He also said that the transfer paperwork would take a couple of days to put together. I left his office elated at the prospect of moving to a helicopter unit actively involved in hunting and killing the enemy.

I continued to fly ass and trash missions with the Rattlers for about a week until my orders came in transferring me to the Warlords. On the next to the last mission that I flew for the Rattlers, the AC and I had just delivered several new guys, the mail, and miscellaneous items to a base called Mihn Long, when a Special Forces Major came out to the helipad and asked us to shut the aircraft down and come to the Tactical Operations Center (TOC) for an urgent briefing.

We went into the TOC where we were told that a village about eight miles to the west had been attacked the previous night, and they'd had no further communications with it. The village contained about forty Vietnamese Regional Forces/ Provisional Forces called "Ruff Puffs" and approximately two hundred villagers made up of civilian men, women, and children.

The major asked us to take eight Special Forces Green Berets out to the village to see what happened. We agreed and then loaded everybody on board. Flying to the village took only a few minutes, but as we got closer we could see smoke rising up from the center. We descended and slowly flew over the village where we saw that everything had been burned down.

In the central open area, there was a large circle of dead Ruff Puff soldiers and village men. Inside the circle was a pile of naked, obviously dead women who had been raped, disemboweled, and mutilated. Several of the women had been pregnant, and their babies had been cut out of their bellies. There also was a group of approximately twenty to thirty small children who had been tied together and burned alive with gasoline. All the animals and dogs had been killed by the NVA and Vietcong. It was apparent the village men had been made to watch as their wives and children were abused, butchered, and set aflame.

After circling for a few minutes at about five hundred feet (to see if we would draw ground fire), I landed the aircraft outside the village perimeter and the Special Forces operators departed the aircraft and went inside the compound with weapons at the ready.

For safety purposes, we took off and climbed to about fifteen hundred feet and circled overhead until we were radioed to pick up the guys on the ground about an hour later. When they climbed aboard, we could tell most of the hardened Special Forces operators had tear streaks down their cheeks and were in a state of shock at what had occurred in the village. They had known the people there personally. We took them back to their base at Minh Long and dropped them off. I was horrified and sickened by what I had witnessed in the village and can only describe the scene as Satan's playground: *straight out of hell!*

I thought of the poem by Aldus Huxley in his book *Apes and Essence*:

> *The leeches kiss; the squids embrace,*
> *the prurient apes defiling touch:*
> *Do you like the human race?*
> *No, not much!* [3]

That day, and forever more, I did not like the Communist

"race" at all and decided I would seek revenge for all the people they had brutally tortured, raped, and murdered.

The next day we were told the NVA and Vietcong had made an example of the village, and the Ruff Puffs living there, because of their support of the Americans and South Vietnamese forces. I knew then that I'd made the right decision to become a Loach pilot and fly for the Warlords.

That incident immediately hardened my heart against the enemy and created an inner rage to kill as many NVA and Vietcong soldiers as I possibly could. Later, I would quietly stand by the LOH and tap into that rage before every flight to prepare myself for what I was about to encounter that day — a perfect killing strategy!

CHAPTER 5

FLYING WITH THE WARLORDS

When I arrived at "B" Company 123 Aviation BN, I was assigned my call sign, Warlord 22, also known as *Skeeter*, to be used when flying missions. The company first sergeant took me to the supply building where I drew my flight gear, 45-ACP pistol, and CAR-16 rifle. He then took me to the officers' area, and I moved my things into a quonset hut. Five other Warlord pilots were living there and over time I became friends with them. Our hooch, as our quarters were called, was on a thirty-foot embankment overlooking the beach, which was on the South China Sea. The view was stunning, and the beach (China Beach) was a great place to go on days off.

Before I began flying low-level reconnaissance missions in the Loach, I first had to transition into the aircraft (learn how to fly it). Then I had to fly with the other experienced Loach pilot until I was proficient at low-level recon tactics. I also had to learn how to operate, dismantle, assemble, and fire the M-60 belt-fed machine gun—a 7.62mm (.308-caliber) that was very powerful (like a deer rifle).

While learning the mission and flying tactics, I sat in the front left seat and held the M-60 in my lap pointed out the open left door of the aircraft. *(I've got a photograph showing me sitting in the aircraft with the gun.)* One of the purposes of the machine guns was to suppress enemy fire and to make them duck for cover. The M-60's all had twenty-four-inch barrels with flash suppressors on the end so the enemy could not see a muzzle flash when it was fired. I got permission to have the company armorer cut the barrel down shorter to where it was even with the gas cylinder plug. This way, when the gun was fired, the flash was probably two feet in diameter and six feet in length and was very loud. This definitely got the attention of the enemy on the ground when it was fired at them and stopped any immediate return fire until the aircraft could safely exit the area.

In order for me to transition into the Loach, an instructor pilot and I spent three days flying in a safe area of the beach at extremely low levels (usually one to two feet above the ground). We flew at speeds ranging from a hover to 100 mph; twisting and turning on points ten to twenty feet in front of the aircraft.

I also learned how to auto rotate the aircraft in the event the engine quit. This maneuver was performed at the Chu Lai base air strip and consisted of approaching the end of the runway at five hundred feet and then cutting the power off to glide down and land to a full stop on the pavement.

When power was cut, the immediate descent was similar to riding steep roller coaster downhill and was actually a lot of fun. We practiced this dozens of times because the instructor told me that I would eventually have to perform it for real someday on a mission. He was absolutely correct!

After my initial Loach training, I spent the next three weeks riding in the left seat holding and firing the M-60 with Warrant Officer Drew Tully piloting the aircraft. As we flew the recon missions, I became very proficient at spotting any anomaly on the ground. Usually, that meant finding gun emplacements, camouflaged enemy encampments or spider holes from which a combatant could pop up, fire his AK-47, and then drop down to safety. Each mission would start before dawn with a briefing at our TOC, usually telling us which free-fire zone we would be flying in that day. We then would go to our assigned aircraft and make sure each was loaded with everything needed for the day's flying.

The Loach crew chief sat on the floor behind the pilot and had an M-60 belt-fed machine gun he fired from the right side of the aircraft if needed. Since I was sitting in the front left seat, the minigun that was usually mounted on the left side of the aircraft had to be removed to compensate for my weight. The Loach took off first, immediately followed by two Cobra gunships, then three UH-1D's, each with eight infantry soldiers called *grunts* who were permanently assigned to the Warlords. The grunts platoon name was "the Animals." One of my roommates was the Animal platoon leader. His call sign was "Animal 6," and he was not a pilot, but rather an army infantry officer who loved being on the ground leading his soldiers.

Altogether, the hunter/killer team consisted of six helicopters, eleven pilots, seven crew chiefs/door gunners and twenty-five grunts for a total of forty-nine people. After takeoff, *Skeeter* would lead all of the aircraft south along the coast line and then inward to a fire base staging area called Quang Ngai or Duc Pho.

From these staging areas, we flew what were called visual reconnaissances (VRs) within the various free-fire zones in which we operated. We returned every three hours to refuel the aircraft and rearm the weapons systems. The staging area was also where we could eat our lunch (if things were slow) consisting of "C" rations and water.

The Warlords hunter/killer team's sole mission was to seek out and destroy the enemy within the Americal Division's area of operation. Our unit was famous for its effectiveness and aggression. The military newspaper, *Stars & Stripes,* and *Time Magazine* had nicknamed us "The Body Snatchers" because on several missions we were able to capture enemy soldiers alive and bring them back for interrogation by military intelligence officers and the CIA.

After the daily missions were finished in the evening, and all the aircraft had been refueled, I would lead the team a few miles east out over the ocean to fly home. En route to "feet wet," a military term used indicate flying over water, we would frequently fly over what appeared to be a mostly deserted Vietnamese village called My Lai.

My Lai was where the Cobras would fire all their rockets so that they did not land at our home heliport (Ky Ha) with any two and three-quarter-inch folding-fin aerial rockets (FFAR) ordinance in the launch tubes.

My Lai would later become infamous in military history because of the shooting of its civilian inhabitants by American soldiers. The massacre was discovered and reported by a Warlord pilot named Warrant Officer Buck Thompson. The incident had occurred a few months before I arrived in Vietnam.

Ironically, the Warlord teams frequently used the village and surrounding area as a target range before it became a restricted zone while General Peers investigated the massacre.

CHAPTER 6

SKEETER FLYING RECONS

"Yea, though I flew through the valley of the shadow of death, I feared no evil, for I was the evilest one in the valley."

Warlord 22

After I flew in the left seat for about three weeks, I was cleared to pilot the Loach. The armorer installed the minigun on the left side of the aircraft and an ammo container with five thousand rounds of 7.62mm (.308-caliber) ammunition in the back with the crew chief. With a warning from Major Maher to me to be careful, I spent the next three days flying the aircraft along a deserted beach near the base and practiced firing the minigun. I fired fifteen to twenty of the ammo containers over a three-day period and became extremely proficient at hitting a target with the first shots.

On several occasions, while flying at the beach, I found very large sharks slowly cruising along the top of the water. The minigun made mincemeat out of them, whenever I fired a two-second burst at them. That was a heck of a way to go shark fishing, but I have to say it was lots of fun.

The minigun is an awesome weapon. It is a Gatling gun similar to that used in the Civil War, but is powered by a GE electric motor instead of a hand-turned crank. On July 25, 1893, Richard Gatling received a patent for an electric-motor version of the hand-cranked Gatling gun that had a three thousand-rounds-per-minute rate of fire! The U.S. Army rejected the design in favor of the gas-operated single-barrel machine gun firing six hundred rounds per minute.

Designated the M134, the minigun is a six-barreled machine gun that is rotated by an electric motor. During each one-sixth rotation of the barrels, three functions are performed; i.e., chambering a live round, extracting the fired brass, moving a live round from the belt feed, and then chambering a live round again. As each of the six barrels is at a different point in the cycle, this sequencing allows the gun to have a very high cyclic rate of fire from between four thousand and six thousand rounds of ammunition fired per minute.

Our Warlord miniguns were calibrated to fire five thousand rounds per minute which was eighty-three rounds per second. The attached ammunition container had five thousand rounds that were belt-fed into the gun. That meant that I could fire continuously for one minute before the ammo box had to be replaced. Each ammo box weighed approximately two hundred-fifty pounds and could only be replaced back at Quang Ngai or Duc Pho, our staging areas. The gun's trigger was mounted on the stick (the cyclic) and had a three-second burst interrupter to prevent the meltdown of the firing barrel. At eighty-three rounds per second, a three-second burst was approximately two hundred fifty rounds on the target (usually NVA or VC soldiers).

I had to be careful with my ammunition conservation on each mission. All 7.62mm caliber machine gun ammo, which the minigun fired, had a tracer bullet inserted every fifth round, so each eighty-three-rounds-per-second fired, contained seventeen tracer bullets. As a result, when I pulled the trigger, I saw a bright solid red line coming from the end of the minigun to the target.

The red line allowed me basically to use the minigun like a water hose and point it at whatever I wanted to shoot.

When I sighted in the gun at practice, I had the crew chief who was flying with me mark a heavy red X on the plexiglass at the point where the gun initially fired in the neutral position. The heavy red X was my reference point, at which I initially looked, when I was shooting the gun.

The sustained recoil of the gun was so powerful that when I pulled the trigger to fire, I had to compensate for the torque by pushing hard right pedal to keep the five-thousand-pound Loach from suddenly and violently turning to the left.

For those of you who have seen Jesse Ventura in the movie, *Predator*, fire a minigun from his hip, I'm here to tell you that is absolutely impossible and only Hollywood fantasy!

Although my flight helmet had noise-attenuating headsets, I had to wear rubber earplugs to keep from losing my hearing when I was firing the gun. The gun would roar like a jet engine when I fired it and did not sound at all like a machine gun going tat-tat-tat-tat. The end of the minigun barrel was mounted approximately five feet slightly down and to the left of me, so whenever I pulled the trigger, the muzzle blast felt like somebody was slapping me rapidly on the left side of my face. It took a while to get used to that, but I did. It's amazing how we can adapt to a situation when we really have to. When I resigned my Army commission in 1974, an exit physical exam revealed a fifty percent hearing loss in my left ear, which I still have to this day.

CHAPTER 7

MY FIRST KILLS

My first solo visual recon began at dawn when I lifted the Loach to a hover and took off from Key Ha helipad followed by two Cobra gunships and three Huey's loaded with the Animals. Although I was in front leading the others, I was not *Lead*. That responsibility (and call sign) was given to the senior aircraft commander flying in the first Cobra. He was in charge of the mission and coordinated everything as we flew to our assigned free-fire zone. The second Cobra call sign was "Two." The first "Huey" call sign was "Slick One" and the remaining Huey's were "Slick Two" and "Slick Three."

Once in our area of operation (AO), I descended from fifteen hundred feet in what can only be described as a controlled freefall. By tilting the rotors on my Loach in a seventy degree bank, virtually all of the lift provided by the blades slipped away and the aircraft descended in a tight spiraling turn at a rate of about six thousand feet per minute. It only took about fifteen seconds to reach the ground, where I leveled off and began to fly slowly looking for the enemy. The purpose of the rapid descent was to stay out of the effective range of small arms fire.

Once at ground level, I armed the minigun and flew a pattern of S-turns, usually at 50-60mph, looking for any sign of enemy activity or terrain anomalies such as .50-caliber doughnut holes, trenches, or camouflaged structures or soldiers.

Within a few minutes of flying at extreme low level (one to two feet), I crested a large hill, chopped power, and rapidly and quietly descended down the other side. Near the bottom was a long sloping grassy area in which three NVA soldiers, carrying backpacks, were crouched down with AK-47s pointing at me. I immediately turned and headed straight for them. To this day, I still remember thinking, *If this is murder by biblical definition, then I may be condemning my soul to hell for eternity, and I am screwed!* As I closed upon them, they began shooting at me, and I fired a two-second burst from my minigun instantly killing all three. So much for worrying about my soul; self-preservation had kicked in big time!

I slowly circled above their bodies, thinking about all the villagers that had been massacred, and knew that only Satan's evil demons could possibly do something like that. Suddenly I felt elated and proud for killing the three soldiers!

The four Cobra pilots and the six Huey pilots, who had been watching me from their safe altitudes above, all got on the VHF radio at the same time and were whooping and hollering about my "kills" on my first solo mission. They gave me lots of "at-a-boys" and "way-to-go's." (*There were also lots of other things they said to me that I will not mention here.*) The moment was one of self-pride and somewhat mixed feelings for me.

Fortunately for my survival, that was the only time I had second thoughts about pulling the trigger and killing anybody. I'd gotten my wish to become a member of an aggressive hunter/ killer team and had proven that I had "the right stuff" to fly in combat as a "Skeeter" pilot.

Later that evening, after we had returned to our Key Ha base,

Major Maher congratulated me at the officers' club and had me buy everyone a beer—a tradition for FNG's. (Definition: "Fine New Guy" or something close to that.) There were thirty or forty people in the club at that time, so the cost to me was a whopping $3 or $4.

CHAPTER 8

ACE OF SPADES

S everal pilots, who had been in Vietnam for a long time, said the NVA and VC were terrified of the Ace of Spades in a deck of cards. I decided to contact the Bicycle Playing Card Company and see if they would ship me several decks of only aces of spades. At the time, I was unaware their company had already been sending decks of cards to American infantry soldiers in the Mekong Delta.

I wrote a letter to the president of the company and asked him to send me as many decks as he could. About a month later, I received two large boxes from his company. Each box contained one hundred decks of cards that were all Aces of Spades. The decks were housed in plain white paper cases, inscribed "Bicycle© Secret Weapon". The cards were perfect for psychological warfare! The NVA and VC were very superstitious and highly frightened by this Ace.

The French previously had occupied Vietnam and in their fortune-telling with cards, the Ace of Spades predicted death and suffering. The enemy even regarded the Lady Liberty statue on the ace playing card as a goddess of death. I started carrying ten decks of aces with me whenever I flew.

The crew chief, who sat behind me on the floor of the Loach, had a belt-fed M-60 that he fired out the right side of the aircraft.

Whenever we killed NVA or VC soldiers, he would scatter a portion of a box of aces of spades over the bodies as I slowly flew low level over them. I did my part to totally mess with the enemy's mind. I don't know if it worked, but I like to think that I scared the holy crap out of some of them. In the course of flying Loaches for sixteen months, I used up all two hundred decks!

CHAPTER 9

CAPTURING SIX NVA NURSES

I mentioned earlier the Warlords' nickname in the media had been "The Body Snatchers." One morning when the team arrived on station, we had the opportunity to reinforce that name once more. On most missions, when we arrived at our free-fire zone destination, I would make my descent from fifteen hundred feet in a fast right-hand spiraling circle down to low level. Depending upon the terrain, sometimes I was able to cut the power back to idle on the helicopter and glide down into a valley or open area. My descent was virtually silent because of that tactic. That was a big advantage when we were in an area in which we suspected (through intelligence briefings) we could catch NVA or VC soldiers by surprise. In those situations, the Cobras and the Huey's would stay behind me about a mile to keep from alerting the people on the ground that I was coming with their rotor noise.

This particular morning, I cut the power and began to glide down a mountainside to a valley with open grassy fields at the bottom. As I neared the fields, I saw movement in the middle and flew slowly in that direction. While circling, with my minigun armed, the helicopter rotor wash pressed the tall elephant grass down flat revealing two people wearing backpacks lying down. I immediately rolled to the right and saw four more people on the ground. I elevated my minigun above their heads and fired a one second burst. Instantly, six NVA female nurses jumped up and raised their hands in surrender. They were dressed in dark green standard issue NVA uniforms with boonie hats. I called Lead and told him what I had just found. I backed off about twenty yards (still pointing the minigun directly at them) and told him I would keep them there until the Huey's could land with the Animals and capture them. Within three minutes, the helicopters landed and "snatched" the six NVA nurses. The Hueys then took off, climbed to three thousand feet, and circled while I continued to search the area.

Obviously, from their presence, there must be a large hospital complex either underground or camouflaged in the nearby jungle. Otherwise, the nurses would not have been there. I spent the rest of the mission looking for the site to no avail. Finally, we left the area and returned to Duc Pho to refuel and rearm. The three Hueys landed at the MACV (Military Assistance Command Vietnam) helipad and turned the nurses over to waiting military intelligence officers and CIA operatives.

We found out later the nurses were part of a contingent of NVA medical personnel who staffed a five hundred bed underground hospital, located approximately one-half mile from where I captured them.

After refueling, we returned to the area, and I spent the rest of the day trying to find evidence of a hospital. I was not shot at, nor did I see anything at all. Knowing we'd learned there was an underground hospital nearby, I'm pretty sure the NVA didn't want us to call in a B-52 airstrike in the vicinity, so they never made any attempt to engage me. A bomb strike would've collapsed the underground facility and killed everyone inside it. *(Too bad I didn't find it!)*

CHAPTER 10

DESCENDING WITHOUT POWER

I used that tactic with great success on many occasions. It usually worked best first thing in the morning when I was descending along the face of a mountain with the sun at my back. On many occasions, I was able to surprise NVA and VC personnel on the ground and shoot them before they could reach their weapons. But not always! The enemy frequently dug what's called a donut hole and mounted a .51-caliber machine gun on the center raised area (where the hole would be in a donut mold). These gun emplacements usually were in open areas on the sides or tops of hills to give them a larger field of fire to shoot at helicopters.

One morning, I found a donut hole with the machine gun tripod in the center (but no gun). As I circled around to the right to get a better view, I saw movement in a hole dug in the side of the trench. When I hovered next to it, a VC soldier wearing black pajamas *(which they all did)* stuck an AK-47 out of the opening and fired at me point blank!

None of the thirty rounds fired struck me, but the bullets ended up blowing out the Plexiglas on the right side of my aircraft, the instrument panel twelve inches above my head, and impacted in my bulletproof seat and the floor panel.

My crew chief, sitting immediately behind me and facing the guy shooting at us, returned fire killing him. Lead had "Slick 1" come in, and land next to the donut hole, and the Animals got out and recovered the .51-caliber machine gun with tripod and lots of ammunition. With a grenade, they also killed another VC hidden far down in the hole. Once they boarded their aircraft, we took off and returned to Chu Lai. I had to fly slower than usual because of the wind blowing in my face without the Plexiglas windshield.

When I landed at the base, everyone with the team came over to look at the aircraft, which was pretty well shot to pieces. I'm amazed that neither I, nor my crew chief, was hit by any of the gunfire. I learned a valuable lesson that day: never hover over a donut hole until you're sure the bad guys do not occupy it.

I also decided to start carrying homemade bombs to deal with situations just like that. To make them I would take an empty standard-sized coffee can and tape a fragment grenade inside, and then pack the remainder with C-4 plastic explosive. I taped the top of the coffee can with high-strength duct tape, leaving the grenade fuse out and its spoon exposed on the side. I started carrying two or three of these bombs with me whenever I flew.

On two different occasions, when I spotted movement in a donut hole, I slowly flew over it (but not exposed to the hole in its side) and had the crew chief pull the pin on the grenade and then drop the homemade bomb in the hole. Of course, I had to get the "hell out of Dodge" immediately so I didn't blow myself out of the sky along with whatever was on the ground. The bombs worked perfectly in demolishing a machine gun position; however, when my commanding officer once saw one in the back of my helicopter, he said they were too dangerous to carry and ordered me to stop. If a bullet had hit one, he explained, the explosion would've vaporized me, the helicopter, and the crew chief. I stopped making bombs then. *(As a fourteen-year-old kid living in Big Spring, TX, I enjoyed building pipe bombs and blowing things up in the country. Today, anyone doing that goes to jail—for a long time.)*

Soon after that incident, while flying on a VR, I found a series of spider holes next to a river bank. The holes were used as entrances and exits to underground complexes, and the enemy soldiers were very adept at camouflaging them. I circled to the right and saw the barrel of an AK-47 poke out of the hole. As the guy fired at me, I pulled maximum power and made a hard left turn to avoid getting shot point-blank again.

I glanced up just in time to hit a very large tree. The tree stopped the forward movement of the helicopter, but I was able to keep it flying, although all the Plexiglas windshields were shattered. Fortunately, the rotor blades were not badly damaged, and I was able to fly the helicopter back to home base at Chu Lai to be repaired.

I started to get a reputation for destroying and damaging Loaches. My CO said I was obviously good at finding the enemy and engaging them, but admonished me for flying the helicopter with damaged blades, explaining that any crack in one or more of the blades could cause the rotor head to disintegrate leaving the aircraft to plummet to the ground. I was more careful after that.

CHAPTER 11

FRIENDLY FIRE (MINE!)

One morning before takeoff, all of the pilots were called in for a special meeting at the TOC. We were told that reliable intelligence sources indicated an NVA command and control headquarters was located on the western side of one of our free-fire zones near the Laotian border. Captain Gordy Hines, who was Lead, got the coordinates of the site, plotted them on his map, and we all flew to that AO. The area was near the Ho Chi Minh Trail, which was used to move supplies from North Vietnam to South Vietnam. Apparently, the NVA command headquarters was instrumental in coordinating supply movements and providing enemy troops.

Arriving on station, I descended in my usual tight spiraling right hand turn down to low level and began my search. Lead, "2," and the three Hueys were at their normal altitudes of fifteen hundred and three thousand feet above me. As I was descending, I armed my minigun. Once at a one to two foot low-level altitude, I began to make lazy S-turns in search of any movement or terrain anomaly on the ground. One thing that I'd recently learned was NEVER to fly in a straight line while low level, but always to turn slowly left or right.

While returning to home base one evening, I was very tired from a long day of flying missions. Since we were nearly *feet wet,* I was flying low and fast straight toward a hedgerow near a coastline rice paddy when a bullet pierced the windshield and struck the overhead center console wall two inches to the left of my head. I learned that lesson quickly!

After about two hours of searching and not finding anything we decided to return to Duc Pho and refuel. I didn't want to keep searching for something as important as the NVA headquarters, and then realize I was low on fuel and had to leave. After refueling, we returned to the same area, and I began my search again. After a few minutes, I saw a nearby outcropping of gigantic boulders on the side of a mountain. When I flew over to look, I saw was a trail leading through the grass into the boulders. I made one fast low-level pass over the top and saw some movement down below. I lowered the barrel of the minigun to its maximum downward deflection, which was at a forty-five degree angle pointing forward and below me. When I came back around, I begin taking AK-47 small arms fire from below and yelled, *"Skeeter's taking fire!"*

I opened fired into the boulders and instantly about thirty ricochets from my own minigun bullets hit the underbelly of my helicopter! It happened so fast I wasn't sure what had occurred. I immediately flew away from the area and then realized I'd almost shot myself down by firing the minigun at the boulders so close below me. I had never before received that many hits on my aircraft, but then no one else had ever shot at me with a minigun.

Needless to say, I had to go back to Chu Lai to get a replacement aircraft and explain why the aircraft had taken so many hits in the undercarriage. Loaches were great little helicopters and could fly with substantial damage. Since it was late in the day, we waited until the next morning to return to that AO.

That night, I received a lot of hazing and good-natured harassment at the officers' club for nearly shooting myself down. None of the other pilots had never heard of, nor witnessed, anything like that before. A few months later, my platoon leader gave me a plaque (that I still have) stating that I was a victim of "very friendly fire." I was unique amongst my peers.

Because the entrance to the NVA headquarters was located in the boulders, and there likely were caves below them, a B-52 strike probably would not have done much damage to the enemy complex. The next morning after arriving in the area at fifteen hundred feet AGL, I began to receive heavy small arms fire while I was descending in my tight spiraling turn. I yelled into the radio, "Skeeter's taking fire!" (Bullets coming close to your head sound like firecrackers popping.) Lead told me to make one fast low-level pass over the boulder outcropping and drop four smoke grenades in the middle. I did as he instructed, got out of there, and the two Cobras began to make gun runs with high explosive rockets, white phosphorus warheads, and their miniguns. Once they had expended about half of their ordinance, Lead cleared me back into the area to see what I could find.

As I flew over the boulders, I again began to receive AK-47 small arms fire. I immediately yelled, "Skeeter's taking fire!" and flew away to let the Cobras make more gun runs. After their second gun runs, I flew back over the area and again received more small arms fire!

"Skeeter's taking fire!" I screamed into the radio. It was obvious the NVA were entrenched in such a way as to avoid being hit by the Cobras' ordinance and machine gun fire. Lead told me to move about a mile away from the boulders and stay low level while he called for help.

Not including being shot at by my own minigun, I was fired upon four separate times by the same NVA soldiers hiding in the boulders. They were determined to shoot me down, but oh, how they would ultimately regret revealing their command headquarters position. Death, like Wagner's flight of the Valkyries, was soon screaming toward their location at nearly six hundred mph!

CHAPTER 12

NAPALM ATTACK

Lead called in two F–4 Phantom jets from the 366th Tactical Fighter Wing, the "Gunslingers," in Danang to drop eight napalm bombs on the enemy position in the boulders. (*Note: Had my father been assigned to that unit as his orders had called for, he could easily have been the senior pilot flying the mission.*)

Napalm is made from a combination of gasoline and thick gelatin that's carried in 110 gallon, six-foot-long aluminum canisters that look like torpedoes. F-4's can carry four of them mounted under the wings, and they ignite upon hitting the ground. One canister can incinerate everything within a fifty-yard by fifty-yard area (about half the size of a football field). The napalm sticks to everything it touches and burns longer than gasoline because it contains gelatin. Lead told me to come up to their altitude, and we moved about three miles away to allow the two jets room to make their napalm runs.

Within thirty minutes of being scrambled, the F-4 Phantoms arrived and the pilots were able to identify the target from the smoke grenades I had dropped and the burning white phosphorus warheads (called "Willie Petes") the Cobras had fired. The jets made direct hits on the boulders with the napalm. Each aircraft dropped four napalm canisters on the target, so the surrounding area, for about one hundred yards by two hundred yards, was instantly engulfed in a huge fireball that burned intensely and sucked all the oxygen out of the cavern.

After the jets made their bombing run, they departed and I was cleared by Lead to descend and return to the area. When I returned, there were dozens of NVA soldiers outside the boulders whose clothing and skin were on fire. They were running around as they tried to escape the burning cave and extinguish the flames.

I immediately opened fired with my minigun and killed all of them. I continued to fly around the flames and the boulders waiting for more soldiers to come out. As they ran out, blindly firing their weapons in all directions because they couldn't see, I shot them too. Anyone left inside the cave died from lack of oxygen after the napalm ignited on top of them.

That was the first time I ever saw napalm burn human beings alive, and I will never forget the sight or smell of their charred and burning flesh. It's a horrible way to die, and I'm glad the enemy didn't have access to it. If they had, I'm certain they would've used it against the American and Vietnamese forces.

As I was leaving the AO, after Lead said it was time to go refuel and rearm, I remembered the village where the small children had been doused with gasoline and burned alive and felt that I had just avenged their murders. (*"He is God's minister; an Avenger to execute wrath on those who practice evil."* Romans 13:4 NKJV) I executed my wrath on the evil ones that day with my minigun! Revenge had the sweet, sickly smell of burning enemy flesh and napalm.

Once we refueled the aircraft and re-armed, we flew back to the boulders to see what we could find. I descended from fifteen hundred feet and began looking for the carnage I thought would be on the ground. To my utter surprise and amazement, I could not find any bodies of NVA or VC soldiers. There were none in or around the boulders or in the open area near the entrance where I had shot so many that were on fire. I soon found footprints and trails in the burned grass going into the nearby jungle.

Apparently, soldiers from the headquarters, who had been away at the time of the attack, had come back and picked up all of the bodies and carried them into the dense vegetation.

No one shot at me while I was flying in the area, probably because they were afraid we would call in more napalm if they did. The air was heavy with the pungent smell of napalm and burned flesh. I searched for about an hour but found nothing more on the ground.

Finally, Lead radioed and quietly said, "Let's call it a day, Skeeter, and head home." I murmured, "Roger that." and climbed back up to fifteen hundred feet where I led the team back to Duc Pho and then further east to the coastline that would take us back to our base. There was no chatter or good-natured banter on the radios going home that evening. Everyone was quietly introspective after watching the awful events of the day.

Knowing I wasn't flying the next day, I got drunk that night! The next day I nursed a hangover and lay on the beach trying to forget the events of the previous day. I'm very glad that I never had the need to call in napalm on a target again. What I'd experienced at the boulders was a stomach churning event I never wanted to repeat.

A few years later, I saw the movie *Apocalypse Now,* and heard Robert Duvall say, *"I love the smell of napalm early in the morning!"* while standing on the beach wearing his black cavalry hat. His words had a very strong and poignant impact on me that the other moviegoers in the theater probably didn't feel.

After coming home from my first tour in Vietnam, I told my

dad that story one night, and he said he had experienced a similar event in May, 1945, while he was on Iwo Jima during WWII. The Marines used flamethrowers to shoot napalm at the Japanese soldiers who were dug in the side of Mount Suribachi. He said the smell of napalm and burned flesh permeated the entire island the whole time he was flying P–51Ds from there and he never forgot it. He was twenty-three years old at the time. What a remarkable coincidence to share a similar experience with my dad, who was the same age as I when he was on Iwo Jima!

CHAPTER 13

SNIFFER MISSION

A couple of days after the boulder mission, I was asleep in my hooch when I heard the screen door open, and somebody say, "Corvin … Corvin! Get up!" I looked up and saw the staff duty officer (SDO). *"What time is it?"* I said. *"It's 0400 hours. You need to get up and come to the operations center for a briefing about a special mission you'll be flying today,"* he answered. *"What's going on?"* I asked. *"Come on, you'll find out."* He just waved and laughed ominously.

I got up, dressed, gathered all my gear and headed to operations. When I got there, several pilots were drinking coffee and looking at a map of our AO that was on the wall. I poured a cup of coffee and tried to wake up so that I could pay attention to what was going on. There was a heavyset captain with them explaining that he needed to fly into a specific free-fire zone area with his equipment. I went over to them, and Captain Gordy Hines (Lead) introduced us and told him I was the Loach pilot that was going to be carrying him and the "Sniffer Machine."

I looked at Gordy and said, "What is a sniffer machine?" He laughed and said, "We are about to find out."

The captain, who was in the chemical corps branch of the Army, explained that an airborne personnel detector, designated the XM–3, needed to be installed in a Loach. Because of its weight, and his too, a minigun could not be carried. The sniffer machine consisted of an upright equipment console sitting in the cargo bay area of the small helicopter with two large flexible hoses running out each side then duct-taped to the skid supports and the forward ends of the skids. The operations officer had already contacted the Warlord maintenance section, and they were working with the captain's assistant to install the equipment on a recently acquired Loach.

The captain explained that he would be riding in back monitoring the equipment, which detected trace amounts of ammonia as the helicopter flew low level over the jungle, and the air entered the mouth of the flexible hoses. Human sweat and urine both emit ammonia. The sniffer machine was sensitive enough to detect trace amounts of the gas through the triple canopy jungle. A positive reading indicated that personnel (presumably NVA and VC soldiers) were hidden below, although out of sight.

He said that he would call out *Hotspot* whenever the machine indicated a concentration of ammonia as we flew over the jungle. Lead's front seat co-pilot, who operated the rocket launchers, minigun, and 40mm grenade launchers called "thumpers," was going to be following me on a terrain map. He would mark an X on the map at the exact location where the chemical captain called out *Hotspot*. Once the sniffer machines had detected enough hotspots in an area, then Lead would call in a B-52 airstrike to theoretically destroy whomever and whatever was under the jungle canopy.

The airstrike was called an "Arc Light" mission and consisted of a "cell" of three B-52s each carrying approximately ninety thousand pounds of bombs. Thus, two hundred seventy thousand pounds of ordinance was dropped in one fell swoop on the Hotspot. I wasn't particularly excited about flying the Loach without a minigun, but thought seeing how the equipment worked and what the Arc Light would reveal would be interesting after I flew in and performed what was called a bomb damage assessment (BDA).

By the time the equipment was installed, all of the pilots had been briefed and were at their aircraft. Although I didn't have a minigun, I did have a crew chief sitting on the floor behind me with his M-60, 7.62mm machine gun. We couldn't carry our normal complement of smoke grenades, hand grenades, and machine gun ammo because of the weight of the sniffer machine and the captain that operated it. But we were flying over triple canopy jungle, and anyone on the ground probably would not shoot at us because they couldn't see us. For the uninformed, triple canopy simply means three distinct dense layers of foliage that have grown up in a jungle area and basically block out most of the light on the ground.

In 1985, a UH1-H Huey helicopter was found in Vietnam suspended twenty feet off the ground in a triple canopy jungle with the skeletonized crew inside still strapped to their seats. This is probably where the writers of the 1987 Hollywood movie, *Predator,* got the idea for the scene where Arnold Schwarzenegger, et al., found a missing helicopter with dead crewmembers inside.

We took off and flew along the coastline until we reached the Hoi An River, where we turned inland and flew for about fifty miles to the designated free-fire zone the chemical captain wanted to search. Once in the AO, I made my spiraling descent down to the top of the jungle. Lead then instructed me to fly a regular grid pattern, using my slow S-turns, for approximately three miles.

At the end of the pattern, I would reverse course and come back, parallel to the track until I had reached my beginning point and then start the other direction repeating this over and over. This pattern was like mowing grass in a yard. The captain, monitoring the equipment, had a canvas hood over his head so that he could easily see the indicator dials. We had only flown the first three-mile segment (constantly making tight S-turns right then left) when the crew chief started yelling (*words I will not repeat here, but rhyme with bucket*) and I began to smell vomit.

The crew chief said the captain had just thrown up all over the equipment, himself, and the entire cargo bay area. I got on the intercom and asked the captain if he was okay. He gurgled and coughed somewhat and said that all of the turning, and the fact that he had a hood covering his head and was unable to see the outside jungle, had given him major vertigo, and he had thrown up his breakfast. I asked him if he wanted to abort the mission and return to base and he very emphatically said, "No!" (I later found out he was a West Point graduate and had played football, so he really believed he was a tough guy!)

Since there were no bases nearby where we could land and clean everything, we continued to fly the sniffer mission. After throwing up a couple more times, he pretty much emptied his stomach out and then all he did was "dry heave" until the mission was completed two hours later. *(With the rotor wash vortices blowing inside the helicopter, everything was quickly covered in the captain's vomit. I didn't like what I was "sniffing" at all, but sometimes you just have to shut up, gut up, and press on!)*

I flew over a part of the jungle containing several tall structures that appeared to be ancient stone towers covered mostly in vegetation looking like Kudzu I've seen in Louisiana and Tennessee. At this point that the captain got on the radio and started saying, *"Hotspot ... hotspot ... hotspot ... hotspot!"* over and over. He asked me to circle around and come from a ninety degree angle to the direction that we had been flying. When I did and approached the same area, he began to say, *"Hotspot ... hotspot ... hotspot!"* again. Obviously there was a huge concentration of ammonia being emitted directly below us in the jungle.

He became very excited and asked Lead to call in an Arc Light at the coordinates of the hotspot. Since we only had about half of our fuel left, Lead suggested that we refuel before calling in the B-52s. We left the AO and refueled at Duc Pho. We were also able to wash most, but not all, of the vomit off the equipment and ourselves.

After cleaning up and refueling, Lead called in the bombers as we headed back to the hotspot location. When we were within ten miles of the target area, we began to circle and wait for the bombs to fall.

Soon the B-52s would drop "dumb bombs," meaning they were five-hundred-pound bombs released in racks from the aircraft that fell on the target in what was called carpet bombing. They were not "smart bombs" that can fly into a target as was done in Iraq during Desert Storm. We watched as the time approached for the bombs to be dropped. The B-52s flew above thirty thousand feet and were barely visible to the naked eye when they dropped their bombs. Within a few minutes, we saw massive explosions in the distant jungle and a few seconds later could hear and feel the concussion from the detonation of two hundred seventy thousand pounds of bombs exploding on the ground.

The B-52 commander leading the flight got on the radio and asked us to perform a bomb damage assessment (BDA) and call it into his squadron so they could find out what they had destroyed. Lead assured him that he would do that later, upon our return to base.

I was then given clearance to return to the hotspot location to see what I could find. When I got there, most of the vegetation and surrounding jungle had been obliterated, and open expanses of dirt were exposed. Expecting to find NVA and VC bodies everywhere, I was very surprised and considerably disappointed to find hundreds of bodies of dead monkeys!

Apparently, the sniffer machine could not differentiate between human ammonia and monkey ammonia! Additionally, the ancient stone towers had for the most part been destroyed, and the surrounding ruins were *ruined* (pun intended)! Had PETA been with me that day, they would've had a "cow", man! We'd accomplished nothing after all the effort! Since it was late, and I was tired of smelling vomit, I asked Lead if we could go home. He agreed, so we returned to Key Ha heliport.

When I landed, the chemical captain got out and said he would never fly another sniffer mission in a Loach again. Although it was nearly dark, I still could see that his face was a pale shade of green except for the parts still covered by vomit.

Later that night, after I'd showered and cleaned up, I asked Gordy if he had called the B-52 squadron commander to give them a BDA. He said that he called them, but only said that no enemy combatants had been found.

He admitted he was too embarrassed to tell the bomber pilots what they had destroyed. (The few remaining living monkeys probably thought *"Holy Crap! We have just met our worst enemy!"* I'm laughing as I write this. *(Skeeter, you devil!)* I've never really liked monkeys, but I didn't mean to wipe out a whole species either. Oh well, that's the way the bombs fall!

While writing about this incident, I went on the web and researched ancient Vietnamese ruins. Wikipedia has an article about the "Ancient Ruins of My Son" where we found the hotspots. It says the ruins are the Cham Dynasty monuments and royal burial grounds of the Champa People dating from the 7th – 13th centuries. They are located in what's called the "Cat's Tooth" mountains. *My Son* translates literally as "Beautiful Mountain." The site is the Vietnamese equivalent of Cambodia's "Angor Wat" and comparable to Egypt's Valley of the Kings. In 1999, USESCO named My Son a World Heritage site.

Wikipedia also specifically says the following, and I quote: *"Until 1968, the Cham monuments remained, remarkably, in almost perfect condition, having been sheltered from the worst excesses of weather by the surrounding hills and jungle. Regrettably, man achieved what nature could not and B-52 bombers destroyed most of the towers when My Son found itself in a free-fire zone during the Vietnam War."* (NOTE: "Man" referred to in the above quote can be replaced with "Warlord 22" a.k.a. "Skeeter.") I was responsible for helping to wipe out a renowned ancient archeological world and almost a species of monkeys too.

I now know how Robert Oppenheimer (the father of the atomic bomb) felt when he first saw the brilliant flash of the exploding Trinity bomb and said, *"Now I am become Death, the Destroyer of Worlds."* This quote is from the *Bhagavad Gita*, an ancient seven hundred verse Hindu Scripture that is part of the epic Indian poem, *"Mahabharata."*

Finally, many years ago at bedtime, I used to say to my four young daughters. *"No more monkeys jumping on the bed!"* Fortunately, they never knew the secret meaning of what I said — until now.

CHAPTER 14

LIVING ON CHINA BEACH

I had been flying with the Warlords for six months, which meant that I'd been in country (Vietnam) for about eight months. I was averaging six to eight hours flying per day. One evening Capt. Barfield, the executive officer (X0), came to my hooch and said that I needed to have a physical exam done by the flight surgeon the next morning. He also said that I was averaging about one hundred seventy hours per month. Army regulations required every combat pilot to be evaluated by a psychiatrist after one hundred forty hours to determine if they were fit for further flying. I was surprised to hear that since none of my friends had mentioned it. However, the pilots flying the Cobras and the slicks were rotated enough that they never approached the number of flying hours I did flying as Skeeter. There were only two of us flying that mission, so we logged more time than the other pilots.

The next morning, I went to the company infirmary and met with the flight surgeon who gave me a complete physical and cleared me to continue flying. Afterward, I met with a psychiatrist who talked with me for about forty-five minutes and also cleared me. I explained that if I could only fly one hundred forty hours per month, then there would be many days when the VR missions would have to cease until I was below that number of hours. He said that he had already discussed this with Maj. Maher. I was going to be given a waiver to allow me to fly more than one hundred forty hours per month. BUT, every fifteen hours over the one hundred forty, I would have to see him and get signed off for another fifteen hours.

He was a good guy, enjoyed flying, and said that he would like to fly with me on a day off so that we could go down the beach and shoot sharks. I wanted to keep him on my good side, so I readily agreed. There were several times in the coming months that we did that.

Part of my flight physical was to be weighed. When I stepped up on the scales, I was astonished to see that I weighed one hundred eighty-five pounds. When I graduated from flight school less than a year earlier, I weighed one hundred sixty pounds. So, in eight months I had gained twenty-five pounds. I knew that I was gaining weight because I had to get larger Nomex flight suits periodically.

A major contributing factor in my weight gain was the fact that we had no running water in our hooch and drank beer all the time (but not within eight hours of flying). The closest water was at the "O" club about a quarter mile away.

For the past six months, several of my roommates who were slick pilots would fly a Huey to the Danang PX and load the cargo bay area with ninety cases of Budweiser beer. Each case cost $2.40 which meant that the total cost was $216. Dividing that by six of us meant that we were each spending $36 on fifteen cases of beer that we consumed in thirty days. (That's one-half case of beer per man per day.) By the end of my tour with the Warlords, I weighed 198 pounds. Rarely does someone go to war and gain weight.

The officer's hooch area was approximately fifty yards

from the beach, which was on the South China Sea. It really was called "China Beach." The water was very clear and perfect for snorkeling. Extending out from the beach for approximately a quarter of a mile was a volcanic reef that was submerged under two feet of water at high tide. The water, on either side of the reef, was about twenty feet deep. At low tide, there were many pockets of water containing rock lobsters and fish, which we frequently would catch and cook in pots at our hooch. I bought goggles, a snorkel, and swim fins from the Danang PX and used them the entire time I was with the Warlords.

Living next to the beach was great fun when I got to use it on my days off. One morning while walking on the reef (in flip-flops because the lava was sharp), I saw an aluminum napalm canister floating in the water near the beach. I went over to it, opened the screw-in cap, and saw that it had never been filled with napalm and was clean on the inside.

Although made from aluminum, the canister still weighed about a hundred pounds and was too much for me to carry back to the hooch. I got some friends to help carry it back. We decided that we could suspend it from a scaffold, insert a valve at the bottom, attach a sprinkler head, and have our own private shower. When I told the company first sergeant what I wanted to do, he said he knew of a base engineering company that had the lumber I could use for the shower.

I checked out one of the headquarters' three-quarter-ton pickups and went to get the lumber. The engineering supply officer traded me the lumber for three bottles of whiskey. (Cheap at twice the price!) Once I got the lumber back to my hooch, several of my roommates and I spent the afternoon building the scaffold and shower. (I have pictures of this.) I then had to figure out how to get water into the one-hundred-ten-gallon tank.

A few days later I saw a potable (drinkable) water truck go to the shower areas and fill up the tanks located there. I went up to the driver and asked him how often he refilled the shower tanks, and he replied, "At least once a week." I offered to give him a bottle of whiskey every time he refilled our shower tank. "No problem!" he said. From then on we had water, albeit cold, at our hooch for showering.

Before starting to build the tank scaffold, I took the tank to the helicopter sheet metal hanger and had them cut a hole in the bottom and install a pipe with a valve attached. I gave them a bottle of whiskey for their efforts too. Liquor was rationed to the enlisted men, so they were very willing to do what I needed in exchange for a bottle of whiskey. *Whiskey talks—BS walks!* The sun heated the aluminum tank containing the water, so we were able to have hot showers in the evening when we came in from flying missions. It worked great! Life was good living on China Beach in a combat zone.

Early one morning, just before I left the hooch to attend the daily mission briefing, there was a loud explosion outside my hooch. At first everyone thought it was an incoming rocket that had exploded between our hooch and the one next to it.

We all hit the deck, waiting for another rocket to land, when suddenly in the distance we heard a muffled voice yelling for help. We got up, ran outside, and saw the latrine was no longer standing between the hooches but was blown to "smithereens."

One of the pilots was lying on the ground with his skivvies around his ankles, covered with dirt, blood, and feces. At first we thought a rocket had landed on the latrine, but oh no, the truth was much stranger and funnier than that.

Before I get into what actually happened, let me explain our bathroom situation. A latrine (outhouse) was built between each two hooches. It consisted of a small wooden building screened in from about four feet above the ground to the top that was eight feet tall and had a tin roof on it. Inside, on a two foot by eight foot ledge, there were two round holes cut side-by-side with commode seats attached. Below the two holes was a fifty-five-gallon drum cut in half around the middle. It was into this container that one person (or two) pooped!

On the backside of the latrine was a hinged four foot by eight foot plywood door. This allowed the Vietnamese "poop burners" (we called them something that rhymes with "spit") to pull the half drums out daily, pour more diesel in, and set fire to the contents inside them. Thus, the eliminated waste was eliminated.

Once everything was burned to an ash and cooled, they poured five gallons of diesel into the empty half drums, readying them for the next poopers. On the day the latrine blew up; the poop burners had poured in five gallons of *gasoline* because the diesel tanks were empty.

The pilot had gone into the latrine and sat down on one of the commode seats. He was a two-pack-a-day smoker and lit a cigarette. He then threw the lit match into the open commode seat next to him. The blast from the ignited exploding gasoline vapors blew the latrine completely apart and propelled him through the air about twenty feet away, where he landed on the ground.

His butt was badly burned, and one arm was broken. Somebody ran to headquarters (HQ) and got the company pickup. The pilot was then taken to the MASH unit about a mile away.

He survived the explosion and was able to fly about six weeks later, but he never lived down the fact that he had blown himself up in the latrine.

I once read that a one gallon can of gasoline, containing a half inch of the liquid, has the same amount of explosive power as one stick of dynamite! The five gallons poured into each half drum in the latrine probably was the equivalent of ten to fifteen sticks of the explosive. No wonder the latrine was blown to pieces. Truth can sometimes be much stranger than fiction.

Living on China Beach was a lot of fun, with all the guys going there on their days off. Drinking and partying went on all day. Today, a large, beautiful, and very exclusive hotel is built there with luxurious and lush landscaping all around. *(No thanks. I don't care to go back.)*

CHAPTER 15

SPRAYING AGENT ORANGE

Periodically, the other pilots and I were required to fly a specially-equipped Huey around the perimeter of the Chu Lai base spraying Agent Orange defoliant. It was made up in fifty-five-gallon drums containing diesel and the defoliant compound. The aircraft we flew had two fifty-five-gallon drums strapped down in the cargo area and hooked up to electric pumps with twenty-foot metal booms extending from each side of the helicopter.

The booms were equipped with nozzles/sprayers every one foot all the way to the end. The mission was to spray all of the weeds and foliage around the base fence to prevent "Sappers" from coming inside. A Sapper was a Vietcong soldier in camouflage concealment, who had been trained to crawl under the fence at an American base, and then use a "satchel charge" of plastic explosive to either blow-up equipment or kill people. They were extremely good at their job, and thus we had to prevent any weeds or foliage from growing within fifty yards of the fence that they could use as cover.

Multiple wooden towers guarded the perimeter manned twenty-four hours a day by soldiers using M-60 machine guns.

Each tower had powerful searchlights to illuminate the open area at night.

The mission consisted of flying a helicopter, which was configured specifically for this purpose, slowly one to two feet above the ground to spray and kill all the ground vegetation. Since we were basically hovering as we flew, the rotor wash and the resulting vortices from the blade tips blew a lot of the Agent Orange inside the aircraft. The chemical soaked the pilot, copilot, crew chief, door gunner, and equipment operator. Usually, the mission took all day to complete and then we would be driven back to our company area where we would shower and scrub the diesel and defoliant off.

Agent Orange got its name from the containers that were black fifty-five-gallon drums that had a six-inch orange stripe running around the middle. The defoliant compound contained Dioxin, which was later determined to be a powerful carcinogen.

Tragically, many pilots and crew that flew the Agent Orange missions later contracted various cancers, leukemia, brain disorders, coronary artery disease, and diabetes. Once the Vietnam veterans returned home, many of their wives had multiple miscarriages, stillbirths, and children born with Down's syndrome, child deformities, and brain disorders.

Finally in the early 1990s, medical science determined that these children's ailments were caused by their fathers having been exposed to Agent Orange in Vietnam. The U.S. Veterans Administration in 1995, (twenty years after the Vietnam war ended) determined that all veterans who served in South Vietnam and were suffering from the above illnesses, were presumed to have been exposed to Agent Orange and thus were entitled to Compensation and Pensions based on the extent of their disease.

In August 2013, my case finally was adjudicated, and I

was granted a 100% disability based upon my coronary artery disease, heart disease, and Type 2 diabetes. The VA pays me a substantial lifelong, tax-free monthly pension, provides me with free medical care, prescriptions, dental care, and vision benefits. (Note: The VA medical care I have received since 2001 is the best health care I've ever received in my life!)

CHAPTER 16

BANGKOK R&R

During the Vietnam War, Army regulations allowed a soldier to take a one-week vacation R&R (Rest and Recuperation) after eight months in country. There were many Southeast Asia destinations available including Bangkok, Thailand, Hong Kong, China, and Sydney, Australia. Several pilots had gone to Bangkok and said that the city was a fantastic place to visit. After I'd been with the Warlords for about seven months, I submitted a request to HQ for an R&R trip to Bangkok. A few days later, it was approved, and I was scheduled to depart Danang early one morning on a Tiger Airlines 707.

Lady Bird Johnson (the President's wife) was the major stockholder in the airline. Tiger Air flew GIs all over Southeast Asia. Several guys had given me information brochures about Bangkok and the various tourist attractions there. First Lieutenant Ted Jenkins, one of my roommates, decided that he wanted to go too. He obtained approval for R&R and early the morning of our departure we were flown to Danang Air Force Base. I was glad to have a traveling companion and thought that we could have a lot of fun together.

Ted graduated from the University of Georgia the year before and was an avid hunter and fisherman. We had a lot in common and were good friends. We were told the Bangkok

International Airport had a U.S.A. R&R center located in the terminal and from there we could reserve hotel rooms.

We boarded the Tiger Airlines plane and settled in for about a two-hour flight. Once at cruising altitude the "stewardesses," as they were called back then, came by and took our drink orders. Everyone traveling on R&R orders was required to wear khakis until they reached their destination, when they could change into civilian clothes. I asked the stewardesses if they could recommend a good hotel and their reply was, "The R&R center will have lots of places from which you can choose." "Where do you girls stay in Bangkok?" I asked. "The Siam Intercontinental Hotel, but it's very expensive compared to the hotels at which most GIs stay," they replied.

Most of the R&R hotels cost between $5 and $10 per night, but the Siam Intercontinental was $25 per night! Ted and I each had about $1,000 cash for the trip and decided that we would go to the Siam Intercontinental and see if we could each get a room.

Arriving at the Bangkok International Airport, we got our bags and then went outside and hailed a taxi. The driver took us to the hotel, which was located on sixty-five acres of luxuriously landscaped gardens, ponds, and greenways. The hotel itself was absolutely beautiful and unlike any hotel I've ever seen. (The year before, it had been deemed the most beautiful hotel in the world by Fodor's *Travel Guide* and *Conde Nash* magazine!)

We walked into the front entrance with our bags, went up to the front desk, and asked if they had any available rooms. They did, and we booked two adjoining rooms that were huge with magnificent architecture and furnishings. The view of the gardens from each of the rooms was stunning. All this for $25 a night!

While we were walking to our rooms, the bellman carrying our bags said there was an Olympic-sized swimming pool in the back with a cabana bar on the side and a floating bar in the middle. Ted and I decided that we would change into our swimsuits and check it out. Once in our rooms, we changed and then walked to the elevators that went down to the lower level where the pool was located.

At the registration desk, they told us there were towels and recliners available at the pool and a fully-stocked bar that served free drinks to anyone staying at the hotel.

When we got to the ground level, we walked outside and along a tall hedge that extended about fifty yards. The pool was on the other side of the hedge. At the end of the lush greenery, we saw the pool, which was huge and surrounded by approximately four hundred women wearing bikinis (except for the pregnant ones). Ted and I stood there for a minute looking in awe at all the females (probably with our mouths open in astonishment). There were no men at the pool—at all. Ted and I were the only ones.

Neither of us had seen any "round eyes" (meaning a non-Oriental woman) except for a few, very unattractive, donut dollies stationed at Chu Lai. We walked to the cabana bar, sat down, and ordered beers. There were maybe a dozen women talking and drinking at the bar, so we asked several sitting next to us why there were so many females at the pool and no men. They laughed and said that a TWA flight had arrived from the U.S.A. the night before carrying two hundred wives and girlfriends of Air Force personnel stationed in Thailand and Vietnam. Their husbands and boyfriends were scheduled to arrive at the Siam Intercontinental Hotel later that night. I asked the woman sitting next to me, "Who are the other two hundred women?" She replied they were for the most part tourists from Canada, Europe, and Australia, who had traveled to Bangkok for a vacation and holiday.

Ted and I smiled at each other, and I thought, *"We are going to have a* really *good time in Bangkok."* We spent the afternoon swimming, drinking beer, and talking with lots of pretty girls from all around the world. They all spoke English except the Sheilas that were Aussies, who spoke their own version of the language.

One of the Warlord pilots told me there was a beautiful Thai restaurant in Bangkok called *Pirans*. He said the food was excellent and that each evening traditional Thai dancers put on a show. At the pool, Ted and I met two girls our age from Montréal, Canada, who spoke English with a very French accent. We invited them to dinner and dancing at the hotel that night, to which they readily agreed. I had brought a navy blazer and khaki slacks with me along with a white shirt and tie. That afternoon, the hotel dry cleaned and pressed the clothes for me.

We met the Canadian girls downstairs at the restaurant and had dinner. We then spent the rest of the evening dancing and drinking at the ballroom dance club located there. Before going to bed, (alone), I asked the girls if they would like to go to dinner with us at a traditional Thai restaurant the next night. They enthusiastically agreed.

The next morning, Ted and I slept late, then had breakfast, changed into our swimsuits, and went out to the swimming pool to relax and get some more sun. The Air Force guys had arrived, and there were lots of women with their husbands and boyfriends at the pool. It was easy now to tell who was there with a male companion.

Throughout the day, Ted and I struck up conversations with several different women from Europe and Australia. All of them asked if we would like to accompany them for dinner that night, but we told them we already had plans. However, not wanting to pass up *targets of opportunity*, we set up dates for the following evenings with girls from Paris, Barcelona, and Sydney. *(I decided on this trip that I wanted to be stationed in Europe on my next flying assignment.)* We spent the rest of the day at the pool flirting with all the girls and drinking beer. As we say in West Texas, *"A good time was had by all."*

Late in the afternoon we went back to our rooms, and I called the restaurant to make reservations for four people. When the phone rang, a man speaking Thai answered. I asked if he spoke English and he answered that indeed he did. I told him that I wanted to make dinner reservations for four people at 8:00 p.m. Then the conversation went something like this:

Maître d' – "Sir, we can accommodate your party of four; however, I need some additional information from you."

I said, "Sure, what do you need to know?"

Maître d' – "What are the names of the four people in your party?"

I said, "My name is Stan Corvin, my friend's name is Ted Jenkins, and the ladies we are bringing are named Chantal and Danielle."

Maître d'- "What are the ladies' last names?"

I said, "They are Canadian citizens, and I don't know their last names."

Maître d'- "What is your nationality and your friend?"

I said, "We are both Americans."

Maître d'- "What brings you to Bangkok?"

I said, "My friend and I are in the U.S. Army and here on R&R."

Maître d' – "Where are you currently stationed?"

I said, "In Chu Lai, Vietnam."

Maître d' – "At what hotel are you staying?"

I said, "The Siam Intercontinental Hotel."

Then somewhat exasperated, I said, "Why are you asking all these questions for a simple dinner reservation."

The Maître d' said, "The King and Queen of Thailand are having dinner here at 8:00 p.m. and we are screening all of the people that will be at the restaurant this evening."

With some astonishment, I said, "Okay, that's interesting!"

The Maître d' then said, "I've made a reservation for you at 8:00 p.m. However, you must arrive by 7:45 p.m., otherwise you will not be admitted to the restaurant after that. Also, you must abide by our custom not to stand with your head higher than the king. Will you agree to that?"

"Absolutely!" I answered.

He said, "Then we will see you at 7:45 p.m."

I hung up the phone and thought, *"This is really going to be an interesting evening."* I called Ted's room and told him about the conversation, and he suggested that we not tell our dates what was going on, but surprise them. That sounded like a great idea to me.

I called my date, Chantal, and told her that we needed to leave the hotel no later than 7:15 p.m. in order to be at the restaurant by 7:45 p.m. She said that she would tell Danielle and meet us downstairs no later than 7:00 p.m.

I showered and dressed in my blue blazer, khaki slacks, and put on a tie. That was the first time I had worn a tie in about nine months. It really felt weird. As my grandson, Noble would say, *"They are my hard clothes!"*

Ted and I met our dates downstairs at the hotel entrance at 7:00 p.m. The bellman signaled for a taxi to pick us up, and we left for *Pirans*. The restaurant was surrounded by a very tall brick fence with wrought iron gates entering into a large courtyard.

The taxi pulled up to the front of the restaurant. There were Thai police cars parked everywhere. I paid the driver, and we all went inside.

Two uniformed Thai police officers came up to us with a clipboard and asked for our names. Chantal and Danielle looked at me with a quizzical expression. I shrugged my shoulders and smiled sheepishly. I gave the policemen our names. Then a man wearing a black tuxedo came up to us and briefed us on the proper etiquette of being in the presence of the King and Queen of Siam. The girls squealed with delight and were thrilled at the prospect of dining in a restaurant with the Thai royal family. The man explained the king, and his entourage, would enter the front door and a gong would sound, at which time we were to stand and face him.

The restaurant dining area was sunken two steps down from the entrance foyer and door; thus everyone in that area was lower than the king when he arrived. We were escorted to our table, which was within a few feet of the stage, upon which the Thai dancers would perform. The large table seated us easily; however, it was only about fourteen inches above the floor. The area under the table was sunken to allow our feet to be placed there. We were sitting on the floor with our feet extending down under the table.

We ordered drinks and discussed how the food could be served without the waiter's heads being higher than the king's. Shortly after our drinks arrived, a loud gong was sounded at the restaurant entrance, everyone stood up, and the king and queen walked in with their two teenage daughters. Everyone quietly applauded. As far as I could tell, there were no other Americans in the restaurant. When the king and his family descended the steps everyone around the sides, which were elevated, began to lie down slowly until they were prone on the carpeted floor. All of us in the restaurant serving area sat down at our tables as the king walked down the steps.

The royal family walked over to where we were sitting and sat down at the table next to ours. Their table was parallel to ours and also faced the stage. The king and queen and their girls looked at us, smiled, and nodded. Of course we, and everyone else in the restaurant, were watching them. A few minutes later, formally-dressed plainclothes security personnel carrying small machine guns, crawled on the carpet to the tables behind, and on either side of us, and sat down.

I wondered, at the time, how any food was going to be served without the waiter's heads being higher than the king's. I also wondered how the Thai dancers could perform on the stage with their heads above his. All would soon be revealed!

In a few minutes two double doors on the elevated sides of the restaurant opened and waiters wearing traditional Thai clothing proceeded to slide large flat trays with water, cocktails, drinks, and appetizers on the carpet until they got to the edge of the steps. Then other waiters, sitting at the steps, took the trays, set them down on the lower carpet, and slid them to our table and the royal family's. The menu contained an assortment of Thai dishes and foods, so there was no ordering of anything else.

The food was wonderful and very tasty. There were several dishes made with hot peanut butter that I didn't particularly care for, but everything else was great. I had ordered a bottle of wine earlier. A waiter brought it to us on a large silver platter, sliding it on the carpet. He proceeded to open it while lying down and then poured some in my wine glass to be tasted. I drank a sip, nodded, and then he crawled around the table and served the wine to each of us. I thought, *"If only the people back in the world could see me now!"*

There was soft Oriental and Thai music playing in the background, which created a very exotic and romantic atmosphere. Soon, a stream of waiters began to crawl along the carpet sliding trays of food to our table and the king's and queen's. This continued on for the next hour until everyone had finished their meals. The security detail, sitting behind us, did not eat, but were constantly looking around the restaurant!

Before the show started, an announcer walked out on stage and said he and the performers were temporarily exempt from keeping their head lower than the king's. He also said the show would begin in about twenty minutes.

While we were sitting there, the king leaned over to me and asked in English if I was an American. "Yes, sir!" I said. He replied that he had been born in Cambridge, Massachusetts, in 1927, and loved America! He asked me what brought us to Thailand, and I told him that my friend and I were in the U.S. Army and flew helicopters in Vietnam. He said that was an extremely dangerous job and hoped that we would be safe for the rest of our tour of duty.

He asked if everyone at the table was American and I explained the two young ladies were Canadians from Montréal. Then, in perfect French, he began to speak to them. They were very excited to learn that he spoke French and had studied engineering at the Sorbonne in Paris. He also had degrees in law and political science from the University of Lausanne in Switzerland.

At that time, he was forty-one years old, very cordial, and friendly. After talking with Chantal and Danielle, King Bhumibol Adulyadej then introduced us to his wife, Queen

Mom Rajawongse Sirikit Kitiyakara. (Queen "Sirikit") They had married in 1950, and had four children. The two teenage girls with him were his youngest daughters.

The announcer came on stage and said the show would now begin. For the next hour, traditional Thai dancers, in very elaborate gold costumes, with small tambourines on their fingers, danced on stage. The show resembled a scene out of the movie, *The King and I*, only the actual King of Siam resembled a wealthy oriental businessman instead of Yul Brenner, the flamboyant, baldheaded Hollywood actor. The evening was a great success, and everyone enjoyed the restaurant and show and meeting the real King and Queen of Siam.

After the king and his family left, we took a taxi back to the hotel where we went to a garden bar and spent the rest of the evening dancing and drinking with the girls. The next morning Ted and I had breakfast, changed into swimsuits, and went to the pool to spend the day.

Later in the afternoon the two girls I met from Paris (Emmanuelle and Marie) came over and asked if we were still going out to dinner with them that night. I said, "Mais Oui!" They thought it was funny that I'd studied French for two years at Texas Tech University and spoke it with a slight Texas accent.

The Canadian girls, Chantal and Danielle, came over and thanked us again for a lovely evening at the restaurant. It was a little awkward because the two Parisian girls now were lying on lounge chairs between Ted and me. To add further to the awkwardness, the two Australian girls came over and said they were going to Pattaya Beach the next morning and invited us to go with them too. Suddenly, Ted and I were outnumbered six to two by scantily-clad bikinied females. (It was a helicopter pilot's dream comes true. I'm just telling you!)

I got up and took the two Australians to the cabana bar next to the pool. Their names were Layla and Mila, and they lived in Sydney, Australia. They told me they had arranged for a car and driver to pick them up at 8:00 a.m. the next morning to take them to Pattaya Beach. Instead of going to dinner that night, they wanted Ted and me to go with them to the beach for the day. I accepted their invitation for both of us (pretty sure Ted wouldn't mind). Pattaya Beach was an isolated and beautiful beach area that was popular with the local Thai people. It was about seventy miles away from Bangkok and about a two-hour drive.

They left the pool area to go shopping, and I went back to Ted, Emmanuel, and Marie (the Parisians - stay with me people!). They had been to Bangkok once before and had eaten dinner at a great restaurant called Nick's #1. They suggested that we go there for the evening.

The restaurant served Japanese Kobe steak flown in daily, along with many seafood dishes. The waitresses were all very tall, blonde, Swedish, and Hungarian girls that wore long black gowns. I called and made reservations, for 8:00 p.m., from the hotel's cabana bar. We spent the rest of the afternoon at the pool.

At 7:30 p.m., we met the girls downstairs and took a taxi to Nicks #1—a beautiful restaurant located in an old French mansion. We had a great time eating Kobe steak and drinking several bottles of Hungarian wine.

The restaurant had a beautiful garden dance floor, with a band, so we stayed until late that evening and then returned to the hotel.

The next morning we met Layla and Mila (the Australians) downstairs at 7:30 a.m. and got into a new Mercedes taxi that drove us to Pattaya Beach. The "Sheilas" (as unmarried girls are called in Australia) had arranged for the driver to stay at the beach for the day and then drive us back to the hotel.

When I was there in 1968, Pattaya Beach was not a developed resort area and nothing more than a fishing village with a few small hotels located near the shoreline. We spent the day swimming and sunning on the beach and had a great time talking with Layla and Mila. We had spent so much time in the sun that I was getting a dark tan. Later in the afternoon, we returned to the hotel in Bangkok, changed clothes and met the girls downstairs at the restaurant where we ate dinner and then went to the hotel ballroom and danced until it closed.

We slept late the next morning, and then I called Elena, one of the girls from Barcelona, Spain, I had met by the pool. She answered the phone and said that her friend Dolores was ill with a stomach virus and asked if I would go sightseeing with her. I said, "Of course," (What else could I say?) and then hung up the phone and told Ted he was on his own for the day and that night.

Elena and I met at one of the casual hotel restaurants downstairs and had lunch. She wanted to see several of the Buddhist temples, including the one of the Reclining Buddha and the Golden Buddha. Our waiter, who was serving us lunch and spoke perfect English, said that in order to enter the temples, I must wear a coat and tie, and she must wear a dress. Before leaving the hotel, we both changed clothes and then caught a taxi to the Golden Buddha Temple.

When we got out of the taxi, I noticed that her miniskirt barely covered her butt when she was standing straight up. We walked across a large concrete park area leading up to the steps of the entrance of the temple. As we approached the steps, two uniformed police officers began walking quickly to us. They started waving and yelling at us to stop.

When they got to us, one said something in rapid Thai and was pointing at Elena's skirt. I asked him if he spoke English, and he shook his head (he understood that much). He continued to shake his head, saying something and was obviously very agitated.

Finally, he motioned with both hands that her skirt was too short to wear into the temple. He made a twirling motion with his hands and pointed to Elena. As she slowly turned around, he shook his head, said something to the other policeman, and said, *"No Go."* It was apparent they weren't going to allow her in the temple. I finally put up both of my hands and said that we would leave.

I learned later the Thai police have a very strict sense of decorum when it comes to tourists entering their temples. Also, public displays of affection (PDAs) will get you arrested. We walked around the temple for a while looking at all of the beautiful gardens and canals. We caught a taxi to the reclining Buddha Temple and got out. As soon as we started walking up the steps, a police officer came running over and started shaking his finger back and forth.

We knew then the Buddhist temples were off-limits if Elena was going to continue to wear her miniskirt. We took a taxi back to the hotel and both changed into casual clothes. Then we left and went to the shopping district where there were many jewelry stores and shops.

Twenty-four karat gold jewelry was very inexpensive, so I bought a heavy gold chain with a circle trident peace symbol to hang on it. (Years later, after I'd returned from overseas, I gave the chain and peace symbol to my sister Penny.)

Elena and I took a dinner cruise on the Chao Phraya River that runs through the middle of Bangkok. There were lots of ferries and long slender boats, used as taxis, called "long tails." The river and surrounding shoreline were uniquely Oriental with thousands of closely packed Thai people living on the boats year-round with their families. The river empties into the Gulf of Thailand.

After the dinner cruise, Elena wanted to go to the "Red Light District" which she had heard about. Our taxi driver, who spoke good English, said he knew just the place for us to go. Upon arriving at the Patpong district, I was amazed to see that it looked like a very sleazy Las Vegas with thousands of bright neon lights and numerous bars and clubs. The driver took us to an upscale Jazz club and go-go bar where we listened to the music and danced. The cocktail waitresses were all very attractive, with lots of makeup, beehive hairdos, and were all transvestites. (Go figure!)

At the bar, several drunken and rowdy American GIs tried relentlessly to pick up Elena, so after a short time we left and returned to the hotel. We spent the rest of the evening dancing and drinking at the outdoor patio bar.

The Bangkok, Thailand, trip was a memorable one that gave me the desire to see the rest of the world. And for several years, I did. Ted and I were scheduled to fly out of Bangkok, back to Danang, Vietnam, the next afternoon. After we had paid our $150 hotel bill, we took a taxi back to Bangkok International Airport and left Thailand, heading back to Vietnam. It had been a great R&R, and I'd really enjoyed it.

But first, this *Amazing Story Related To Bangkok!*

In 1984, a friend of mine in Austin, Texas, Colonel Don Hobart, USAF (Ret.), told me a story about being stationed in Bangkok in 1969, as the senior military attaché to the Thailand Air Force. While there, he spent a lot of time with their commander, a four-star general, and they became friends. After his two-year tour was over, and on the morning he was leaving, an official Thai government vehicle pulled up to his aircraft, a C-141 Starlifter (part of the US Military Air Transport Command). Two Thai military police unloaded a small wooden crate from the car and asked Don if they could load it in the aircraft cargo bay. They gave him a note from his friend saying that he was retiring in a few months and asked him (Don) to keep the crate until he (the general) picked it up when he moved to the U.S.A. permanently. Don agreed to carry the crate with him

Don flew home, and the aircraft landed at McCord Air Force Base in Seattle. Because it was a military flight with only American military personnel on board, U.S. Customs did not have jurisdiction to inspect the passengers, baggage, cargo, or the crate.

He said that he got his bags off the aircraft and had a couple of airport workers load the heavy crate into his car and took it home. Two months after giving Don the wooden crate in Thailand, the general died in a plane crash. For the next three years, the crate stayed in his garage, at his home at McCord AFB, unopened.

One day while cleaning out his garage, he noticed the crate under an old tarp and decided to see what was inside. Once opened, he found a wooden box about two feet by three feet. Inside the box was straw packing material protecting a solid jade elephant encrusted with large diamonds, rubies, emeralds, and other precious jewels. He said the statue weighed approximately fifty pounds, and he'd later learned it was part of the Thailand National Treasury. Apparently the Thai general had somehow stolen it and gave it to Don for safe keeping. Upon calling the

Thai Embassy in Los Angeles, California, he learned the eight hundred-year-old stolen elephant statue was priceless.

That afternoon, the embassy sent a jet, with a Thai envoy, to McCord AFB to retrieve the stolen artifact. As a reward for returning the statue, they gave Don a large engraved Asian ivory elephant tusk.

One evening a few days later, the U.S. State Department sent a couple of investigators to his home unannounced, and informed him that possession of Asian elephant ivory was a serious crime, and unless he gave it to them, he would be charged with a felony.

He immediately gave the tusk to the State Department people. He told me he was happy to be rid of the elephant and the tusk, but always wondered what it would've been like had he kept the stolen jade elephant and sold it on the black market. Don was too honest to do that really. He died in 2008, at age eighty-three, from lung cancer and was a great American fighter pilot.

Don worked for me for three years while I was the Texas Vietnam Veterans Leadership Program's director. Don also introduced me to Ross Perot and Brigadier General Robbie Risner, who had been a POW for seven years in the infamous "Hanoi Hilton" prison. Three of those years were in solitary confinement where he was tortured frequently. He died in his sleep October 2, 2013, at the age of eighty-eight, and was buried on January 23, 2014, at Arlington National Cemetery. He was a giant among U.S. Air Force pilots having flown in WWII, Korea (where he became an "Ace"), and finally in Vietnam. *May God Rest His Soul!*

CHAPTER 17

NIGHT FLARE MISSION

After returning from Bangkok, Thailand, I wasn't scheduled to fly for a couple of days because of a maintenance stand-down for the Cobra gunships. That was fine with me because I needed the time to recover from my Rest & Recuperation!

Two days later I was playing cards with friends at the officers' club when Maj. Maher came in. He walked over to our table and said that there was going to be a flight briefing in the tactical operations center (TOC) at 2100 hours. He looked somewhat grim as he told us this, so we were really curious to find out what was going on.

When we got to the TOC just before the briefing was to begin, we saw two civilians were there with a U.S. Army major. After all the pilots were seated, Maj. Maher stood up next to the maps of our free-fire zone AO's and told everybody the following night we were going to fly a type of mission we had not flown before.

He said the two civilians were intelligence officers (CIA) that worked with the major at Military Assistance Command Vietnam (MACV) in Danang. He then introduced Major Gomez and turned the briefing over to him.

The major spent the next hour explaining that credible

intelligence had been obtained, from a captured high-ranking NVA officer, about enemy troop movements. He revealed that several large convoys of ammunition, troops, and crew-served 37mm weapons (used to shoot down helicopters and jets) were being transported the following night along the Ho Chi Minh Trail, one mile inside the Laotian border, and southwest of Danang. That put the target area nearly eighty-five miles west northwest of Chu Lai. (About a forty-five-minute flight.) The terrain was very rugged, with mountains reaching heights of five thousand to six thousand feet. Major Gomez explained that virtually all convoys and personnel traveled at night along the trail, which was wide enough for trucks to traverse. However, it passed under dense jungle cover, between tall mountain peaks, which also made it almost impossible to be seen from the air.

The Warlords had been given the mission to find the convoys at 0200 hours the next night and mark their exact location, so a B-52 Arc Light bombing attack could be called in to destroy everyone and everything.

As the Skeeter pilot, it was my job to fly low level, just above the jungle, find the enemy, and mark their location with thermite grenades dropped by my crew chief. These grenades did not blow up, but burned magnesium powder at four thousand degrees and emitted a brilliant white light. (I once saw a demonstration where one was placed on top of a disabled truck engine, and it burned completely through the block, the oil pan, and fell on the ground still burning.) At night, they would easily be seen by Lead, who then would mark the coordinates on his map and call for the B-52 Arc Light bombing run.

None of the helicopters, including the Loach, Cobras, and Hueys were designed to fly in IFR (Instrument Flight Rules) conditions. They all were equipped with artificial horizons, vertical speed indicators, turn and bank indicators, and electronic compasses, but they were never intended to fly on instruments for very long. (Usually long enough to fly into an area with a visual reference to the ground.)

The only true helicopter night flying I had ever done was ten hours in a Huey at Hunter Army Airfield during my flight training.

While in college, I received an instrument rating for airplanes in 1965, shortly after I got my pilot's license, but I had never flown in actual IFR conditions. The only night flying experience I had in a Loach was when we were returning late in the evening to our base at Key Ha heliport after we completed our missions.

Major Gomez explained that an experienced Huey flare ship and crew would accompany us to the AO and drop parachute flares so that I could see the terrain where I was to fly, just above the jungle treetops. They would drop the flares at twenty-second intervals providing a string of very bright illumination flares in a line for about two miles.

The flares burned for approximately ten minutes and were suspended below a fifteen-foot parachute. The flares each weighed approximately forty pounds. There was definitely a lot of "murmuring" amongst the pilots as we listened to the briefing. Finally the major said this was a very important mission, and although a very dangerous one, he was sure the Warlords could succeed.

He and the two civilian CIA agents left, and we all sat there talking about what the mission was going to be like the following night. Capt. Barfield, the XO, got up and said the flares should provide sufficient light for me to see what was below the jungle canopy and all I had to do was drop the thermite grenades at the first sign of any enemy activity on the ground. Then I was to climb back up quickly up to four thousand feet and lead everyone east at least ten miles away from the area. He said that once we left the AO, Lead was going to call in the B-52s for their bombing runs and give them the coordinates for the target.

The mission sounded pretty straightforward to me and with the flares illuminating everything, I didn't think I was going to have a problem with the mission. *But oh, how wrong I was to think that!* Maj. Maher got up and said that all the pilots flying the flare mission the next night were ordered not to drink any alcohol after 1500 hours the next day and no smoking at all after dark. (Both alcohol and smoking dramatically diminish a pilot's night vision.) He then dismissed us and we all went back to our hooches and went to bed.

Lying in bed, I got a queasy feeling in my stomach, my heart was racing, and I realized for the first time since arriving in Vietnam, I was afraid! Flying at night, just across the border inside Laos, and low level over the Ho Chi Minh Trail, had all the elements of a disaster if everything didn't go perfectly right. There were tall mountains all around me. If I were to be shot down, I probably would not survive crashing through the jungle canopy. If I survived the crash, I was sure to be captured by the NVA soldiers on the trail and then become a POW. Needless to say, I didn't sleep very much.

I awoke early the next morning, had breakfast, and tried not to think about the night mission. I spent the day writing in my journal and trying to relax on the beach. Late in the afternoon I met the Loach crew chief at the aircraft, and we pre-flighted it. I made sure the minigun barrels and the electric motor were coated in LSA (a heavy duty lubricant), and the ammunition box was full. I also checked to make sure that he had plenty of M-60 ammunition, thermite grenades, and an armor plate on which to sit. There had been many aircraft and helicopters shot down over the Ho Chi Minh Trail.

That evening I went to the officers' club, had dinner, and played cards with my friends. Normally the club closed at 2300 hours, but this evening Maj. Maher kept it open until 2400 hours serving only coffee. One hour before we were to take off, I gathered all my flight gear and made sure I had twenty magazines of 5.56mm ammo in bandoliers for my CAR-15 rifle and ten magazines for my .45-caliber automatic pistol. Then I went to the aircraft to wait and allow my night vision to become acclimated to the dark.

The night was clear and moonlit with lots of stars overhead. The South China Sea was beautiful with the moon and stars reflecting on its calm surface. I wondered if I would ever see it again! I still had butterflies in my stomach, but was ready for the mission. My fear had diminished as I prepared for the flight.

At 0100 hours, we started our engines, took off, and I led the team northwest from Chu Lai. Lead gave me a magnetic heading to fly to the AO and told me to climb to six thousand feet. There was enough ambient light from the moon and stars above and the villages below that I could fly without any difficulty.

Before takeoff, I turned on the interior instrument night lights, which were red, and turned off all the exterior lights. The other aircraft did the same. I was glad that I was in front, leading everyone, and not having to worry about hitting another helicopter or its blades.

Approximately thirty minutes into the flight, the Huey flare ship from Danang called Lead on the assigned radio frequency and said they would intercept our flight in about ten minutes, and take us into the Ho Chi Minh Trail target area. Since they were experienced at dropping parachute flares around mountain fire support bases, I didn't think we would have any trouble with the mission. They rendezvoused with the team and got about a mile in front of me. A few minutes before we reached the AO, they briefly turned on their exterior lights so they could be seen. From that point on every helicopter was blacked out so the enemy on the ground could not see us.

Soon the flare ship called Lead and said that we were nearing the area where they would begin to drop the flares. Lead told me not to begin my descent over the Ho Chi Minh Trail until the second flare had illuminated. He really didn't have to tell me that because I wasn't about to descend into pitch black darkness with mountain tops all around.

(There's a pilot joke that says. "If you are flying at night and your engine quits, turn your landing lights on. If you don't like what you see below, turn them off.")

At approximately 0200 hours, the first flare was dropped, then the second twenty seconds later. When they ignited, the light was brilliant bluish white and lit up the jungle and everything below for about a quarter of a mile. The flare parachute opened at about one thousand feet above the ground. As I began my rapid spiraling descent, they dropped a third flare, then a fourth. The swinging of the flares created lots of shadow movement below them.

I now could easily see the jungle and treetops below and part of the mountains on either side. I armed the minigun and told the crew chief to get ready to drop the thermite grenades. Once I flew under the first parachute flare, I immediately started seeing red machine gun tracers being fired up through the jungle at me.

"Skeeter's taking fire!" I yelled on the radio.

"You don't have to tell us that Skeeter, we can see it," he

said. Then, as they say, *"All hell broke loose!"* From multiple points on the ground, I could see red machine gun tracers coming at me. It dawned on me that I was silhouetted against the flares above me and was an easy target for the NVA soldiers shooting at me from below. Then, large green tracers, from a .51-caliber machine gun position on a nearby mountainside, started being fired down at me. The tracers looked about the size of basketballs and were only a few feet away from the helicopter as they missed. They were very distinct from the smaller red AK-47 tracers being fired at me from below.

Lead told me to stay as close to the jungle canopy as I possibly could to avoid being hit by the intense machine gun fire from above and below. I started flying back and forth in rapid S-turns in the direction where the flares were illuminating the treetops. Since the Cobras and the Hueys did not have any exterior running lights turned on, the NVA under the jungle canopy and on the mountainside could only shoot at me. Suddenly, I was plunged into total darkness flying only a foot above the trees.

"Lead, what's happening?" I yelled on the radio. "I don't know!" he said, and then the flare ship aircraft commander answered saying sometimes the flares did not ignite because they were wet or defective.

I immediately began to climb to a higher altitude and then realized that I couldn't see anything outside of the helicopter because my night vision was totally destroyed because of the bright flares.

I was surrounded by several mountain peaks that were thousands of feet higher than my current altitude. To make matters worse, the flare ship AC screamed at me on the radio, "Don't climb straight ahead because there are three un-ignited flares floating down in front of you." I was flying at seventy knots, the flares each weighed forty pounds, and my windshield was quarter inch Plexiglas! I made an immediate ninety degree turn and started to climb even though I could barely see the red illuminated gauges on the instrument panel and nothing, including the mountains, outside the helicopter. As combat pilots often say, *The pucker factor was then at its max!* At least with the flares not silhouetting me, the NVA with AK-47s and .51-caliber machine guns couldn't see where to shoot. They could, however, hear all the helicopters flying above and were firing at the rotor sounds.

As I was gaining altitude, two flares ignited below, and Lead said, "Skeeter, will you try again?" I hesitated a moment and then with a somewhat shaky voice said, "Yeah, I'll give it one more shot!"

Someone keyed the mic and laughingly said, "No pun intended, right, Skeeter?" I said "Yeah, right." *(I won't describe what else I said.)*

I started my descent again down to the jungle canopy covering the trail. As soon as the flares silhouetted me, the red and green tracers began to be fired in my direction. *(Between each tracer were four bullets that were not tracers!)* On the intercom, I told the crew chief to get ready to drop two of the thermite grenades. Then several AK-47 rounds, fired from below, struck the left side of the helicopter, the cargo bay area, and the minigun, rendering it useless. I yelled at the crew chief to drop the grenades, which he did and began firing his M-60 continuously at the trees below.

I made a ninety-degree right turn and began climbing away from the jungle canopy. I glanced at the instruments and saw that everything was in the green meaning the engine had not been hit. Lead saw me make the turn and marked the coordinates on his map. He told me to climb to five thousand feet (to avoid the mountaintops) and head east southeast while he called in the B-52 Arc Light bombing run. After a few minutes, Lead got on the radio and said, "Let's go home." I called him back and said, "Are we going to wait and watch the Arc Light?" Lead answered with a terse, "NO!" Then he said, "I'll brief all of you at the TOC when we get back to the base."

Leading us back to Chu Lai, I called the Warlord maintenance section so they could assess the damage to my Loach and minigun when we arrived. They were waiting at the helicopter revetment when I landed. After shutting the aircraft down, I walked around to the left side and saw several bullet holes in the gun, the fuselage, and cargo bay floor. All of the bullets had missed the vital control linkages, rotor hub, and engine, which was why I was able to fly the helicopter home. We'd had a very close call indeed. I left the revetment and with the other pilots went to the TOC.

Once inside, Capt. Gordy Hines (Lead), told us that when he called the B-52 squadron operations on the UHF radio he was told to "Wait one." They came back to him almost immediately and said they could not fly the bombing mission. The target coordinates were too far inside the Laotian border and at that time Laos was a restricted "no fly" zone.

They apologized but said there was nothing they could do. We sat there in stunned silence for a few minutes then somebody asked Gordy, "So what did we accomplish?" He said, "Absolutely nothing!" I was furious that I'd risked my life, and my crew chief's, on such a gross misadventure. I realized the political situation in Vietnam might ultimately get me killed.

We left the TOC and went back to our hooches as the sun began to rise out of the sea. What a waste! But it would not be the last idiocy of the war. I went to bed and slept late. I awoke and lay on the beach and drank beer all afternoon until dinner time. It took me several days before I calmed down from the stomach-churning anger at the failed mission and the gut-wrenching fear I had experienced while flying it.

As we often said in Vietnam, *"I know I'm going to heaven because I've already spent my time in hell!"*

CHAPTER 18

STRANGE VISUAL RECONS

The day started, as most did, with me leading the team south to our staging area at Duc Pho. From there, we headed west into a mountainous region that was a newly assigned free-fire zone. This day we had no special assignment other than to see what we could find. I began my descent at the top of a four thousand-foot mountain, cutting my power back, so that I could silently approach a small valley that had some rice paddies built in the flat bottom land.

We had been in that area on a few occasions, but I had never found anybody, although I could see that rice had been planted in the three small paddies. However, this time as I got closer I could see a herd of approximately thirty water buffalo standing in the middle of one of the paddies. They were unattended and stood still. "Lead, can you see the animals in the rice paddy?" I asked. "I sure can, but are there any people with them or nearby?" he said. "Not that I can see," I answered. Had there been anybody with the animals I would have killed them first.

As I flew over the water buffalo, they milled around somewhat but didn't leave the middle of the rice paddy. I flew to the edge of the jungle trying to see anybody or any structures that might be cover and concealment for NVA or VC soldiers. There was no one in sight and more importantly I didn't receive any ground fire from machine guns.

After a few minutes, I flew back over the animals. "Lead, what should I do?" I asked. "Do what you do best, Skeeter," he said. When I came back around and lined up to fire my minigun at the water buffalo, Lead said, "Hold on just a minute, Skeeter." He called the other Cobra and said, "Let's make a couple of gun runs on the buffalo firing only flechettes at them." Cobra "2" answered saying, "Roger that. I'll roll in and fire after you make your first run."

Lead called me and said, "Skeeter, How about moving away from the rice patties about a half-mile so we can kill the water buffalo with our flechettes rockets." I said, "Sure thing." Then I moved away from the rice paddies to give the Cobras a wide berth while they made their rocket runs. The rice paddies had a few inches of water in them so the impact of the flechette darts could easily be seen. I was curious to see what the effects of the three-inch-long metal darts hitting such large animals would be.

Lead began his dive on the water buffalo and at an altitude of about a thousand feet he fired two rockets at them. The rockets burst open and released their twenty-five hundred flechettes about three hundred feet above the buffalo. When the metal darts hit the buffalo, the surrounding water erupted in a frenzy of splashes, so I knew they had been hit. The animals began to mill around, but then stopped. I waited for them to collapse, but all they did was stand there! Then Cobra 2 began his dive and fired two more flechette rockets at the buffalo. Again, the water surrounding them erupted with thousands of small geysers from the impact of the metal darts. Once more, the buffalo moved around some, but then stood still. Both Cobras climbed back up to their normal fifteen hundred feet altitude and asked me to look at the water buffalo. I flew back over the water paddies and the buffalo.

Astonishingly, none of the animals were injured at all; however, there were hundreds of metal flechettes sticking out the backs of each of them like thorns on a cactus. *(Four rockets contained about 10,000 flechettes!)* Apparently the hide of the water buffalo was thick enough to stop the flechettes from penetrating more than about an inch.

I called Lead and told him what the animals looked like and asked him what to do next. "Go ahead and kill them with your minigun," he said. I hovered to within thirty feet of the herd, and pulled the trigger. Immediately the animals began to fall. Within ten seconds all of them were lying down kicking their legs. I continued to fly around the downed water buffalo and let the crew chief shoot them with his M-60 until they were all dead. During this whole encounter, no NVA or VC fired a shot at me or the Cobras, which was surprising.

Water buffalo were used to plow the rice paddies by the indigenous Vietnamese people. They also were used to carry weapons and supplies by the enemy troops and soldiers. Thus, they were a valuable and cherished asset. I was amazed that we had not received any ground fire as we killed the animals. We never did learn how the water buffalo ended up in the rice paddies, where they came from, or who owned them. It definitely was puzzling!

Lead got on the radio and said, "Let's go back to Duc Pho and refuel and rearm." I climbed up to my normal altitude and headed back. Once there we shut the aircraft down, got out our "C" rations and ate lunch, while we discussed what had just occurred. The consensus regarding the use of flechette rockets was that against a human target they were okay, but obviously not against any animals with thick hides.

After eating and refueling, we took off and flew back west to another free-fire zone. This one had more open terrain and in a shallow flat valley there were several abandoned village huts surrounding a large open area that had once been rice paddies. Approaching the dried paddies, I saw a small white object lying in the middle of one. I armed my minigun and immediately turned to fly to it. When I got closer, I could see that it was a very small young girl wearing a white Ao Dai and pink flip-flops on her tiny feet. She was lying flat on her back with her hands placed over her stomach. She appeared to be about three or four years old and had no visible wounds or blood on her clothing. Her skin was very pale white, with no evidence of decay or rictus, so she had apparently been killed shortly before I got there.

She looked like she might be alive, although she never moved as I flew closely overhead, and the rotor wash blew her clothing. I noticed the ground around her had been dug up and replaced, and that she was lying on a slight earthen mound.

There were footprints and tire tracks leading from where she lay to the tree line and jungle foliage about a hundred yards away. At fifteen hundred feet altitude, Lead could see everything around me. I called him and told him what I'd found, and he said, "We can see her lying there." He also said to be very careful because *"She may be booby-trapped and explode if you try to pick her up or move her."*

The NVA and VC were notorious for placing explosives under a body and wiring it to detonate when someone disturbed it. I flew back over to the tracks where they entered the jungle, but couldn't find anyone or anything else. I went back to where the little girl lay, climbed to about ten feet and fired a one second burst from my minigun over her. She didn't move or flinch when I did that, so I was certain she was dead. The sound of the minigun firing at that close a distance was like standing next to a jet engine running at full power. As I flew around the child, I could not figure out what was going on. Lead got on the radio and told me to get out of there because in all likelihood she was lying on a bomb that could be remotely detonated. I climbed to my cruising altitude, and we went home.

About a week later we were flying near the AO's where I'd killed the water buffalo and had found the little girl. Lead said, "Skeeter, let's go check out the dead water buffalo and where you found the child." I said, "Roger that, let's do it." And then I headed in their direction.

As I descended down to where I'd shot the buffalo, I began to smell the putrid stench of decaying flesh. All of the dead animals lay where I had shot them and were rotting in the hot sun. There was no indication that anyone had been around them, so I climbed back up to altitude and flew to the nearby valley where I had found the little girl.

As I approached the dried rice paddies where she had been placed, I saw a huge crater where her body had been lying. About fifty feet away from the crater there were two bloated, black, naked bodies lying face down in the dirt next to each other. One had long hair, the other short. Again, there were no obvious wounds on either of their bodies, but it was impossible to tell because of their decomposition. When I flew over the crater, I estimated it to be approximately twenty feet in diameter and probably six feet deep. Lead said that it looked like a crater made by a thousand pound bomb exploding.

My crew chief then said, "Sir, there's something off to the right laying on the ground." I turned the aircraft and flew to where he was pointing. Arriving there, I saw several blood-stained, shredded pieces of white silk cloth caught in the dried rice stalks and one pink flip-flop laying nearby. I called Lead and told him what I found. "I'm not surprised," he said. I was sickened to think that a small child had been used as bait. It also strengthened my resolve to kill as many of the inhumane and murderous NVA and VC "vermin" as I could and "avenge" her death. We continued on with the VR of the surrounding area, but found nothing more and never learned the identity of the two bodies—probably her parents. Finally, we headed back to Chu Lai.

I was haunted by the death of the little girl for some time afterward. I still am, to some extent; however, I'm no longer surprised by *"Man's inhumanity to man."* If Shakespeare were alive today he would comment: *"Cynicism, thy name is Stan."*

I've never forgotten how beautiful the dead little girl looked wearing her white silk Ao Dai and pink flip-flops, nor, how sad she appeared lying alone in the middle of the dry rice paddy. When she died, I'm sure *Jesus wept*, as he did in John 11:35 NKJV. I know I did that night after I went to bed!

In 1977, Richard Bach wrote a beautiful book entitled *Illusions*. One of the quotes from his book applies perfectly to the child's untimely death. It says: *What the caterpillar calls the end of the world; the Master calls a butterfly.*

CHAPTER 19

NVA ANTIAIRCRAFT WEAPON

Earlier, I described making homemade bombs with C-4 packed into a coffee can. My commanding officer told me never to do that because they were too dangerous; however, I came up with another idea I thought would also work on stationary targets and was relatively safe.

The grenades used in Vietnam were designated as M-61 fragmentation ordinance. (Occasionally, when an officer was "fragged", it was with this type of grenade.) They were round and had smooth sides, unlike the pineapple grenades used in WWII and earlier wars. Inside the casing was a serrated coil of stainless steel wire wrapped tightly around an explosive charge. When the grenade detonated, the serrated wire shattered becoming thousands of projectile fragments flying in all directions. It had an effective range of approximately fifteen to twenty yards. Unlike in the movies, which usually show a huge flame rising from a hand grenade blast, the real thing only made a loud *whoomp* sound and had no flame at all. The M-61s had the traditional ringed-pin stuck in the top of the fuse and a safety lever running down the side that was called the "spoon."

An added feature to the grenades used in Vietnam was the

"jungle clip." The clip was a wire that had to be bent away from the detonator to allow the spoon to fly off in order for the grenade to explode.

This wire clip was added to prevent accidental detonations if a grenade pin was inadvertently pulled away from a soldier's belt or shoulder harness by jungle vegetation. (Several people had been accidentally killed in this manner before the U.S. Army R&D units came up with a solution to the problem; i.e. adding the jungle clip.) In basic training, at Fort Polk, Louisiana, I had learned how to use the M-61 fragmentation grenade and thought it was fun to throw them at downrange targets.

One afternoon, while cleaning out my Loach, I was looking at the contents of the wooden box the crew chief kept behind him in the cargo bay area. In this box, he carried long belts of 7.62mm ammo for his M-60 machine-gun, colored smoke grenades, CS teargas grenades, and M-61 fragmentation grenades. After holding one of the grenades a minute, I came up with a brilliant, albeit dangerous, idea of sliding several armed grenades down a plastic pipe and dropping them on a ground target.

In order to do this, I took a two and one-half inch diameter PVC pipe and placed several grenades inside (the diameter of an M-61 grenade is two and one-quarter inches) with the pin pulled and wire clip removed, but the safety spoon held in place by the inside of the plastic pipe. A metal pin with a ring attached at the bottom of the pipe held them in place. Tying a piece of parachute cord to the metal pin and pulling it out over a target would cause all the grenades to slide out the bottom, the spoons would fly off, and a cluster of grenades would land on the ground at same time. A three-foot length of PVC pipe held six grenades.

The Warlord maintenance department had no PVC pipe, but

I was told the nearby engineer company next door had plenty of it.

I went to HQ and borrowed a Jeep. At my hooch, I picked up a bottle of whiskey and drove to the Engineer unit and saw a stack of PVC pipe next to a maintenance shed. I walked in the nearby office and asked if they had any two and a half inch PVC pipe. The sergeant in charge said he thought they did, but he couldn't give it to me without an official requisition form being signed by my CO. I told him I only needed six feet of pipe, and explained what I was going to build, and how I was going to use it.

He thought it was a great idea, but was still hesitant to give me the pipe until I pulled out the bottle of bourbon from the paper sack I was holding. The sergeant was the only one in the office. He grinned at me and said he thought there might be some spare scraps lying around the maintenance shed that I could have.

I gave him the bottle and he took me outside, where he measured the diameter of a thirty-foot length of pipe to make sure it was the right size and then cut four three-foot pieces for me. He asked if there was anything else I needed and I told him if he could drill two quarter-inch holes, one inch from the top and bottom of the pipes that would be great. He did so and then told me good luck with my new contraption.

I drove back to my company area and went to the sheet-metal department at the hangar to see if they had any pins that would work at the bottom of the PCV pipe. The maintenance officer was a close friend of mine. He rummaged around in a big box with all sorts of metal cotter pins and parts used to hold down portable seats in the back of helicopters.

He found some that worked perfectly and already had a ring

on one end. I took everything back to my hooch and assembled my newest contraptions.

Early the next morning, I took two of the PVC pipes with me and went to the Loach. I explained to the crew chief what I planned to do. He thought it was a great idea and found some aviation-grade duct tape (called 100 mph tape) with which we could strap the pipes to the struts of the helicopter. He then tied a parachute cord to each of the rings and tied the other end to a cargo hook on the floor next to where he sat. He went to the armament shed and brought back a box of twelve M-61 fragmentation grenades.

I carefully (very, very carefully!) pulled out the pin on one, removed the jungle clip and, tightly holding the spoon by the side, slid the grenade into the PVC pipe until it rested on the removable pin at the bottom. *Whew, so far so good!* I did the same thing with five more grenades and slid them on top of the first one I had placed in the pipe. I then duct-taped the PVC pipe to the skid strut so that it was held vertically in place.

When the parachute cord was pulled, all the grenades would fall out the bottom. I did the same thing with the other PVC pipe, and duct taped it to the one already attached to the strut.

So now I had the ability to drop either six or twelve fragmentation grenades on a target by having the crew chief pull either one or two of the parachute cords. He thought it was a *"groovy idea."* (Remember, it was the '60s!) I told him to be careful about getting his feet tangled up in the lines and accidentally pulling the removable pins. He assured me that he would not do that. I also told him that if we got to drop the grenades on a target, I was going to pull maximum turbine power instantly and get the hell out of the area. Since he rode with his legs dangling outside the right cargo bay door, he thought that was a "very good" idea. Later that day we got to test the contraption!

The North Vietnamese Army (NVA) had for many years used an antiaircraft weapon that fired a 37mm projectile (approximately one and a half inches in diameter) to shoot down helicopters and American jet fighters. The explosive projectile weighed one and seven-tenths pounds, had a muzzle velocity of nineteen hundred feet per second and a range of thirty-thousand feet.

The barrel of the gun was nine feet long and was mounted on a towable shooting platform. The barrel could be elevated eighty-five degrees perpendicular to the ground; however, it could not shoot straight up in the air!

The gun was a crew-served weapon composed of a gunner, a loader, and an azimuth operator. (He was the person who quickly could rotate the weapon on the shooting platform.) The guns cyclic rate of fire was approximately ninety rounds per minute; *i.e.*, one and one-half rounds per second. It was a very dangerous weapon, used against all types of aircraft.

By the time the crew chief and I finished taping the grenade contraption to the skid support, everybody else was at their aircraft and were starting their engines. I started mine and led the team to Duc Pho.

Once there, we turned west to fly to a free-fire zone AO near the Laotian border and the Ho Chi Minh Trail. Intelligence reports showed recent ground activity had been detected by electronic sensors scattered along the trail. *(The battery-powered sensors were made from brown plastic and shaped like dog poop!)*

When we arrived in the area, I began my rapid spiraling descent into the valley where NVA activity had been detected. While descending, I armed my minigun and asked the crew chief if he was ready to pull the pins on the grenade pipes if we found a target. "Yes, sir, I'm ready!" he answered enthusiastically.

I reminded him that if he dropped the grenades on a position, I was immediately going to pull maximum power and get away from the grenade blast, which would occur within three to five seconds. *(That wasn't much time to get away from multiple grenade detonations.)*

Arriving at low level above the ground, I began to make a series of S-turns looking for anything that might indicate enemy activity. I flew for approximately thirty minutes without finding anything or seeing anyone. Then while flying near a small hill, I suddenly saw the reflection of something under the green foliage. I circled back to my right and slowed down to 40 mph to get a better look. As I circled, I could tell there was something directly below me but couldn't make out exactly what it was.

Suddenly, the green foliage opened up, in a clamshell manner, revealing the long barrel of a 37mm antiaircraft gun. I saw the three-man NVA crew quickly raising the barrel and aiming it in my direction. As I hovered directly above the gun, they began firing. Since I was only five feet away from the end of the barrel, the muzzle blast was deafening. "Pull the pins!" I screamed at the crew chief. But nothing happened! I spun the aircraft around on its center axis and screamed again, "Pull the pins, now, dammit! The crew chief could not hear me at first because of the deafening blast continuously coming from the weapon. This time he heard me and jerked on both parachute cords tied to the ringed retaining pins. When he did that, I dropped the nose of the helicopter, pulled maximum power, and flew down the side of the hill.

Seconds later, I began to hear the *whoomp ... whoomp ... whoomp* of the twelve grenades exploding. Suddenly, there was a very loud explosion as the ammunition for the 37mm gun detonated as the grenades went off. Dirt and debris flew up in the air as I watched from about a hundred yards away. I asked the crew chief if he was okay and with a "quivering" voice he said he was.

I started to fly back over the "big gun," when I came under fire from an NVA .51-caliber machine gun located on the side of the adjacent mountain. "Skeeter's taking fire!" I yelled on the radio. Then I reversed course one hundred eighty degrees and flew further down the valley. "We'll make a rocket run on the machine gun position," Lead said. As he and the number two Cobra dived straight for the .51-caliber machine gun, two other 51-cal's opened up on them from other positions. Both Cobras each fired four rockets, broke away from their run, and immediately started climbing away from the valley as the .51-caliber machine guns continued to fire them. "I'm hit!" Lead yelled. "But everything's in the green," he said.

I called him and said that I wanted to go back into where the 37mm AA gun was located to see the damage. "Absolutely not, Skeeter!" he said very emphatically. "This area is too heavily defended by multiple weapon positions for us to keep flying above them. Head back to Duc Pho immediately," he ordered.

I flew further down the valley and then began my climb to a higher altitude. While en route, Lead asked me to come next to his aircraft and see if I could find the bullet holes. I flew there and could immediately see where the bullets had hit the engine air intake housing just below the main rotor hub.

I told him what I saw and he said that everything seemed to be all right, but we needed to land at Duc Pho as quickly as possible.

Once back at our staging area, I refueled and parked the

Loach on the tarmac. Lead landed and inspected the damage. One of the control rods, attached to the main rotor hub, had been pierced by a .51-caliber bullet so he couldn't fly the aircraft back to Chu Lai. It had to be sling-lifted back by a Chinook. *(I also have a picture of that.)*

Then Capt. Gordy Hines came over to me as I was standing next to his Cobra and said "What did you do to cause the secondary explosion of the AA gun's ammo?" I could tell that he was still shaken up by what we had just gone through. "Let me show you," I said. I then took him to the right side of my Loach and showed him the two PVC pipes duct taped to the skid strut. By then the other pilots had come over and were looking at my contraption too.

Gordy stood there for a moment and then said, "What the hell is that?" I said, "It's my new secret weapon." I took the two pins the crew chief had yanked out of the PVC pipes and inserted them back into the holes at the bottom of the empty tubes.

I proceeded to explain to everyone how my new *secret weapon* operated as they stood there dumbfounded. Gordy finally said, "Corvin, you are one crazy SOB!" He then turned and walked back to his Cobra. I stood there grinning from ear to ear.

After we finished eating our "C" rations, we took off (minus Lead's Cobra) and flew back to Chu Lai. Later that evening as I was eating dinner in the officers' club, Maj. Maher came in and walked directly to my table. *Great, I'm in big trouble now!* I thought. "Gordy tells me that you blew up a 37mm antiaircraft gun. Did you do that with another homemade C-4 bomb?" he sternly asked. "No, sir," I replied looking somewhat sheepish. "Okay, then how did you do it?" he asked. I told him about my grenade contraptions and assured him that I had not made any more coffee can C-4 bombs.

He listened with a surprised look on his face. "You know if a bullet had hit the grenades they would've blown you out of the sky," he said. "I know that, sir; however, we generally carry about a dozen fragmentation grenades in a wooden crate next to my crew chief and behind my seat, so that can happen any time I fly."

Maj. Maher thought about what I said for a moment and then he said, "I guess that's true, but be careful!" Then he turned and left the club.

Everyone agreed the only reason I survived was because the 37mm AA gun barrel could not elevate ninety degrees straight up. When I was flying five feet directly over the gun barrel, the NVA could not hit me because it would only elevate eight-five degrees vertically. Had they shot at me while I was hovering on either side of them, when the camouflage first opened, my crew chief and I would have been killed.

My Guardian Angel was looking after me once again! (My wife, Peggy, says that when I arrive in heaven, he's going to come up to me all battered, beat up, and shot to pieces and say, "Stan, what in the world were you doing down on earth?" All I'm going to say is, "Just doing my job, Bro! Just doing my job!")

Tapping into my MacGyver-inspired ingenuity had worked perfectly, although I have to admit the grenade contraption looked more like a Rube Goldberg rig. (Jerry-rigging is better than no rigging at all!) I continued to use it on other missions, but never with such spectacular results as with the NVA big gun.

CHAPTER 20

SEE DICK & BOB *SCREAM!*

One evening Maj. Maher had an impromptu briefing for all the pilots in the officers' club at Ky Ha airfield. He explained the Americal division commander had recently met with the U.S. Air Force Vietnam (USAFV) commander, and they concluded that it would be helpful if the fighter pilots had an *up close and personal* experience with Army tactical flight operations.

The CO explained the "Gunslinger" jet jockeys from the 366th Tactical Fighter Group, located on the main airfield in Danang, were going to arrive the next afternoon. He said each would fly with me (Skeeter); one on a morning mission and the other on an afternoon mission. In order to do that, the crew chief had to be left behind to meet the max gross aircraft limit.

Additionally, to balance the load with the USAF pilot sitting in the left seat (with the minigun on the same side), the ammunition container had to be moved to the far right side of the cargo area where the crew chief normally sat.

I wasn't particularly happy about the arrangement because the extra set of crew-chief eyes looking out the right cargo bay door was helpful on a VR. I asked Maj. Maher about the fighter pilot sitting only three feet away from the muzzle of the minigun.

"That's better than him sitting behind you where the crew chief normally sits. Isn't it?" he replied.

I agreed with him, but said the fighter pilot was probably going to be temporarily deaf, at least in his left ear, after the mission was over if I had to fire the minigun. (At that moment, I decided I would DEFINITELY find an excuse to fire the gun, knowing it would scare the hell out of the USAF pilots.) Good natured inter-service rivalry was strong among all the military branches.

Maj. Maher told us to be on our best behavior around the Air Force guys, probably knowing that we were not going to be on purpose. As Army pilots, we had all heard stories about how well the fighter pilots lived. At Danang airfield, they had air-conditioned rooms to themselves and steak and lobster at their officers' club at least once a week.

I was at their officers' club once, when a drunken pilot friend of mine, who played football at West Point, stood up at our table and said, "I'll buy a beer for anybody in here that's not a queer!" That promptly started a fight that got us kicked out of the Club and banned forever.

The next day I lay on the beach all day, sunbathing and snorkeling, while the Warlord maintenance section moved the Loach's minigun ammo container and feed chute and installed lap and shoulder harnesses in the left front seat.

Late in the afternoon, a Huey landed at the heliport, and two young Air Force captains got out each carrying a RON bag and wearing their flight suits. Little did they realize the "fun" they were about to experience with me! Maj. Maher hosted them at our officers' club where we had a steak cookout (one of the first) on the patio overlooking China Beach.

They were both experienced F-4 Phantom pilots who had

been in country about nine months and were good guys. That evening, before going up to dinner, I went to the supply room and found the oldest-dated "C" rations case available. (I think they were from the Korean War!) I took them to my Loach and tied them down in back so the Air Force pilots would have a "yummy" field lunch the next day.

At 0500 the next morning, the two fighter pilots, with Maj. Maher and Capt. Barfield, had breakfast at the "O" club with the rest of the team. I tried to get them to eat a big breakfast of scrambled eggs and bacon, but the CO had already warned them not to do that. (I was just trying to help!) The supply sergeant brought in two SPH-4 flight helmets for them to use that day. After eating breakfast, we all went to the flight line and got ready to take off. The USAF pilot's names were "Dick" and "Bob." I thought *This is going to be so much fun; I can barely contain myself!* We took off, and I led the team to an airfield on the western side of Quang Ngai city which was slightly north of Duc Pho.

Lead had decided to stage from here because it was closer to the first free-fire zone in our AO, which meant I could spend more time flying low level on the VR.

After takeoff, I climbed to fifteen hundred feet and cruised along at 150 mph. An F-4 Phantom has a maximum rate of climb of 41,300 ft./m., a top speed of Mach 2.23 (1,472 mph) and a cruise speed of 506 knots. Dick, the first pilot to fly with me, got on the intercom as we were flying to my first VR AO. "This is great not having any doors and being able to see the ground so well!" I looked over at him, smiled mischievously, and said, "You ain't seen nothing yet." Lead got on the radio as we neared our objective and said, "Skeeter, go ahead and start your VR." I abruptly pushed the cyclic stick hard to the right and put the aircraft into a ninety-degree descending, spiraling turn. It took less than fifteen seconds to go from fifteen hundred feet above ground level to one foot. When I started my tight spiraling turn, "Dick" grabbed an overhead handhold and the right side of his seat as if he might be thrown out the open door. Once low level, I slowed the helicopter to sixty mph, armed the minigun, and began making my lazy S-turns.

The area had numerous hills and open valleys covered with lots of vegetation. "Do you always fly this slowly?" Dick asked. "This is faster than I normally fly," I replied. Then I slowed to forty mph and began to fly in right-hand circles over the trees. By the way that Dick was squirming and fidgeting in his seat, I could tell he was scared. Suddenly, I saw movement in a tree line in front of me, leveled the helicopter, and fired a three-second burst from the minigun. Dick screamed and grabbed the left side of his face! For a second, I thought something had malfunctioned with the gun, and bullet fragments had hit him. I pulled up, swung to the right, letting go of the trigger. "Are you okay?" I yelled. He gurgled something unintelligible into the microphone and nodded his head.

"Look at me!" I said. He did as I instructed, and I could see that he was white as a ghost, but there was no blood on his face. "I wasn't prepared for how loud the minigun was going to be sitting this close to the barrels. I also didn't realize you were going to begin shooting as soon as you armed the gun," he said. I looked at him with all the sincerity I could muster (which wasn't much) and said, "Sorry about that, guy. I'll try to give you a heads-up before I shoot again," knowing that was *never* going to happen.

We continued on with the VR as I flew over to the tree line where I'd seen movement. There was nothing below, but I spent some time flying in circles trying to see if there was any more movement or any structures. Once I determined there was nothing there, I headed back up the valley making rapid S-turns and circling to the right every few minutes. Dick got on the intercom and said, "I think I'm going to throw up!" I yelled at him, "Lean out the left door as far as you can!" He leaned out and began to hurl. Of course with the rotor wash, and the slow speed, it all began to blowback on him, the ammo container behind us and me. He continued to vomit for probably five minutes until he was dry heaving. "Are you going to make it?" I asked. He looked at me and nodded. I've never seen anybody whose face was as pale green as his. I told him that we would head back to the staging area in about an hour and to hang on until then. "Is there a bathroom with water where I can get cleaned up?" he asked. I told him no. The only water was in his canteen. "I didn't bring one," he said. I told him there were plenty of people on the team who would give him water once we landed. Then he leaned out the door again and started dry heaving. I continued flying the VR making S-turns and circling but didn't find anything and finally told Lead that I needed to head back to Quang Ngai to refuel and rearm.

He said, "Okay" and I climbed back up to altitude and headed east. Once we got to the refueling area and landed, Dick unbuckled his harness and got out. He was really wobbling, and I thought for a minute he was going to fall down. His face, flight suit, and the minigun were splattered with vomit. The crew chief from the slick refueling next to me ran over to Dick and gave him a towel and a canteen full of water.

After refueling, I moved the Loach to a nearby revetment, shut it down, got out and found my canteen full of water and cleaned up as best I could. Then I cleaned the minigun and made sure there was plenty of LSA on it for lubrication. (I wasn't sure vomit was a good lubricant!)

Dick came over and apologized for making such a mess. I assured him that it was okay. "How about some "C" rations?" I asked. He looked at me. "No thanks. I'm not hungry," he gurgled. We walked over to the nearby slick. I ate my "C" rations and talked to the other pilots. Dick's buddy, Bob, could tell things had not gone well. A few minutes later, the two of them walked a short distance away and had a hushed discussion. Lead saw them and went over and told Bob he was on deck or some baseball metaphor like that.

In a few minutes, they came back. "I'm ready whenever you are," Bob said to me. Frankly, I was surprised that he didn't say something along the lines of *No way am I going to fly with you!* He had a lot more guts than I gave him credit for.

After everyone had finished refueling, eaten, and I had rearmed the minigun ammo box, we took off. I climbed to fifteen hundred feet and headed west to an adjacent free-fire zone AO. As we neared the boundary I rolled the helicopter to the right ninety degrees, cut power, and began a rapid descent down to low level. Bob, having been warned by Dick, was already holding on to the overhead handhold and the right side of his seat. On the ground, I began to make my S-turns and circle turns at sixty mph as I flew over the rice paddies. Suddenly, I heard a single crack sound near my head. I immediately armed the minigun and told Bob that I might be shooting soon. Then I started receiving AK-47 fire from the left front side of the aircraft. I turned the aircraft to the left and opened up with the minigun for about a three-second burst. I thought Bob was going to unbuckle his harness and jump out when I did that because he was climbing all over the place trying to get away from the muzzle blast. I keyed the intercom, "Be still, dammit!" I yelled at him.

His flailing arms and legs were causing control issues with the helicopter as he kicked the floor pedals. I saw two black-clad VC firing AK-47s at us from a distance of about forty feet. I fired two long bursts into them, and their bodies basically disintegrated, splattering blood on the Plexiglas windshield. Bob had finally gotten control of himself and was holding on tightly and watching everything unfold. "Are you okay now?" I asked him. "I think so, sorry," he replied. He was still shaking like a leaf. I spent most of the next hour seeing if I could find anything more in the area.

I continued to make S-turns and circles, but Bob hung in there and didn't get sick. After a while, Lead called on the radio. "Let's head home, Skeeter." "Roger that," I responded and turned east to the South China Sea coastline.

When we got back to Key Ha heliport, and I shut down the Loach, Dick came over and shook my hand. "I wouldn't do what you do for any amount of money. It's the most dangerous thing I've ever experienced, and I'll never do it again." "Are you usually that close to a target when you shoot at it with the minigun?" Bob said while sitting in the left seat. "Yeah, that's usually the distance when I pull the trigger," I replied. "Do you see the blood splatter on the Plexiglas?" he asked. "Yes, I do, but don't worry— the crew chief will clean it up tonight. He's used to it," I said. He stood there shaking his head. "You guys have to be crazy to do what you do, but I'm glad you do it, and I don't have to!" I laughed, "It certainly helps. How's your hearing?" "What hearing? We can't hear anything out of our left ears. Hopefully, it'll come back soon," Dick said. I smiled. "I hope so."

Maj. Maher pulled up to my Loach in a jeep. "You guys

ready to head back to Danang? he asked. In unison, they both exclaimed, "ABSOLUTELY!" We shook hands; they jumped into the jeep, and he took them to a waiting Huey that would fly them back to their 366th Gunslinger unit.

Later that evening the CO came into the officers' club and announced that there probably would not be any more flights with Gunslingers riding as passengers. The two fighter pilots told him they were going to recommend to their commanding officer that further flights with the Warlords be canceled because the low-level missions were too dangerous. Maj. Maher came over to me, "Corvin, I don't know what you did out there today, but you scared the holy crap out of those two guys, and they won't be back. Grinning, I looked at him and said, "I just did what I do every day—my job." He started to say something but didn't.

He laughed, went over to the bar, got a beer and began playing cards with Capt. Barfield and two other senior pilots. Periodically, they would look over at me while they were talking, shake their heads, and laugh. It had been a fun day with "Dick" and "Bob." No one got hurt, and I got two more confirmed kills.

CHAPTER 21

TEST PILOT

One morning, after I had been flying Loaches for eight months, I was summoned to the CO's office. When I got there, Capt. William ("Wild Bill") Roberts, the head of Warlord maintenance, was sitting in Maj. Maher's office. When I walked in the front door, they waved to me to come in. I sat down. "How would you like to become a Loach test pilot?" Maj. Maher asked me. I told him I didn't know anything about it, but was willing to learn. He said that I had almost a thousand hours flying time in the Hughes OH-6 LOH, and Captain Roberts needed somebody to fly the Loaches on a test flight after routine maintenance and repairs were performed. The other high-time Loach pilot was leaving soon to return to the World and would be unavailable to fly them. My CO laughingly assured me that it would not cut into my beach time or mission availability. "Wild Bill" said that usually a test flight took about one hour and if all went well I could then sign off on the helicopter's airworthiness.

He said I probably would fly one or two times per week. Maj. Maher said that if I agreed, he would immediately have the orders prepared authorizing me as a designated test pilot. I thought *This probably will look good in my flight records and on my 201 personnel file.* So I agreed.

Captain Roberts asked me to come by his office in the

maintenance hangar and he would give me a couple of operating manuals with specific instructions detailing what flight tasks must be performed on the OH-6 before it could be cleared for flight. After leaving HQ, I went by his office and picked up the manuals and spent the rest of the afternoon reading them. It was pretty simple stuff, and there was a checklist used for each test flight to make sure everything was performing as required.

For several days, I flew my normal recon missions. Then one evening, when I was having dinner at the officers' club, Capt. Roberts came over and said that he had two Loaches that needed to be signed off by me before they could be flown on missions. I went over to the operations officer sitting nearby and asked if I was flying recon's the next morning.

"No, the Loach you were flying today is due for regularly scheduled maintenance and won't be ready for a couple of days. There are two more that need to be test-flown and then we can put them back on the flight line." I told him that I would fly them the next morning. Turning to Wild Bill I said, "I'll be at the maintenance hangar at 0800 tomorrow morning to fly and sign off on them." He said, "Great! I'll see you then."

The next morning I went to the maintenance hangar where the two Loaches had already been pulled out and were sitting, ready to be flown. Both crew chiefs and a maintenance mechanic were standing next to the helicopters. I pre-flighted the aircraft, got in, and strapped on my harnesses. Then I waited for the crew chief to sit down behind me and strap in. He came over and explained that until I performed the test flight and signed off on the airworthiness form, no one could ride in the aircraft with me. I thought about it a minute and then said, "Okay, no problem!" I started the engine and went through my normal pre-takeoff flight checks. As I was about to pick up to a hover, I noticed the foot pedals (that turn the helicopter left and right) felt unusually heavy even though they were hydraulically-powered.

I looked at the crew chief and shook my head indicating I was not going to take off. Then I shut the engine down. He came over to me and asked what was wrong. "The pedals don't feel right; there's some sort of friction when I try to move the left one," I said. Captain Roberts was watching from the open door of the hangar and came over when I shut everything down. "What's up?" "We've got some sort of a problem," I replied. He instructed the crew chief and a mechanic standing nearby to pull off the floorboard inspection panel that provided access to the control rods to the pedals.

When they unscrewed everything and pulled the left floor panel off, we found an eighteen-inch crescent wrench lying on top of the left control rod. I was stunned! So was Wild Bill. He turned to the crew chief. "Is this your helicopter?" The crew chief answered, "Yes, sir, but I didn't do any of the mechanical work on it. I just performed the engine maintenance." "I want to know who did this," Captain Roberts stated. I said, "Let's pull all of the inspection panels off to make sure everything's okay." For the next hour, the crew chief and two mechanics pulled off all the panels, but found nothing else. When they replaced all the panels and tightened them down, I got back in the helicopter, strapped my lap and shoulder harnesses, and performed my pre-takeoff checklist again. I took off and spent approximately two hours flying around the heliport and down the beach, but everything seemed okay.

When I landed at the maintenance hangar, Captain Roberts came over and said that he couldn't find out who left the wench on the control rods. He said they had several new mechanics that had recently arrived in country and were new to working on the

Loaches. I told him everything seemed like it was okay and that I would sign off on the airworthiness form. He assured me that nothing like that had ever happened before, and absolutely would not happen again!

If the crescent wrench had become wedged between the control rods, I wouldn't have had any way to turn the helicopter while flying. This undoubtedly would have resulted in me crashing. I decided to be *very* cautious with my preflight of any helicopter before I took off and flew it. Since it was late in the day, Captain Roberts suggested that I return in the morning at 0800 to test-fly the other Loach. I thought that was a great idea and left.

The next morning, I was back at the maintenance hangar and began my preflight inspection of the second Loach. The crew chief was there, but there were no mechanics around. After checking everything around the lower part of the helicopter, I got up on a short ladder to inspect the air intake chamber. Much to my surprise, I saw an electrical cord down near the intake to the engine. I told the crew chief to bring me a flashlight, which he did. When I shined it in the intake, I could see an electric drill. (I have censored the many "expletive deleted" remarks I made as I pulled the drill out of the intake.) I couldn't believe it! There was a metal grate that prevented large objects from being sucked into the engine; however, the electrical cord could easily have become entangled in the engine or the main rotor transmission attached to it.

Such an event would've have disastrous results had I been flying. I turned around to the crew chief who was standing there and could see that he was shaken too. Immediately he said, "I didn't put it there, sir. I swear!" I remarked, "Go get Captain Roberts and bring him here immediately." A few minutes later

Wild Bill walked over. "The crew chief just told me what happened." Two mechanics were with him, and he told them to take all the inspection panels off and remove all the engine shroud covers. Then he and I went back into his office while they did what he instructed. After about an hour, the crew chief came in and told us the helicopter was ready for a complete inspection.

We went outside and looked everything over. There was nothing else to be found, so it was put back together and tightened down. I went over to the right side of the helicopter and climbed in, but before I started the engine, I motioned for the crew chief and the chief mechanic to come over. They did as instructed. "Get your flight helmets, guys. You're going with me!" I told them. The chief mechanic was an E-6 staff sergeant and immediately said, "Sir, we can't do that!" "Sergeant, if you and the crew chief don't go with me, I'm not flying this helicopter," I said. By then Captain Roberts had come over to see what was going on. I told him that I wanted both the chief mechanic and the crew chief assigned to the helicopter to fly with me on the test flight.

"That definitely is against army regulations. They're not supposed to fly with you until you sign off on the aircraft airworthiness form," he said. "Then I'm not going to perform any more test flights. I'm not going to risk my life because of negligent maintenance." I replied. He was fuming with anger and said, "Corvin, wait here, I'll be back in a few minutes." About ten minutes later, a jeep pulled up next to me with Maj. Maher and Capt. Roberts inside. Maj. Maher got out and came over to me. "I hear you're not going to fly unless the chief mechanic and crew chief are with you. Is that right?" he asked.

"Yes, sir," I replied. He said, "Captain Roberts told me what happened yesterday and today so I can't really blame you for being reluctant to do the test flights." Before he could say anything else, I said, "Sir, it's dangerous enough for me to fly low-level recon's and get shot at all the time, but to crash and burn on a test flight because of negligent maintenance is just crazy!" He looked at me for a moment and then said, "Okay, I understand." He then turned to Wild Bill and told him to have the crew chief and chief mechanic fly with me under his authorization temporarily waiving the existing regulation against it. The maintenance guys were not happy campers at all!

For the next two months, whenever I had to test-fly a Loach, the crew chief and the chief mechanic flew with me. However, before each flight they spent several hours going over the helicopter with a *fine toothed comb* making sure everything was in order. Their attention to detail was great! I never had any more issues with sloppy mechanical work or willful negligence.

One evening Wild Bill came to my hooch and said that a new pilot had just arrived from the stateside maintenance school located in Corpus Christi, Texas. He was going to take over the Loach inspections and test flights.

Capt. Roberts asked me to come to the maintenance hangar the next morning to meet the FNG and brief him on where I flew along the beach for the test flights. I told him that I would there bright and early the next morning.

I arrived at the hangar where Captain Roberts and a second lieutenant I didn't know were standing outside talking. I walked over and introduced myself to 2nd Lt. Craig Jeffers. He was not the new pilot that was going to be flying the test flights and did not have pilot wings. He was also one of the few second lieutenants I had ever seen in Vietnam.

He wore the crossed flags of the signal branch on his collar and said that he was going to be the new communications officer at our heliport. He and a team of "commo" personnel were going to be responsible for maintaining all of the complex radios used in the helicopters. As we were standing there talking, two UH1-D's (Hueys) taxied nearby, about seventy-five feet away, going in opposite directions. Suddenly, there was a loud bang as they passed each other. Instantly, the second lieutenant fell to the tarmac. At first I thought he was ducking to avoid incoming rocket fire, but when I reached down to help him up, I saw a large jagged hole in his forehead between his eyes, with blood pouring out.

Capt. Roberts knelt down and rolled him onto his back. His eyes were wide open, fixed, and fully dilated. He was totally limp, perfectly still, and stone dead! I ran into the maintenance hangar and yelled for somebody to call an ambulance immediately. Then I ran back outside to where Capt. Roberts was gently closing the lieutenant's eyes. The two Huey pilots had shut their helicopters down and came running over to see what was going on. One of the pilots said the tips of their blades had struck each other while they were passing. Within a few minutes, a military ambulance arrived and took the dead lieutenant to the MASH unit a mile away.

A couple of days later, we learned that when the tips of the helicopter blades had impacted, a small titanium metal piece broke off and flew away. The shard struck the lieutenant between the eyes, piercing his brain and killing him instantly. Wild Bill and I were standing on either side of the second lieutenant when it happened. As they say, *There but for the Grace of God, go I.* What a harsh reminder there were many accidental ways to die in a combat environment. The second lieutenant had recently graduated from college, married his high school sweetheart, and had been in Vietnam less than ten days. He was twenty-two years old. What a pity!

CHAPTER 22

ROLLING DOWN
THE RIVER

One cold, rainy, and windy afternoon, I flew down a steep valley. I was wearing my nylon flight jacket to stay warm. In the monsoon season while flying in the mountains, the temperature was often fifty degrees. The team and I were flying a normal VR in one of our free-fire zone AOs, and I was flying low level over a deep and fast moving river. Before takeoff that morning, I helped my new crew chief, SP4 Charles "Charlie" Robinson, restock his wooden box of fragmentation grenades, tear gas containers, and smoke grenades. We loaded five two-hundred-round metal containers of 7.62mm machinegun ammo for his M-60. With all his gear, the minigun, and the weight of the five thousand rounds of its ammo, my helicopter was at its maximum gross weight.

The Hughes OH-6 Light Observation Helicopter (called a Cayuse) was an incredibly fast, turbine-powered aircraft, easily capable of spinning in circles, flying backward and sideways. It was perfectly suited for low-level visual reconnaissance missions; however, it had one design flaw that was potentially deadly.

If the helicopter was slowly flying at its *maximum gross*

weight in windy conditions, sometimes the tail rotor was not sufficiently effective to keep the aircraft from spinning around uncontrollably in clockwise circles. This phenomenon was known as the "Hughes spin." I had never experienced the spin before but was about to soon, *with disastrous results*!

Shortly after I began flying Loaches for the Warlords, I cut up an old pair of boots left by a former hooch mate, and sewed the leather tongue inside my right combat boot with a large needle and dental floss. This became a "boot scabbard" for an M-16 bayonet I found laying on the ground one day. I took the knife to the maintenance hangar and cut off the ring used to attach it to a rifle. (I thought I was very "cool" walking around with a knife stuck in my boot. I didn't realize it would save my life one day.)

The day was very windy. Flying through the deep valley and maintaining flight control was somewhat difficult. At the bottom, where the two mountains came together, was a fast-flowing river with steep rocky sides along each bank.

I was slowly flying a couple of feet above the water when my new crew chief yelled on the intercom. "There's a "dink" to the right with an AK-47!" (Dink is a pejorative name for an oriental, similar to "gook" and "slope.") I pulled maximum power and quickly spun the helicopter to the right to aim the minigun at him, but the helicopter continued turning and then picked up speed. I pushed in full left pedal to stop the turn, but couldn't stop the spinning. I tried to gain altitude because my skids were only inches above the water, but the helicopter was beginning to spin faster and faster and descend!

Lead called on the radio, "Skeeter! … Skeeter! What the hell are you doing?" "I can't stop the Loach from spinning!" I answered. He started to say something, and then my skids touched the swiftly flowing water, and I yelled, "Mayday! Mayday!

Mayday! Skeeter's going down!" My aircraft had already made ten or twelve very fast clockwise turns, and I was getting dizzy. I shouted at the crew chief to unbuckle his harness and jump into the water, which was only two feet below. He screamed, "… swim!" but I couldn't understand what he was saying because he wasn't using the intercom. Then the dink on the nearby riverbank began shooting at us with an AK-47 and his bullets started hitting the helicopter as we spun around in circles.

The helicopter dropped into the river as I fought to keep it level. The rushing water hit the fuselage and pushed the aircraft over on its right side, where I sat. The main rotor blades hit the water and instantly exploded in all directions. Then I was underwater, rolling down the river, trapped in the dark and completely flooded helicopter. I tried to unhook my shoulder and lap harnesses, but couldn't because my flight jacket was jammed in the release! (Flight harnesses are made of two heavy nylon straps that go over each shoulder and attach to a lap belt at a single point.) As I frantically pulled on the harness release, I was choking on water, couldn't see anything, and couldn't breathe. For a moment, I thought, *I'm going to drown!* Then I remembered, reached down to my right boot, and pulled out the bayonet. With it, I was able to cut the lap belt loose, which released the shoulder harnesses. The whole time I was struggling to get out, the fuselage had been rolling and bouncing along the rocky river bottom. Once freed from the harnesses, I dropped the bayonet and tried swimming out, but realized the thirty-pound chicken plate strapped to my chest was preventing me from exiting the aircraft. I pulled the vest off and somehow got out of the cabin.

Once out, I started to swim to the top of the rushing water, but my leather combat boots, wet flight suit, and soggy flight jacket were dragging me down. I managed to pull off my boots, get out of my clothes, and swim to the surface where I started coughing violently and vomiting up water. I was being swiftly carried downstream by the strong river current, but managed to swim to some boulders near the right bank—the same side where the dink had been shooting at me.

After coughing, sputtering, and vomiting more water, I started to breathe better and crawled to the river bank wearing only my green army skivvies, T-shirt, one sock, and my dog tags. I couldn't see my helicopter or crew chief anywhere. I started to call out to him then remembered the dink shooting at us from somewhere upstream, not far from where I was. I crouched down in the cold water and looked around. There was dense vegetation and large rocks along the river's edge. I couldn't see or hear any of my Warlord team. I thought, *Man, I'm really screwed now: no clothes, no boots, no weapons, and no survival radio to call for help!*

I stayed there for a while and then from downstream, I heard the "wop, wop, wop" of an approaching Huey with its M-60 machine guns firing from each side. *Thank God!* I thought. They obviously were looking for me. As it sped past, going upstream, machine gun bullets began striking the vegetation and rocks all around where I was hunkered down. I could hear the two Cobras firing their miniguns somewhere upstream, near where I crashed.

As I looked around, I thought, *Great! How am I going to get out of this situation?* Then I heard the Huey coming back downstream, but this time not firing its machine guns. I quickly pulled off my white T-shirt and waited for the helicopter to fly nearby. As it got closer, I waded away from the shoreline to some big boulders and got ready to either duck down if they were shooting, or wave my T-shirt at them, if they weren't.

The Huey slowly came into view, flying low level over the middle of the river, coming toward me. Grasping the boulder with one hand, I frantically started waving my T-shirt back and forth with the other. The Huey was about fifty yards away when I saw the crew chief (who sits on the right side of the aircraft) point his machine gun straight at me and then a second later started waving his hand. He had seen me! I realized I was going to live, after all!

The aircraft, hovering just inches above the water, flew sideways over to me. The main rotor blades began to strike several small tree limbs hanging over the water. The pilot slowly continued moving until I was able to stand on the right skid and crawl onto the cargo bay floor. Inside, there were seven Warlord Animals pointing their M-16 rifles at me.

I cannot begin to describe the tremendous joy I felt at that moment! Cold and wet, I sat shivering on the metal floor as we took off downriver and began to gain altitude. I looked up at the pilot, who grinned and gave me thumbs up. I realized he was my hooch mate and close friend, Warrant Officer James T. Bateman a.k.a. Batman.

I put on a headset with a microphone and asked him if they had found my crew chief and helicopter. Batman looked at me and shook his head. "Can we go back upstream and look some more?" I asked. "No, there are too many NVA and VC camouflaged along the banks for us to search any longer. We were getting shot at continuously, searching for you, until Lead and "Two" rolled in and started firing their miniguns and rockets on either side of the river, where you crashed," he answered. "Have you seen *any* sign of my crew chief at all?" I asked. Batman shook his head again. "No, he didn't make it out of the Loach." Then he turned around, and we began to climb faster.

I asked him to let me talk to Lead. He nodded his head and flipped a toggle switch on the center console, so my mic was "hot". "Lead, let's go back to base. I'll get another Loach, and then we can come back and look for my crew chief," Lead quietly answered, "Skeeter, it's no use. It's getting dark; the river is too swift, and there are too many dinks with AK-47s on either side of the river where you went down." My heart sank, as I sat there a moment, and then said, "Roger that." Then Lead said, "Let's head home, guys."

As we flew back to Ky Ha heliport, SFC James Gordon, the Animals' platoon sergeant, handed me his field jacket because I was soaking wet, half naked, and shivering violently from the cold. I thanked him and put it on. I closed my eyes, lowered my head, and began to sob from overwhelming feelings of relief at being saved from such a harrowing ordeal, and immense grief and guilt at losing the young crew chief. After a while I stopped sobbing and lay down on the metal floor, bone weary. Everyone averted their eyes from me for the remainder of the ride back to our home base.

Once we landed, I went to my hooch, picked up some clothes, and headed to the showers. It was 1900 hours and dinner was still being served at the officers' club. I dressed and walked up there. When I entered the door, several friends came over to me, put their arms around my shoulders, and told me they were glad that I'd made it. "Thanks, but I need to be alone," I mumbled.

I got a food tray, went to a corner table, ate dinner, and drank a bottle of scotch by myself. I passed out at the table. Later, my friends carried me to my hooch and put me to bed.

The next afternoon, at HQ, I met with Major Maher; the XO, Capt. Barfield; and an old gray-haired Hughes Aircraft,

Inc. civilian field rep. I told them the details of the crash. After discussing the loading of the aircraft with me, the field rep said that I undoubtedly had exceeded the maximum gross weight of the Loach, and that was what caused the "Hughes spin." I told him the loading for that flight was the same as on all the previous flights, with no problems encountered. He looked at me, "Son, you have been very lucky in the past. Yesterday, your luck ran out!" I was so angry at the guy I was ready to punch him and jumped up. Captain Barfield quickly stood up in front of me and said, "Corvin, it's okay. But I want you to go to the infirmary and let the flight surgeon take a look at you. After a couple of days of rest, you can go back to flying VRs if the doc thinks you're okay." I reluctantly said, "Yes, sir."

I left headquarters, went to the infirmary, and got checked out. Physically, I was okay; however, mentally I was a wreck! Gradually, with the consumption of lots of alcohol, I was able to suppress my feelings. But I never was the same again. I became sullen, withdrawn, angry, and depressed. I stayed that way for many years.

For the next week, although I was shot at repeatedly, I flew VRs along the river with the Warlord team, but never found the helicopter wreckage or the crew chief's body. Finally, we moved on to other AOs and stopped searching.

Over the past forty-nine years, I have often wondered what the crew chief said when I told him to jump out of the helicopter and into the river. I now believe he was screaming, "I can't swim!" (As I write this, I feel an intense sense of sadness and am choked up.) What a horrible way to die. But at least now he's with his band of brothers!

Soon, the hooch mate who saved me, Warrant Officer James T. Bateman and ten others, including SFC Gordon, would join their ghostly band of brothers too! But that's another story and chapter in this book.

CHAPTER 23

GRENADE PROBLEM

While flying VRs, the crew chief occasionally used an M-79 grenade launcher to shoot at targets. The M-79 was a single-shot, shoulder-fired, break-action grenade launcher that fired a 40mm (1.75 inch) grenade. The crew chief, sitting behind me, always carried the gun in his wooden box with the fragmentation grenades, ammo, and other paraphernalia. The launcher looked like a big sawed-off shotgun with a fifteen-inch long single barrel that was one and three-quarters inches in diameter. It broke open like a single shot shotgun and then a grenade round was inserted. The recoil was similar to a shotgun. The minimum arming range of the grenade was ninety feet. Its blast radius was the same as a fragmentation grenade, i.e., ten to fifteen yards.

One morning, while flying on a routine VR, the crew chief asked me if he could fire the M-79 to see how it performed when shot from the helicopter. "Sure, let's try it out," I said. He put his machine gun down, got the grenade launcher out, and fired at a rock on the hillside a hundred yards away. The effective range was about three hundred fifty meters. When the gun went off, it made a sound something like "whomp." It wasn't as loud as I thought it would be; however, when the grenade hit the ground it exploded with the force of a fragmentation grenade. As we flew along in an open area, the crew chief practiced shooting at various targets. Then he said, "Sir, I see somebody off to the right about a hundred yards!" I immediately made a hard right turn in order to aim the minigun, which dropped the rotor blades almost to ground level. As I did, I heard the grenade launcher go "whomp" and the crew chief say, "Oh, no! Sir, I just fired a grenade through the rotor system!" When he said that, I suddenly felt a heavy vibration in the cyclic stick that meant the rotor blades were significantly out of balance. The Loach was now shaking so violently I could not read any of the instruments on the panel. *This is not good!* I thought.

I called Lead and told him what had just happened and that I needed to land the aircraft immediately. Suddenly, from the tree line where the crew chief had seen somebody, several NVA started firing AK-47's at me. I turned the Loach away to avoid getting hit by the bullets. I was barely able to maintain flight control of the Loach because of the violent shaking. "Skeeter, can you make it back to Duc Pho?" Lead asked. "I think so, if this thing holds together that long," I answered.

"It's about twenty minutes away. Stay low level and land if you have to. But we need to get away from these hills and mountains, into open country, so the Animals can set up a defensive perimeter around you if you have to land in the boonies!" "Roger that," I replied.

I got on the intercom with the crew chief and told him to put the M-79 in the box, secure his M-60 machinegun, and hold on. "Sir, I already have," he replied. "Be sure to sit in the middle of the cargo bay and don't dangle your legs out the right door, in case we crash and roll the Loach up in a ball!" I said. "I'm really sorry, sir," he rather sheepishly said. "It's okay. I'll try to get us home," I told him. I kept the airspeed at fifty mph and flew back to the staging airfield wondering what was going to happen when I shut the engine down, and the rotor blades stopped turning.

Lead called me saying. "Skeeter, I've talked to the airfield tower and they've instructed me to have you land alone in one of the open fields, next to the runway, away from any other aircraft. Once you shut the engine down, you and the crew chief need to get away from the Loach immediately at least a hundred yards!" "Roger that, Lead, but what about my aircraft?" I asked. "The control tower's calling EOD (explosive ordinance detail) people right now and they'll be waiting for you when you land. They will see if there's a live grenade lodged in one of your rotor blades. It may be that the blades are just severely damaged, and that's what is causing the vibration." I double clicked the transmitter button, which meant that I understood. I continued to fly with the helicopter shaking badly. Frankly, I expected it to fly apart at any second, but I knew the "egg" shape of the Loach would probably protect us if we crashed. At least I hoped so!

Soon, I saw the hill overlooking the runway at Duc Pho and the control tower. Lead and the Huey's were behind me about a half-mile at fifteen hundred feet altitude. He called me and said "The tower has cleared the flight pattern and runway of other aircraft, and you can land perpendicular to its heading in the open field nearby." "Roger," I replied. On the intercom, I told the crew chief, "Once I land in the open field, I want you to jump out and run like hell away from the Loach at least a hundred yards." His only comment was, "Yes, sir."

As I approached the field, I could see several vehicles standing by with two fire trucks next to them. I flew between the guard towers and over the concertina wire (surrounding the base perimeter) and hovered to the middle of the open field. I got on the intercom and told the crew chief, "When the skids touch down, I want you to jump out and run to the fire trucks." He said he would. I gently descended until the skids were on the ground. I yelled, "Go!" and the crew chief took off running.

I unbuckled my lap belt and shoulder harnesses. Then I called Lead and said, "As soon as I shut down the engine, I'm going to exit the Loach and get away from it while the blades are still spinning." He said, "Okay, we are going to park in the revetments next to the runway and come over to the fire trucks." I told him I would meet him there. I turned the fuel system off, tightened the collective down, climbed out of the helicopter, and quickly walked away while the blades were still turning.

Walking to the vehicles and the fire trucks, I saw the two Cobras and Hueys were on short final to the runway. There were several people talking to the crew chief when I arrived. An ordinance branch first lieutenant walked over to me and said, "This has got to be a first for us. We've disarmed all sorts of bombs and booby-traps but never have we had to remove a grenade from a helicopter blade!" I looked at him, laughed and said, "Just think about the stories you'll be able to tell all the people back in the world." He replied, "You know something, I hadn't thought of that. You're right!"

In a few minutes, all the pilots and Animals from the Warlord team walked over. Captain Gordy Hines (who was Lead) came over to me, and in his best Stan Laurel and Oliver Hardy imitation said, "Stanley, look at the fine mess you've gotten us into this time." I said, "Of course, Ollie!" and grinned.

By now, the Loach's rotor blades had stopped turning, and I asked the EOD lieutenant what they were going to do. He said, "We have an M-114 armored personnel carrier (APC) that will be here in a minute, and we then can go see what we're dealing with." I said, "We need to take the crew chief along because he's responsible for the maintenance of the Loach." Gordy said, "I'll go too so that I can report back to Major Maher. He's already been told about the incident." I looked at him, and he said, "Two called HQ and told the CO what was going on." I said, "Okie Dokie." The APC pulled up next to us and lowered the rear ramp. The driver came over and said that he would take us over to the Loach, next to the blades, so we could see them up close. He was laughing as he said this. I could tell that pretty much everybody at the airfield knew what was going on.

We climbed into the APC, sat down, and the driver raised the ramp. When we got near the Loach, the driver said to me, "If you will open the top hatch, there's a bulletproof guard that protects the .50-caliber machine gun when it's mounted. You should be able to see the rotor blades because they're the same height as the top of the APC."

He stopped the vehicle. I went over to the hatch, pulled the release, and the spring-loaded door popped open. Carefully, I stuck my head out to look at the four blades that were about six feet away. At first I couldn't see anything wrong. Then I saw the grenade projectile embedded in the titanium-covered leading edge of the blade that was directly over the tail. It was located halfway between the tip of the blade and the rotor hub. I asked Gordy to come see, which he did. "Will you look at that!" he said. "What can we do?" I asked. "I have no idea!" he replied. "Do you think the grenade is armed?" I asked. "I really don't know," he answered. We drove back to where the fire trucks and other vehicles were located and got out. I asked the ordinance lieutenant if he knew anything about an M-79 grenade projectiles. "I think it has to travel some distance away from the barrel before it is armed," He said. "How far?" I asked. "I don't know, but I'll find out," he replied.

He went to his Jeep and called his headquarters on the radio. After a few minutes, he came back and said, "It has to travel about eighty to ninety feet before it's armed. But with it hitting the blade and embedding on the leading edge, I don't know if it's armed or not. We have to assume it's armed and can explode at any time or somebody could really get hurt." "Let's get our maintenance section to come here and remove the blade," Gordy said. "We can pull the APC under the blades and pile sandbags around the projectile to protect your people while they work to remove the blade," The lieutenant said.

Gordy and I agreed that would probably work, so he went back to his Cobra to use the UHF radio to call maintenance. A few minutes later he came back and said they were already on their way. He laughed and said, "Corvin, you will never live this down, I promise you that!" We caught a ride with the lieutenant who took us up to the officers' club where we ate lunch. My crew chief and the Animals stayed with the choppers and had C-rats. After lunch, we drove back to the fire trucks just in time to see the APC driving over to the Loach.

When it got next to the rotor blades, a guy stuck his head out of the hatch and slowly rotated them until the one with the embedded projectile was parallel to the tail rotor. The driver moved the APC under the blade as one of the ordinance guys held it up with a pole. Gently, he set the blade down on the roof of the tracked vehicle. Then one by one he slowly began to pile green colored sandbags on the blade on either side of the grenade.

In a few minutes, he had sandbags piled two feet high. We saw the rear ramp slowly drop to the ground. An EOD First Sergeant came strolling over to us and said, "It's all yours, sir. Just tell the mechanics to approach the aircraft on the opposite side of the sandbags so that if the grenade explodes, they'll be protected."

The Warlord maintenance Huey had flown in while we were at lunch. The officer in charge (OIC) went over to the mechanics, talked for a few minutes, and then they carried a couple of ladders with their tools to the Loach. In less than forty-five minutes, they had the blade detached from the hub—a record time for removing a blade!

The driver gently backed the APC away from the Loach, which suddenly freed the blade from the aircraft. He slowly maneuvered his tracked vehicle about a quarter of a mile away to the perimeter concertina. When he got there, he lowered the rear ramp, and the EOD lieutenant got out with a coil of heavy wire in his hands. Being careful to walk up to the blade from behind the sandbags, he attached one end of the wire to the blade and then tied the other end to a stake holding up part of the concertina wire. After the lieutenant got in the APC, the APC driver slowly backed away until the wire was extended to its full length, about a hundred feet. Then he began to inch backward, and the blade began to slide to the edge of the APC. Suddenly, the driver gunned it, and the blade fell to the ground and lay there. He drove back over to us and said, "It doesn't look like the grenade was armed." Then we heard a loud "whoomp" and saw a dirt cloud, and parts of the blade fly up into the air. Everybody started laughing, and I thought, *Yeah, right!*

The mechanics had brought an extra Loach blade with them and installed it in about an hour. The OIC got in the helicopter, started it, and they balanced the blades. When he shut the aircraft down, the crew chief and I went over to him, and he said, "It seems to be working fine. You can have it now. But take it easy coming back to Key Ha and land at the maintenance hangar so we can make sure you didn't shake something loose."

I assured him that I would be careful and then turned to the crew chief and told him to pull all the inspection panels and do a very thorough preflight check. The crew chief looked down and said, "Yes, sir. I'm sorry for all the trouble I've caused." I laughed and told him, "But think of the story you'll have to tell everyone back in the world!" I could tell that he was relieved I wasn't angry at him, and that he wasn't going to get into trouble.

I said to him, "I want you to ride in one of the slicks going back to the base." He protested, but I was adamant that only I was going to fly in the Loach. I walked over to Gordy and told him what the maintenance officer had said about taking it easy flying the Loach. Gordy said that they would slowly follow me back to Key Ha. After the pre-flight was finished, everyone returned to their aircraft and we headed for home. Watching the sun set as I was flying alone along the beach, I chuckled to myself and thought, *What an adventure!*

All in all, it'd been an interesting day and, as they say, *A good time was had by all - well almost!*

CHAPTER 24

CHINA NIGHT BAR & SKY PILOT

While flying with the Rattlers, I met Command Sergeant Major George A. Vidrine, the senior noncommissioned officer (NCO) for 5th Special Forces (SF) headquartered in Danang. He was forty-five years old and from Port Arthur, TX. He had a son who attended the Virginia Military Institute (VMI) and was very proud that his son was about to graduate as a second lieutenant. He said he wasn't sure how he would feel about having to salute his son, after having changed his dirty diapers when he was a baby! He told me that I reminded him a lot of his son. I took that as a compliment. The Sergeant Major and I soon became good friends.

Many times we flew him to the 5th Special Forces compounds as we headed to our free-fire zone AOs nearby. He met there with the Mnong and the Degar, also known as Montagnards (A French term meaning Mountain People). Both of these minority groups were despised by the Vietnamese population because of ongoing conflicts dating back to the 9th century. Neither group spoke Vietnamese—only their own language derived primarily from Malaysian-Polynesian and Khmer origins.

American Protestant missionaries converted most of them

to Christianity in 1930, which made the Communist Party suspicious of them during the Vietnam War since they thought the Montagnards would be more inclined to help the American forces who were predominately Christian (mainly Protestant). And the "Commies" were right.

Military Command Vietnam (MACV) and the CIA sponsored the training of these two groups in unconventional warfare by American Special Forces. Because the Ho Chi Minh Trail was near their mountain compounds, both groups fought alongside American soldiers and became a major part of the U.S. military effort against the NVA and VC. The Montagnards were ruthless guerrilla fighters and were very adept at ambushing enemy troops along the trail. They enjoyed beheading fallen enemy soldiers (dead or alive!) and impaling the heads on sticks stuck in the middle of the trail. That practice was more intimidating than dropping Aces of Spade cards on bodies as I always did.

Whenever I saw the Sergeant Major, he always came up to me, shook my hand, and warned me to be careful flying Loaches. I assured him that I would. On several occasions, while waiting for Lead to finish up his discussions with the SF commanders, I would fly the Sergeant Major around the mountain top bases in my Loach. He enjoyed sitting in the open door (where the crew chief usually sat) and shooting at rocks and other targets on the ground. Other times, he would take me to the edge of a base perimeter and would let me shoot various machine guns and suppressed weapons including a small, 9mm Swedish K sub-machine gun. (That's what I carried with me when I flew on my second Vietnam tour.)

One day, while flying with me, he asked if I would like to join him and a group of Special Forces personnel for a "counterpart" function at a Chinese restaurant in downtown

Danang. I said, "Great, I would really like that," but had no idea what a "counterpart" was! He said that he would call my First Sergeant when he knew the date and time. I told him that I would ask my CO for permission when I got back to Chu Lai that evening. Lead called me on the radio and said they were ready, so I took the Sgt. Major back and dropped him off.

We flew a routine mission in our AO and then returned back to Key Ha heliport. I saw Maj. Maher at the officers' club having dinner and asked him if I could attend the SF party in Danang. He looked at me and said, "How did you swing an invitation to party with the Special Forces guys?"

I told him about flying the Sergeant Major around in the Loach and letting him shoot the M-60 machinegun out the side door. He laughed and said, "Okay! You can help with our relationship with the SF guys by doing this." He also warned me not to do anything stupid or get into trouble that would make him, or the Warlords, look bad. I assured him that I would not. He told me that as soon as he heard from the Sgt. Major, he would make sure I was not scheduled to fly for two days, and that I could take a Loach to the 5th Special Forces headquarters, located on China Beach. I was very excited about going!

In about a week, a clerk from Warlord HQ came to my hooch and said that I was to go to Danang in two days. I thought *This is going to be such fun!* I didn't realize that soon I would become embroiled in a standoff involving twenty lightly-armed American Military Police (MP's) against two hundred thoroughly pissed-off, heavily-armed Mnong and Montagnard guerrilla fighters.

At noon on the following day, I loaded my overnight bag in the Loach and flew to Danang about fifty-five miles north of Chu Lai. The 5th Special Forces' compound was located on China Beach next to Marble Mountain and the airfield. It had its own defensive perimeter with concertina wire and elevated guard towers for protection. The trip took about thirty minutes to reach the Special Forces camp heliport. When I landed, the Sergeant Major pulled up next to the Loach in a jeep and came over and shook my hand, saying, "Glad you could make it. It'll be fun. I think you'll enjoy the evening, Stan." (He always called me "Stan," and I always called him "Sergeant Major!")

Command Sergeant Major George Albert Vidrine was a living legend in the 5th Special Forces. At the age of fifteen, after lying about how old he was, he enlisted in the Texas National Guard in 1939. He received his army training at Camp Bowie in Austin, Texas. Five years later, he was one of the first soldiers to land on Omaha Beach (in Normandy, France) on D-Day during World War II. After the war had ended, he was discharged as a sergeant and returned to Texas where he finished high school, graduated from college, and got married. He re-enlisted in the Army in 1950, and was assigned to Fort Bragg with the 82nd Airborne Division. He went to Korea with the 4th Airborne Ranger Company in 1951, and was wounded twice during two combat tours while there. In 1965, he went to Vietnam on his first tour of duty. He was wounded twice and sent to the Philippines to recover.

He spent two more tours in country as the Command Sergeant Major for the 5th Special Forces in Danang. During his career, he was awarded the Army Distinguished Service Cross, one Silver Star, six Bronze Stars, ten Purple Hearts, six Air Medals and the Legion of Merit. He died in 2004, at the age of eighty, from cancer caused by his exposure to Agent Orange in Vietnam. (What enemy bullets could not do, chemical agents did!) He was a very humble man and truly a great American hero.

He was a good friend of mine, whom I admired and respected tremendously.

After he took me to their air-conditioned VIP quarters to drop off my overnight bag, the Sergeant Major and I went to their Special Forces Officers/NCO club. It was early afternoon, and only a few people were there. The place was very well-outfitted with plush chairs and couches around the central floor which had about a dozen tables. The bar was huge and on the wall, over the bottles of liquor, was a giant anaconda skin about three feet wide and twenty feet long. He told me the snake had been killed after attacking an SF soldier who was hidden in the jungle while on a long-range patrol with four other soldiers. He said the guys had been concealed at night while waiting to ambush enemy troops coming up a footpath. The snake weighed about two hundred pounds. In order not to give away their position, two other SF guys crawled over to the soldier that was being crushed by the anaconda and silently stabbed it to death with their K-bar knives. Later, after the ambush, they left the bodies of the NVA and VC, but recovered the dead snake. They brought it back to the SF compound, skinned it, dried the skin, and then nailed the skin to the wall. He said the Mnong and Montagnard guerrilla fighters ate the snake leftovers—a delicacy to them they did not want to waste! We sat in the cool, dimly lit bar talking and drinking beer.

The door opened, and several Special Forces guys walked in and came over to where the Sergeant Major and I were sitting. He introduced me to everybody including the "A" team leader who was an African-American major named Jackson. Jackson was rugged looking and very big—probably six foot six inches and weighing two hundred seventy-five pounds. He had spent the last six months living in the field (meaning in the jungle) with several companies of Mnong and Montagnard guerrilla fighters. Their sole objective was to ambush NVA and VC soldiers silently at night and without being detected. This long-term mission bonded Major Jackson with all the indigenous fighters to the point where they would follow him into *Hell* without hesitation. Because of his size and the color of his skin, which was similar to theirs, they viewed him as a *god* to be trusted implicitly.

We sat drinking beer until late in the afternoon with the SF guys telling war stories about their recent experiences. They asked me what I did flying helicopters, and I explained about the low-level flying and shooting NVA and VC with the minigun. They all agreed they never wanted to do that. I told them I never wanted to do what they did. There was mutual respect between us.

After a while, Command Sergeant Major Vidrine looked at his watch and said, "It's time for everyone to get cleaned up and head to the restaurant in downtown Danang. Let's all meet in front of HQ in forty-five minutes, and we will convoy down there in jeeps and pickups." Everyone left, and I went back to the VIP quarters to get ready and put on a clean flight suit. (Military personnel were not allowed off base in civilian clothes.) I walked over to HQ and soon about a half-dozen SF guys, including Major Jackson, showed up. Then about a dozen Mnong and Montagnard senior commanders arrived to go with us. They were the counterparts with whom we were going to have dinner. Because of their ethnicity they were not allowed in the Vietnamese restaurant except in the company of the Special Forces personnel. (Sort of like the American south in the 50s.)

Just before sunset, we arrived at the restaurant appropriately called the *China Night Restaurant and Bar.* After parking the jeeps and the pickups in a secure area, guarded by Vietnamese soldiers wearing "QC" armbands (signifying they were MPs), we walked into the restaurant, which was lavishly decorated with red and gold Chinese lanterns and furnishings. In the back were several tables pulled together with white table cloths on top, and seating for about twenty people. Major Jackson sat at the head of the table with the Sergeant Major and me on one side and the other SF guys arranged opposite to us. The counterparts all sat around the rest of the table.

Soon, several waitresses came over carrying large trays of Vietnamese Ba Muoi Ba beer (pronounced Ba Me Ba) that tasted a lot like Shiner Bock beer from Shiner, Texas, and was kind of "skunky." The American GIs called it "Tiger Piss." (After hearing that name I didn't want to know how they made the beer.) They served the cold beer to everybody sitting at the table. Soon everybody was talking, laughing, and having a good time. Two waiters came over to Major Jackson and in Vietnamese discussed the food that had been previously ordered. The major spoke fluent Vietnamese with them.

I learned that he also spoke fluent Cantonese Chinese, Russian, French, German, and the Malaysian-Polynesian and Khmer dialects the counterparts spoke. He was a 1960 West Point graduate, born in a little town near Tupelo, Mississippi. He had a bachelor's degree in chemical engineering and a Master's degree in International Studies. He was working on his Ph.D. in economics. He was a very intelligent man!

Once the food had arrived at the table, he stood up, raised his beer bottle, and spoke to the Mnong and Montagnard guerrilla fighters. They instantly jumped up and raised their beer bottles too. As the major was speaking, a young American MP second lieutenant, with two MP Sergeants, walked in the front door and came over to our tables in the back of the restaurant. They stood there silently while the major was speaking.

When he was finished the second lieutenant said, "Everyone, please sit down, I need to talk to you." Everyone did as they were asked, except the Major. He said, "Son, you need to get out of here and leave us alone!" The lieutenant replied, "Sir, this restaurant is off-limits, and you all have to leave immediately." The Major walked over to him and said "Lieutenant, this is a counterpart function, and we will leave when the party is over."

With that, the lieutenant said, "Sir, may I speak with you outside?" The major looked at him in disgust and said, "You better get out of here right now, lieutenant!" The MPs stood there a moment not saying anything and then left the restaurant.

About fifteen minutes later, we heard vehicle tires screech to a stop in the front of the restaurant. The doors opened and in walked six really big MPs, carrying large white night sticks, and led by their battalion commander, a U.S. Army colonel wearing a Ranger tab on his left shoulder and jump wings over his left pocket.

He walked over to Major Jackson and said, "You are all under arrest and are coming with me right now!" Major Jackson said, "Let's go outside, Colonel, and talk about this." The colonel turned to his men and said, "Put this major in handcuffs and then in the back of my car." The major stood silently there as they handcuffed him. When the counterparts saw what was happening, they jumped up and started speaking rapidly in their dialect. The major started shaking his head vigorously and spoke to them for several minutes. They left the restaurant and only the MPs, SF personnel, and I remained.

The MP colonel told us to get in our vehicles and follow him to his headquarters. We all walked out of the restaurant. Major Jackson, with his hands handcuffed behind him, was put in the back of the colonel's car.

We drove for about fifteen minutes and then came to the MP headquarters inside a high-walled compound with two large steel reinforced doors at the entrance and concertina wire strung all around the top. As we were driving, I told the Sergeant Major that I had applied to the Department of Army for a direct commission to commissioned officer and hoped this incident would not hurt my chances of getting it. He assured me that any correspondence relating to the matter would come across his desk, and he would take care of it. Then he said, "Don't worry about it, Stan, everything is going to be okay." He said it with such confidence that I believed him.

The two large metal front doors swung open, and all the vehicles drove into a big courtyard area with several MP jeeps and cars parked around the sides. Then the doors were shut. The Sergeant Major and I got out of the jeep and walked inside the headquarters office. Two MPs walked over to us, told us to sit down, and asked for our military IDs. Then they walked to the other SF guys and did the same. After a while, they came back and gave us our IDs after writing down all of the information. The office had no air conditioning and we were hot so the Sergeant Major asked if we could go outside where it was cooler. The MP Staff Duty Officer (SDO) said that would be okay, but not to leave the compound. We went outside in the cool night air. "Don't worry, Stan, it'll be okay," the Sergeant Major said again.

As we were standing there, we heard several heavy trucks coming down the street to the entrance of the MP headquarters. The steel doors were closed, barring entrance to anyone outside. Then we heard the trucks stop at the doors, followed by loud banging on them from outside. We could hear loud voices yelling in the street, but not in the Vietnamese language. "What's going on now?" the Sergeant Major said. The two MP guards at the front gates looked through a peephole in the steel doors, turned around, and started running to the entrance of their headquarters. I thought *This can't be good!* Within a couple of minutes, twenty MPs armed with M-16s began running out the front door and formed a semi-circle around the two steel reinforced doors with their weapons pointed at them.

The MP colonel came outside and walked over to the peephole in one of the doors. He stood there a moment, then turned and came back to where the MPs had formed a semi-circle. He told a captain to unlock the doors and swing them open. When he did that, we could see two big deuce and half trucks backed up to the MP entrance with their tailgates down. Inside each was a manned .50-caliber machine gun mounted on a tripod pointing at us. In the truck, behind the 50-cal's, were Mnong and Montagnard guerrilla fighters dressed in full battle gear pointing their M1 carbines at us. Then from either side of the trucks more of them ran around and knelt down and pointed their weapons at us too.

Apparently the counterpart commanders had rushed back to the Special Forces compound and loaded up two hundred of the guerrilla fighters living there. All of them drove to the MP headquarters to demand the release of Major Jackson. The MPs were outnumbered ten to one. The guerrilla fighters not only had the 50-caliber machine guns, but five of them were holding shoulder-fired light antitank weapons (LAW) capable of penetrating three inches of steel!

Sergeant Major Vidrine told me not to move, and then he slowly walked over to where the Mnong and Montagnard guerrilla fighters' commanders were standing. He said something to them, turned, and walked over to the colonel, who had drawn his .45-caliber automatic pistol. They talked for a few minutes and then the colonel went inside his office. A few minutes later, he came back outside with Major Jackson walking in front without handcuffs. The major walked over to the counterpart commanders and spoke to them at length in their language. When he finished, the commanders turned around to their soldiers, yelled something, and everybody loaded up in the trucks and left. (I started to breathe again at that point.) The major walked back into the headquarters with the MP colonel. After the trucks had left, the gates were closed, and the contingent of MPs filed back inside leaving me outside.

Soon, Major Jackson and the other SF personnel walked out of the headquarters building and told us to get in our vehicles and go back to their headquarters. We left together and drove back to Marble Mountain. On the way back, Sergeant Major Vidrine assured me that this incident would in no way affect my receiving a direct commission. Then he said with a laugh, "I told you it was going to be fun, didn't I, Stan?" I replied, "You were absolutely right, Sergeant Major!"

The next morning I had breakfast with the Sergeant Major and several of the Special Forces NCOs that worked with him. We talked about the MP incident the night before, and I laughingly said it was an event that would stay with me the rest of my life. After we had finished eating, I told the Sergeant Major that I needed to head back to Chu Lai. He told me that he would pick me up at the VIP quarters and drive me to my Loach. I went and gathered up all my gear, then went outside and waited. In a few minutes, he drove up with a passenger sitting in the right side of the jeep. Sergeant Major came up to me and introduced me to the passenger who was a U.S. Army major who was a Baptist chaplain. In Vietnam, members of the chaplain corps were called "Sky Pilots."

The chaplain said to me, "I understand you are flying back to Chu Lai. Can I hitch a ride with you to the Americal Division Headquarters on Freedom Hill? I said, "Yes, sir, I'll be happy to drop you off there." He laughed and then said, "You will land first, won't you? I grinned and said, "Well, maybe!" I thought that he was a pretty cool guy. The Sergeant Major took us to my Loach, and we put our gear in the back. I shook hands with him and said "I appreciate you inviting me to the counterpart function, Sergeant Major, it was "really" fun like you said it would be!"

He said, "We'll have to do it again soon." I replied "Not that soon, please. I'm still shaky from last night!" The chaplain also thanked him, and they shook hands.

When I met Chaplain Frank McLeod at the jeep he was wearing a steel pot on his head, web gear shoulder harness with extra M-16 magazines pouches, and a forty-five automatic in a holster on his belt. He was carrying a small bag (presumably with extra clothes) and a bag with his communion paraphernalia. He was also holding an M-16 rifle. He got out of his web gear and secured it in the back of the helicopter, then climbed in the front left seat and strapped in.

I started the engine, called Marble Mountain tower, and told them I was departing the 5th Special Forces compound and was heading south. They cleared me, and we took off flying over the beach to Chu Lai and Americal headquarters. As we were flying, I told him about the missions I flew with the Warlords and how rewarding it was being involved in the day-to-day killing of NVA and VC soldiers. "Isn't it dangerous to be flying on the low-level missions? he asked. "I suppose it is, but my minigun is the great equalizer!" I replied.

Then I asked Chaplain McLeod why he was wearing the steel pot, web gear, and carrying a sidearm and an M-16. "I thought the Chaplain Corps could not carry weapons," I said. He answered "We are not supposed to; however, several weeks ago I spent the night in the field with a bunch of soldiers that had set up a defensive perimeter on a hill. In the evening, we ate our "C" rations, and I performed communion for them. Later, after dark, I lay down on my poncho to sleep. About 0300 hours, I heard shooting, screaming, and then all "heck" broke loose. The VC had managed to crawl into one of the perimeter foxholes and killed the two GIs in a there. Somebody saw them and started shooting.

"That's when everybody but me crawled to the perimeter defensive positions and a firefight began in earnest. All I could do was stay low on the ground as bullets and mortars began to impact in the middle of the defensive area. I began to pray that I would survive the night and vowed if I did, I would never go out in the field again unarmed. That's why I carry all the gear!" I asked, "Doesn't the Geneva Convention forbid chaplains from carrying weapons?" He answered, "It does, but what are they going to do to me if I'm caught, *send me to Vietnam?*" Then he started laughing.

I laughed too and said, "So, let me get this straight. Are you going to kill a Commie for Christ?" He looked at me, smiled, and said, "Absolutely, if I have to." I told him, "Right on, Padre, right on!"

By then we were approaching the Americal HQ, and I landed but kept the engine running. He unbuckled his seatbelt and got out of the left seat and came around to my side of the aircraft. He yelled, "It's been a pleasure. I hope we can fly again." Then he shouted, "Son, are you a Christian?" I said, "Yes, sir, I've been baptized twice, so I guess I am." He put his left hand on my shoulder and loudly said, "Will you let me pray for you?" I said

"No, sir! I don't need you to because my rod and my staff they comfort me, and they're called an M-134 GE powered minigun!" He grimaced, shook his head, put on his gear, waved at me and walked up the hill.

I flew back to Key Ha heliport, landed and went to headquarters. Only Capt. Barfield was there, and he asked, "How was the SF party?" I said, "It was so much fun that I'll never forget it." And to this day I haven't!

CHAPTER 25

B-52 ARC LIGHT RECON

At an 0500 hours briefing in the TOC one morning, the operations officer announced that in two hours, at 0700 hours, a three-plane cell of B-52s planned to bomb an area along the Ho Chi Minh Trail. The target area was in our AO and the Air Force asked us to perform a bomb damage assessment (BDA) and let them know what we found. They had called just an hour before to let us know about the Arc Light bombing run. The briefing officer said we would have just enough time to get to the area if we left immediately.

Since the aircraft are all pre-flighted by the crew chiefs, the pilots, including me, ran to the helicopters and started them. Lead got flight clearance from the Key Ha tower, and I backed out of my revetment and took off south along the beach. Within minutes, the two Cobras and three Hueys had climbed to their altitudes and were behind me. I climbed to fifteen hundred feet, got on the radio, "Lead, what's the plan?" "Skeeter, let's go directly to the Arc Light target area and once we are near, I'll call the Air Force guys and let them know we're ready to go in and perform the BDA once the bombs have been dropped." He then gave me a heading to fly directly to the target.

I've mentioned before that the B-52s dropped their bombs from above thirty thousand feet, and the jets could barely be seen and could not be heard because of the altitude. Consequently, when the two hundred seventy thousand pounds of bombs struck the ground, they were a complete surprise as they made no sound falling from that height. One second was a normal cool morning in the target area and then suddenly the world erupted with over a quarter of a million pounds of explosives hitting the ground. The bomb track usually was about a quarter of a mile wide and two miles long with everything obliterated in that area.

As we neared the western edge of the free-fire zone that was one of our AOs, Lead called me saying, "Skeeter, we need to hold in a daisy chain pattern for about ten minutes while the bombers arrive and drop their payload." I said, "Roger that. I'll begin a right-hand turn now." Within a few minutes, all six helicopters were flying in a large right-handed circle. After about twenty minutes, Lead called me and said "Skeeter, the bombs will strike the target in one minute. You'll have no trouble knowing when they hit because you'll see the blasts." We were about ten miles away from the target just as a safety precaution.

Suddenly in the distance I saw bright flashes as the bombs began to strike the ground and could hear the rumble of the bomb blasts. Then a giant invisible concussion wave began to move through the jungle towards us, which dissipated before reaching our flight.

"Alright, Skeeter, go ahead into the area and see what you can find," Lead said. As I flew to the bomb target area, there were still giant clouds of dust and dirt up in the air. I began my descent in my usual spiraling right turn until I was over the jungle tops a few hundred yards away from where the bombs had first hit. I armed my minigun and told the crew chief we were about to enter the blast area. "How many boxes of Aces of Spades do you have?" I asked him. "I have about fifteen," he replied. I thought about that a moment, then realized that I only had about twenty decks of cards left in my hooch. I told the crew chief, "We are running low, so let's disperse them carefully if we find any bodies." He said, "Yes, sir, will do!"

As I entered the blast area, the clouds of dust began to settle, and I could see debris from the forest and jungle lying all around the ground. I got on the radio saying, "Lead, what am I supposed to be looking for?" He replied, "Skeeter, all they told me was there will be multiple large underground structures that contained an NVA division headquarters." I said, "Okay, I'll keep looking." Then in an open area in front of me, I saw nine standing figures totally covered in dirt.

As I flew over them, I could see blood coming out their ears, noses, and mouths. They made no movement to hide when I flew over them. When I came back around, I could see they were wearing NVA green and khaki uniforms, but carried no weapons or helmets. As I approached, I realized they couldn't hear me, probably because their ear drums were burst from the bomb concussions. I hovered down thirty feet in front of them, and they all looked up at my face. I deliberately smiled widely and pulled the minigun trigger killing all of the enemy soldiers. The crew chief got on the intercom "Sir, there are more dinks crawling out of a mound of dirt to the right." When he began to fire his M-60 machine-gun, I circled to the right and said, "Lead, I am starting to find people crawling out of piles of rubble totally covered in dirt and without any weapons." He said, "Skeeter, it's kind of like shooting fish in a barrel, isn't it?" I replied, "A dirt barrel!" He keyed the mic and laughed, saying, "Go get them, Skeeter!" And I did.

For the next hour, I continually fired my minigun at dirt-covered NVA soldiers as they crawled and walked away from their destroyed headquarters. I told my crew chief to spread out only a few Aces of Spades over each of the bodies. At the end of fifty-five minutes, I was out of ammunition (five thousand rounds), and he had gone through fifteen hundred rounds of his M-60 ammo.

He got on the intercom, "Sir, that's the last of the playing cards, and I'm out of ammo." "That's okay, I'm out too," I answered. I called Lead and said, "We are out of ammo and need to return to Duc Pho to rearm." He and the other pilots had been watching me kill the enemy soldiers for almost an hour without receiving any return fire from them. Lead said, "Go ahead and climb up to altitude and we will head back to rearm. Then we will return." I said, "Roger," and began to climb to fifteen hundred feet to head back to our staging area. On the way back, Lead asked, "Skeeter, how many NVA soldiers do you think you killed?" I answered, "I don't know, but we used up all my Aces of Spades and threw out only a few over each group of bodies I shot." He said, "How many boxes of cards did you have." I told him fifteen. In a moment, he got on the radio and said, "Way to go, Skeeter! Maybe you can add more to your total when we return from rearming." I responded, "I sure hope so."

After rearming and refueling, we headed back out to the Arc Light bombing run. When I could see the blast area, I began my descent and armed my minigun. Once I was at a low level, I began making my usual S-turns looking for more NVA "targets of opportunity." By now, several hours had passed since the bombs had first hit, so the dust and dirt had completely settled to the ground.

As I flew low level around the area, I found many of the bodies of the soldiers I had just killed with Aces of Spades scattered about them. I spent about forty-five minutes on the recon, but found only two more NVA soldiers both slightly wounded and unarmed. As I flew past them, my crew chief asked, "Sir, can I shoot them? I said, "Sure, go ahead." I then turned the aircraft for him to have a clear shot. He fired a long burst from his M-60 machine gun and both of the enemy soldiers fell to the ground. As I flew over their bodies, I saw that both were wearing NVA green pith helmets and had officer ranks on their epaulets. I said to the crew chief, "Do you want a souvenir?" He said, "Absolutely, sir!" I said, "I'll land next to the bodies, and you can get the two helmets, okay?" I quickly set the helicopter down; he jumped out, picked up the helmets, and jumped back in the aircraft.

I took off and headed back to where the bombing run had started. He said, "Sir, can I really have one of the helmets?" I replied, "You sure can. But I want the other one." Lead called me on the radio and said, "Skeeter, what are you doing?" I said, "Picking up a couple of souvenirs." He replied, "Okay, just be careful."

Once we got back to the start of the bombing run, I could tell that we were probably not going to be able to find any more NVA soldiers and told Lead that I thought we were finished.

He said, "Skeeter, let's head back to the staging area, refuel, and then go home." I double clicked the mic and began to climb to cruising altitude and head to Duc Pho. After refueling, we flew back to Chu Lai. Lead called the Air Force guys and told them what I'd found and how many NVA soldiers I had killed. They were thrilled to get the BDA.

After arriving at Key Ha heliport, we parked in the revetments, went to our tactical operations center (TOC), and told the operations officer all about the bomb damage assessment. Major Maher was there listening to everything. In a minute, he came over to me, and I stood up. "Outstanding job, Corvin. You've significantly added to the Warlords' body count." He shook my hand and then left the building.

Later we all were at the officers' club having dinner and drinking beer. Several guys came over to the table where I was sitting with Batman and said, "Way to go, Corvin! Congratulations on getting all the kills." One of them said, "I don't think I would have the stomach to do what you did today." I smiled and replied, "I was just doing my job and I love my job!" I thanked them but saw that they glanced at me in a strange way as they left the table.

Afterward, and for the remaining time I was in Vietnam on my first tour, I was treated very deferentially whenever I was around a group of pilots at the officers' club or the TOC for morning briefings. When I mentioned this to Batman, his response was, "They probably are wondering how you can do what you do, every day, without it appearing to affect you." I thought about that a moment and then told him about my belief that I was an incarnated biblical "Avenger." He laughed and asked, "Are you sure you're not an Avenging Demon?" I slowly shook my head and said, "No, I'm no demon, but it's fine with me if the NVA and VC believe that they have encountered one!"

When I departed Danang airfield at the end of my tour, an MP inspecting my baggage saw the NVA pith helmet with the red communist star on the front. He told me that the helmet was considered enemy contraband and I could not take it home. He picked it up and put it under the counter upon which my bags had been laying. Because it was in pristine condition and unique, I'm pretty sure that he took it home or gave it to one of his superiors as a gift. Later I realized that I didn't need a memento of that day to remind me of all the enemy soldiers that I killed.

After all these years I can remember that day as if it were

yesterday! The smell of the five-hundred-pound bombs' explosive cordite, newly churned up earth, wood smoke from cooking fires, and flying through all the dust!

My dad once told me the same thing about incidents that he experienced during WWII on Iwo Jima and the Korean War. Some memories *never* go away for combat veterans!

CHAPTER 26

BROKEN ARROW
(1ST DFC)

During the Vietnam War, the code words, "Broken Arrow," were an urgent call for close air support, by all available forces, to come to the aid for an American military unit on the ground that was in grave danger of being overrun and destroyed by the enemy.

On November 1, 1969, I was flying a low-level reconnaissance mission twenty miles west of Quang Ngai City. The primary terrain in that area was made up of large hills and valleys covered with tall grasses and short scrub brush. I had been flying for approximately thirty minutes when suddenly I heard on the emergency guard channel of my UHF radio, "Broken Arrow, Broken Arrow, Broken Arrow!" Then the voice said, "Any aircraft in the vicinity of grid coordinates BS7635, please come up Guard." "Guard" was two radio frequencies used only for emergencies. The VHF channel was 121.5. (Still is.) The UHF channel was 243.0. (Still is.) All United States military aircraft, regardless of the service branch, continuously monitor these two frequencies while in flight.

I knew that *Broken Arrow* was an emergency call for help

from a ground unit under attack, and everyone was about to be annihilated, but I had never heard one called—until now!

Lead got on the UHF radio frequency and told the caller that our Warlord hunter/killer team was only ten minutes away from the grid coordinates. The caller said, "There are two platoon-sized ground elements (approximately one hundred soldiers) that have been in a firefight with NVA soldiers for the past eight hours. The fighting has been so intense they are almost out of ammunition, and no resupply has been able to reach them. One Huey attempting to help has already been shot down with everyone on board killed in the crash and subsequent fire. Can you help?"

"Affirmative, we are on our way now," Lead answered. "Skeeter, did you hear that last transmission?" "Yes, I did. I'm climbing to altitude now and will head to those coordinates if you give me directions." "Before I direct you to the grunts' location, you need to land at Gia Vuc, the Special Forces compound, and pick up four wooden cases of M-16 ammo and two cases of grenades to give them," he said. "I've burned off enough fuel to compensate for the weight of the ammo crates, so I guess I won't have any issues with max gross weight," I said. "I think you'll be fine, but hurry, they are in serious trouble," Lead urged.

I had flown into Gia Vuc on many occasions when I was flying Huey's for the Rattlers and knew that it was only a few miles from my current location. I pulled maximum power and reached a top speed of 180 mph. "Can you have them waiting at the helipad so that they can load the ammo and grenades in my Loach as soon as I touch down?" I asked Lead. "I've already arranged that, Skeeter," he said. Within three minutes, the mountaintop compound came into sight.

Approaching the Special Forces helipad, I saw six guys next

to a "mule" (a small utility transport vehicle like a Kawasaki) carrying ammunition boxes. I landed, and they drove up to my Loach and quickly began loading four wooden crates of M–16 ammo and two boxes of grenades in the cargo bay. After the load was tied down, I took off. "Lead, which way to the grunts' location?" I asked. "Head due east for about ten miles and when you get close, 1 will have them pop smoke," he said. I turned to a heading of ninety degrees and reached my maximum speed within a few seconds. At 180 mph, I was flying three miles per minute, so I took about three minutes to reach their location.

When I got close, I could see smoke rising from the burning helicopter that had been shot down. "The ground commander can see you and is going to pop yellow smoke," Lead said. "Roger that," I replied as I armed my minigun and began my spiraling descent. I saw bright yellow smoke coming from a large depression near one hill. The downed helicopter was burning on the top of it.

As I neared the ground, suddenly I heard lots of AK-47 rounds being fired at me. "Skeeter's taking fire! Skeeter's taking fire!" I yelled. By the time I said that, I was already low level near the yellow smoke that was pouring out of a grenade. When I flew over the smoke, I saw dozens of GIs huddled down in foxholes dug in a large circle as a perimeter defense. Everyone was looking at me and waving. Then a U.S. Army infantry captain covered in mud and dirt jumped out of a foxhole and started waving both arms at me. I turned the Loach to him and heard several loud "bangs" as enemy bullets impacted the side of my Loach. I glanced at my instruments and saw that the engine was okay and then stopped my forward motion as I flew over the captain. I yelled into the intercom for my crew chief to drop all of the crates of ammo and grenades next to the commander who was standing there.

I heard a hail of AK-47 rounds all around me and more "bangs" as the bullets hit my Loach. The control panel in front of me exploded from rounds striking it and glass went flying everywhere. "Skeeter's taking hits! Skeeter's taking hits!" I yelled. I saw a large hole in my UHF radio which was about four inches away from my left knee. I felt something hit my right leg just above my knee. Then I saw a bullet hole in the lower right side of the center control console. I looked at my right pants leg and saw blood spreading from a hole in my flight suit. "Lead, I have been hit by a bullet or a piece of metal from the console." He didn't answer.

I turned the radio selector switch and called Lead saying, "Can you hear me on my VHF radio?" Before he could answer, more AK-47 fire was directed at me, and I pulled away from the center of the defensive position and the captain now crouching there. When I flew over the foxholes where the GIs were dug in, I saw numerous NVA soldiers crawling up to the American perimeter. They immediately began shooting at me as I flew over them. My crew chief started firing his M-60 machine gun at them as I spun the Loach to the right and began firing my minigun too. Suddenly bullets were flying at me from enemy positions on both sides of my Loach and below it.

I rolled away in a tight turn, flew about a hundred yards and saw even more NVA soldiers. It was obvious they had surrounded the American troops and were closing in to slaughter them. I began firing my minigun continuously and saw enemy troops start to run and fall. I turned the aircraft in the opposite direction and flew back over the GIs in their foxholes. As I crossed over the top of them, I could see them yelling at me and pointing in one direction. I was then over the top of the other NVA soldiers, and they began shooting at me. I opened fired with my minigun and saw many of them fall, but also many more opened up at me with their AK-47s.

Lead called me on the VHF radio. "Skeeter, get out of there and let us make rocket runs with both Cobras." "Man, am I ever glad that I can talk to you! I'll make another run and drop smoke on the targets and then leave," I replied. I turned the Loach around and told the crew chief to get all the red smoke bombs out of his box and be prepared to drop them. I flew back over where I had just shot some of the NVA soldiers, and they fired at me again. Then I saw two white streaks coming fast at me from the right. *Holy crap! They're firing rocket-propelled grenades (RPG's) at me!* I rolled the Loach in a hard left turn and saw the helicopter blades clip the tops of the grass.

Both RPG's passed under my fuselage and between the skids and missed! I continued turning and flew over the two NVA soldiers that had fired them at me. "Drop two red smoke grenades, NOW!" I yelled at the crew chief. He did as I ordered, then I flew back over the GIs and told the crew chief to get ready to drop the other smoke grenades. Once I was over the other NVA positions, I screamed, "Drop them!" He did, and I hauled ass!

When I was about a hundred yards away, I began receiving more AK-47 fire from an even larger group of NVA soldiers. "Skeeter's taking more fire over here!" I yelled. Then I heard the Cobra rockets impacting the ground behind me. I made a hard right turn and yelled at the crew chief to drop more red smoke, which he did. "Lead, I've dropped red smoke on the NVA positions over here," I yelled. "We'll be right there," he said. "Affirmative." I turned around and flew away from that area. I watched as the two Cobras made rocket runs firing at the positions I had marked with the smoke grenades. After several runs there, they flew over to where I had marked the positions with the other red smoke and started firing rockets at those NVA. I watched as they made their minigun runs.

"We don't have enough ammo to keep the NVA from overrunning these guys, so I'm calling in artillery now," Lead said. I began to climb and turned east. "I've just called in a fire mission and four 175mm howitzers will begin shooting in one minute, so everybody move to the east so that we are clear of the incoming artillery rounds." Lead said. By then I was at normal altitude flying away from the American GIs dug in on the ground. "Everyone move further away because the 175mm rounds are about to impact the target," Lead said. Within a few seconds, huge geysers of dirt began to fly up into the air as the artillery rounds hit the NVA soldiers surrounding the grunts.

The artillery firing continued for about thirty minutes with the rounds impacting within fifty yards of the GIs in the foxholes. The infantry captain on the ground had taken control of the fire mission and was directing the artillery onto the NVA positions from his "Prick" 25 radio carried by his "RTO". (PRC-25 is a backpack radio with long range capabilities and an RTO is a "Radio/Telephone Operator.)

"We are all running low on fuel so let's head back to Quang Ngai airfield to refuel and rearm," Lead said. I turned east and headed to the staging area. Once I landed, I shut the engine off and pulled up my right pants leg that was soaked in blood. Just above my right knee, about six inches, there was a small hole in the skin with blood oozing out. My crew chief came over and saw the blood running down my leg. "Sir, when did that happen?" he asked. "The last time we started taking hits in the aircraft," I answered. "I'll go get Captain Hines," he said. Then he took off running to where the Cobras were hot refueling at the POL area. After refueling, they moved into revetments and shut down their engines. I had already gotten out and found thirteen bullet holes in my Loach; including three in the engine compartment!

In a few minutes, Lead came over and looked at my right leg. "Do you think it's a bullet wound?" he asked. "I don't know. It doesn't hurt very badly. Sort of aches and stings a little!" I answered. By then most of the other pilots had come over to look at the Loach and all the bullet holes.

They were surprised that I could still fly the aircraft. (I was too!) Lead walked around the helicopter and came over to me. "Corvin, since you are wounded, and the aircraft is shot up so badly, you can't fly this back to Chu Lai. I'm going to call maintenance and have them come down here and sling load it back to Key Ha heliport."

I agreed entirely as I was picking broken slivers of glass out of my flight suit and left leg that was also still bleeding. "Sir, I'll stay with the Loach and ride back with the maintenance flight," the crew chief said. I shook his hand. "You did well today, dropping the smoke grenades. I appreciate how you held it all together," I said. He shrugged and smiled at me sheepishly. I picked up my CAR-15 machine gun and flight helmet and limped over to one of the Hueys and climbed in. When we arrived at Key Ha, Major Maher was at the flight line in a jeep. He drove over to me as I was getting out of the slick. "Hop in, and I'll drive you to the infirmary," he said.

At the infirmary, the flight surgeon had me remove my bloody Nomex flight suit and examined my left knee and right leg. "I need to inject the site with Novocain to deaden it and then remove whatever is inside," he informed me. "Do whatever you have to, Doc, just don't ground me from flying because of this!"

After a few minutes, the Novocain had deadened both areas. He took a thin metal probe and stuck it in my right leg wound. After pulling it out, he took a metal instrument that looked like long, skinny needle-nose pliers, inserted it into the wound, and pulled out a small piece of bloody gray metal.

"That's not part of a bullet. It looks like a piece of shrapnel," he said. "I think it's from the gray center console that was shot up," I said. "Probably so," he grunted. He took the thin metal probe and searched for more pieces but could not find any. After closing the wound with three stitches, he bandaged it, gave me a tetanus shot and some antibiotics. Then he took some long tweezers and pulled several slivers of glass out of my left knee. He put ointment on a large gauze bandage and taped that to my leg saying, "You'll be able to fly in a couple of days, but take it easy." I thanked him, and Major Maher drove me back to my hooch where I showered and limped to the officers' club.

It had been a good day. I was glad that we had helped the American GIs on the ground that were facing total annihilation by a much superior force of NVA soldiers. The four bodies of the helicopter crew who had been shot down on the hill near the American GI's under attack were never recovered. When an investigation team went to the crash site, the bodies had been removed, presumably by NVA soldiers. It was never determined if the crew had died in the crash and subsequent fire, or had survived, albeit injured, and were taken prisoner. (They are still listed as MIA.)

Four months later on February 18, 1970, the Warlord Commanding Officer, Major James C. Maher, and I were notified by Headquarters, Americal Division, that I was awarded my first Distinguished Flying Cross (DFC) for my actions in saving the lives of the American soldiers that day.

For those of you unfamiliar with the DFC award, it is given by order of the U.S. President to individuals for extraordinary bravery while participating in aerial flight. One of the first ever given was to Captain Charles A. Lindbergh of the Army Corps Reserve in 1927 for his solo flight across the Atlantic Ocean.

Another DFC was awarded to Commander Richard E. Byrd of the Navy Air Corps in 1927 (the first man who flew to and from the North Pole). Both of these famous aviators also received the Congressional Medal of Honor.

Amelia Earhart was given one for her flight around the world. At the time, hers was the first such awarded to a civilian. A Presidential executive order issued in March, 1927, ruled that the Distinguished Flying Cross should not be conferred on civilians.

Estimates now are that in the past eighty-eight years, approximately seven thousand DFC's have been awarded to military personnel. I have been awarded two Distinguished Flying Crosses (the next chapter describes how I received the 2nd DFC), and I am listed in the National DFC Society's honor roll of recipients.

CHAPTER 27

MEDEVAC MISSION
(2ND DFC)

ontrary to what people think about medical evacuation
(MEDEVAC) of wounded soldiers in Vietnam, most were
done by armed UH-1 Hueys that happened to be flying
nearby and responded to an urgent call for help. The designated
Army MEDEVAC units, located at MASH hospitals, were flown
by pilots specifically trained in picking up injured soldiers. The
helicopters they flew were unarmed UH-1 Hueys with large red
and white crosses painted on either side. They were frequently
called to pick up the wounded, and sometimes the dead, but
would only do so if the landing zone was not "hot." In other
words, all of the fighting and shooting had to be over when they
picked up the casualties. Of course, it didn't always work out that
way!

The Geneva Convention of 1954 specifically stated that no
vehicle (later including helicopters), painted with red and white
crosses on either side, was to be fired upon while picking up the
wounded. The MEDEVAC pilots usually would not respond to
a call for help if there was any chance they would be shot at.
Consequently, during the Vietnam War, most of the injured

soldiers were picked up by helicopters that were not MEDEVAC aircraft.

This story is about one such event in which I participated. On January 14, 1970, I was flying a Loach on a VR operation ten miles west of Quang Ngai City. The Warlord team had been asked to provide landing zone security for a large helicopter assault (nine aircraft) that was going to put about one hundred American ground forces into a hotly-contested AO controlled by NVA and VC forces.

When I arrived at the coordinates for the LZ, I began a routine search of the perimeter of the grassy field to see if I could find any indication that the NVA or VC were present. I called Lead after searching for approximately ten minutes. "Everything looks okay so far, but there are several areas that I'm not sure about," I said. "Skeeter, why don't you go ahead and recon by fire to see if someone will shoot at you," Lead responded. "Roger, I'll see if that stirs things up." A recon by fire simply meant that I would find an area where enemy combatants were likely to be camouflaged and hidden and then shoot into it with my minigun. They would think their position had been compromised and would shoot back at me. I flew to several areas that were covered in dense vegetation and fired into it for a couple of seconds. At no time did anybody shoot back at me. So far so good!

The helicopter assault Aircraft Commander called Lead and said they were inbound to the LZ and would land in about five minutes. I moved away from the large grassy field, in which the nine Huey's would land, and continued to look for enemy combatants. The goal was for all of the Hueys to land at one time and have the "friendly" troops (meaning American soldiers) quickly unload, spread out, and form a defensive perimeter. The nine Hueys were flying in a "V" formation of three aircraft in a triangular pattern, followed close behind by three more, and then finally the last three. This formation was Standard Operating Procedure (SOP) for a helicopter combat assault. It was a proven method of quickly landing large numbers of troops in an area without endangering the helicopters in collisions with each other.

Within a few minutes, Lead got on the radio and told all the Warlord pilots that the combat assault team was on short final to the LZ. "Skeeter, move off to the side of the field and give these guys plenty of room to land," he said to me. I replied, "Roger, that." (Wow! As I'm writing this, a group of six Fort Campbell helicopters, flying in two "V" formations, just passed over the top of my house. Talk about being in the moment—that will do it!) I flew to the side of the grassy field and then watched as the nine helicopters approached and landed.

All of the soldiers on board the helicopter assault jumped out and started setting up a perimeter defense. Then I heard AK-47 machine guns being fired (they have a very distinctive sound that's easily recognized by combat veterans) at the helicopters and the soldiers on the ground. I flew to the end of the field where the lead aircraft was positioned and saw dozens of NVA soldiers kneeling down firing. They were wearing tan-colored camouflaged Ghillie suits that allowed them to blend in perfectly with the tall grass. I immediately maneuvered my Loach between them and the lead helicopter and began firing my minigun at the NVA. They stopped shooting as I fired into their ranks; then a .51-caliber machine gun began firing at me from one of the areas I had shot into as a recon by fire. The bullets going by me were much louder than an AK-47 bullet as I turned my Loach and attacked the machine gun position with my minigun. At fifty feet, I saw the orange line of my tracers hit the crew-served weapon and the guys shooting at me. As I passed over, I could see the bodies of four NVA soldiers in their green uniforms.

Then I heard more AK-47 machine gun fire from the other end of the field where the last helicopters had landed. I turned and flew down there and was met by a hail of enemy bullets, several of which impacted the front of my Loach shattering the lower Plexiglas at the passenger-side pedals. I opened fire with the minigun and continued firing eight three-second bursts. That amounted to nearly two thousand rounds of ammo! That stopped the enemy from firing anymore.

Lead got on the radio. "Skeeter, stay clear of the assault team helicopters because they are all taking off now." He didn't need to say that because I could see they were all starting to move forward in formation. They took off and left all the grunts on the ground. Suddenly, from both sides of the landing zone, I heard AK-47's firing into the soldiers and their M-16's firing back. It was obvious this site was being used as a "killing zone" for the American troops that had just landed. I saw several GIs fall and lay still as blood flowed from their wounds. I flew over the top of them and found a group of ten or twelve hunched-over NVA soldiers slowly advancing, firing their weapons at the Americans. I opened fired with the minigun and killed them. "Skeeter, there are multiple injured grunts that need to be immediately Medevac'd out! The lead Huey's returning and will land to pick them up. Try to cover him as much as you can." Lead yelled at me.

"Roger, that, but there are lots of NVA and VC hidden on both sides of the LZ, and a major firefight is going on down here with me caught in the middle," I said. "I know, I can see that, but hang in there if you can." Lead said.

The helicopter assault leader came in very fast and flared

in the middle of the LZ. GIs started running to his helicopter carrying the wounded lying on nylon ponchos. From the right side, where I had just flown, several NVA started shooting at them. I turned and flew straight at the enemy soldiers and opened fire. Behind them were probably thirty or forty more enemy combatants running to the landing zone. I begin firing at them and saw many fall, and the rest scatter in retreat.

Then I heard the Huey take off, and Lead screamed, "Stay low, Skeeter, the sonofabitch is going to overfly you." I spun to the left just in time to see the Huey fly over me about four feet away from my blades. He was close enough that I thought his skids would hit my rotors, but they didn't! "Skeeter another Huey's on short final to pick up more wounded. Do you think you can cover him?" Lead said. "I'll try. But I'm not sure how much ammo I have left. I've lost track of how many times I've pulled the trigger," I replied.

American GI's jumped up from the shallow foxholes they had dug and began running to the helicopter carrying the remaining wounded soldiers on green ponchos. I flew beside the Huey and positioned my Loach so that neither the NVA nor VC could shoot at the soldiers loading the wounded. I expected to start receiving AK-47 fire at any second; however, nothing happened! I flew over the area where I had seen the large group of NVA, but there was no one there except for the bodies of the ones I had already shot. I continued to fly around the area, but didn't get shot at anymore. I flew to the other end of the landing zone, but again no one shot at me. I found the bodies of the NVA I'd shot earlier, but couldn't find any more enemy troops. Then I saw the Huey take off with the wounded soldiers and start climbing to a higher altitude to head east to the MASH hospital.

I continued to fly over the dug-in American troops and their perimeter defense but did not receive any more incoming fire. After a few minutes, Lead said, "Skeeter, there's a resupply Huey landing in a few minutes that's going to offload more ammo, mortar tubes, and mortar rounds. I'll let you know when he's on short final." I double-clicked the mic indicating I had heard him.

I flew around the edges of the landing zone but could not find any more NVA soldiers. I told my crew chief to break out the boxes of Bicycle Aces of Spades cards and be prepared to throw some out on each of the NVA bodies. He did as I asked, and soon he had thrown out all of the cards in twenty decks.

Lead called me and said the resupply Huey was on short final and would touch down in a minute. I made sure I was far enough away that I could avoid him flying over me if he started getting shot at and panicked. The aircraft landed, and the grunts ran over and unloaded all of the supplies. There were no more AK-47's firing at the helicopter or the grunts on the ground. *This is great; so far so good!* I thought. The Huey took off straight ahead, and I flew all around the American troop's defensive perimeter, but couldn't find any more NVA or VC soldiers that were alive!

I glanced down at my fuel gauge and saw that it was nearing the twenty-minute fuel warning indicator so I called Lead to let him know that I needed to refuel soon. "Let me know when your low fuel warning buzzer starts to beep, and we will leave then," he said. "Roger that," I answered and continued to fly around the LZ looking for someone to shoot and waiting to get shot at, but there were no more NVA or VC in the area.

I called Lead and told him that it looked like the enemy combatants had all left. Then my low fuel warning buzzer started to beep loudly. I told Lead that we needed to leave. "That's fine, Skeeter. Let's go back to Quang Ngai. I'll call the grunts CO and let him know we are departing the area. Do you have enough fuel to make it there?" He said. "That's affirmative, but I also need to check out the bullet holes in the left side of the aircraft," I answered. "Take it easy and stay low in case you have to land quickly before we get there." Lead said.

I slowly flew over the GIs in the foxholes one more time. They were all jumping up and down, yelling, smiling, and waving wildly at me. I climbed to about twenty feet and then did two fast three hundred sixty-degree spins to the right, took off low level, and headed east to our staging area. The enemy had been completely routed and left the area, leaving their dead comrades behind. It felt good to know that I'd helped the guys on the ground, and I wished there were more opportunities to do that.

When we arrived at our staging area in Quang Ngai, I hot refueled, moved into a revetment, and shut the Loach engine down. My crew chief and I crawled under the left side of the helicopter and found four bullet holes in the bottom. It didn't appear they had hit any of the control tubes or linkage surfaces, so I decided to head back to Key Ha heliport. Lead came over and asked me for a damage assessment. I told him that the crew chief and I thought everything was okay to fly back to our base. He said, "Okay then, let's head home." We all took off and landed just as the moon was rising in the east. That was the most rewarding day of my life! There have been others since, but that was very special, and I've never forgotten how I felt.

Six months later, on June 16, 1970, while I was stationed at Schweinfurt, Germany with D Troop, 3rd Brigade, 7th Cavalry, 3rd Infantry Division, my Commanding Officer, Major George Kyle, and I received notification from our Commanding General that I had been awarded my second Distinguished Flying Cross (with First Oak Leaf Cluster) for my actions in saving the American lives and protecting the wounded soldiers on the ground.

CHAPTER 28

"BATMAN" CRASHES AND BURNS

A t 0800 on February 17, 1970, I was packing up all of my gear in preparation for leaving Vietnam and returning to the United States two days later on the 19th. Batman walked to the end of my bed and shook my hand. "In four months, I'll be heading home too, and I promise you that I will not extend my tour here in country!" he said. "Man, I was having so much fun flying Loaches I didn't want to stop. Besides, if you stay in country more than 510 days, all of your income tax being withheld is refunded." I said. Batman replied, "No amount of money can keep me in this hellhole, separated from my young wife and two little kids!" I laughed and said, "Different strokes for different folks. I'll see you later when you guys get in." He turned and headed for the screen door saying, "I shall return!" as General Douglas MacArthur had famously said when he left the Philippines during World War II.

Batman returned to Ky Ha heliport two days later in a body bag—dead and burned beyond recognition, on the day I left from Danang Air Force Base.

On February 18, 1970, Linda Bateman heard two car doors slam shut on the front street outside as she laid her new baby girl down in the crib. She had just finished feeding her. It was 6:00 a.m. and she wondered who could be coming to her parents' house at this hour. She was living with them in Eugene, Oregon while her husband, James Bateman, was flying in Vietnam as a U.S. Army helicopter pilot. She walked to the front window and peeked between the blinds in time to see two Army officers walk up to the front porch, one clutching a Bible in his hand. Her heart started racing as she went into the hall and screamed, "NO! NO! NO!" Her mother and father came running out of their bedroom, looking confused and distraught. They saw Linda and came over saying "What's wrong?" The doorbell rang, and she cried, "Jim is dead!" and collapsed into the arms of her parents.

Linda Bateman was twenty-one years old, the mother of a little boy, a two-week-old baby girl, and she was a war widow! Up to 1970, scenes like this had played out all across America 53,849 times as families of soldiers were notified of their loved ones' deaths. By the end of the war in 1975, another 4,344 American troops would die. The total number of American deaths during the Vietnam War was 58,193.

By comparison: the total number of American military deaths over the past thirteen years in the Iraq and Afghanistan conflicts currently is 7,115, with Iraq deaths at 4,800 and Afghanistan deaths at 2,315.

Warrant Officer James (Jim) Terrence Bateman was born August 23, 1947, in Portland, Oregon. He married his college sweetheart, Linda, in 1968 when he was first drafted into the U.S. Army. They both had been attending the University of Oregon in Eugene. Jim said that they were planning to marry after graduation, but decided not to wait since he was about to be inducted into the Army. While in basic training, he got a letter from Linda announcing that she was pregnant. He told me it was the greatest day of his life when he read the letter. He was very excited about being a father.

After basic, he went to Advanced Infantry Training (AIT) and learned about the Warrant Officer Rotary Wing Aviation Training. He applied for flight school and was accepted. His primary helicopter training was at Ft. Wolters in Mineral Wells, Texas, where all new pilots went. His pregnant wife, Linda, joined him and soon had a baby boy at Beech Army Hospital.

From there he went to Fort Rucker, Alabama, for advanced helicopter training. After graduating from flight school in May of 1969, as a Warrant Officer, Jim, his wife, and little boy drove back to Portland, Oregon. He spent five weeks with his family then took Linda to her parents' home in Eugene, Oregon, where she would live until he returned from overseas. Jim left from McCord Air Force Base in Washington State for Vietnam. He arrived in Danang on June 17, 1969, and was assigned to B Company 123rd Aviation Battalion, 23rd Infantry Division (The Warlords).

Jim was a good-natured, affable, funny person who loved flying helicopters. He was soon dubbed *Batman* because his last name was Bateman. Upon arriving at the Warlords, he was assigned to my hooch and moved into the metal bed next to mine. I first met him at the Key Ha officers' club the day of his arrival. I had been in country for almost a year and was flying visual reconnaissance nearly every day as a Loach pilot. *Batman* began flying as a peter pilot (co-pilot) on a UH-1D Huey (slick) carrying seven Animals. After three months, he had flown almost three hundred sixty flying hours and was promoted to Aircraft Commander (AC). That meant he was in command of his helicopter as it flew with the hunter/killer team. (He was also the AC who picked me up in his Huey after I crashed into the river.)

We became close friends because we were hooch-mates, flew together daily, and played cards at the officers' club in the evening. He was a great bridge player and a fierce competitor playing Spades. We had many good times together in Vietnam.

At 0700 hours on February 17, 1970, eight months to the day after arriving in country at the Warlords, Batman walked to his Huey and greeted First Lieutenant Arlen Richardson, his new peter pilot. Batman asked him if the pre-flight had been completed and if everything was all right. The lieutenant assured him that UH-1H tail number 67-17175 was in tip top shape and mission ready.

First Lieutenant Arlen D. Richardson, twenty-seven years old, was from Lawrence, Kansas. He had been in the U.S. Army for four years as an infantry officer and had graduated from helicopter flight school in late November, 1969. He arrived in Vietnam at the Warlords on January 8, 1970. Richardson grew up in Lawrence, was a 1961 graduate of Lawrence High School and the University of Kansas in 1965. He was married and had a six-month-old son named Ryan.

In addition to First Lieutenant Richardson, Batman's helicopter was crewed by SP4 Jack Drye, the crew chief, and SP4 John Mitchell, the door gunner. Flying as passengers aboard the slick were SFC James Gordon, the Animal platoon sergeant, SP4 Carl Brown, SP4 Samuel James, Cpl. George Grover, SP4 Thomas Frazier, Cpl. Ronald Means, and SP4 Theodore Williams.

Batman flew with the rest of the team to Quang Ngai airfield. There, he and the other pilots were briefed about the visual reconnaissance mission that would take place twenty miles to the west of the airfield. They departed and flew to the western AO where the first VR took place. Afterward, they returned to the staging area and refueled. The team, including Batman's helicopter, departed Quang Ngai at 1030 hours to begin the next VR. Halfway through the mission, Batman called Lead and reported a loss of main rotor transmission oil pressure and a maximum transmission oil temperature on his instruments. Lead suggested he immediately land the Huey in an open rice paddy. Batman said that he thought the problem was with his instruments and not the main rotor transmission, so he continued on to Quang Ngai airfield.

Batman turned his aircraft to a general heading of northeast towards the airfield. His flight path was curved to avoid various hilltops that were obscured by low cloud cover that day. He was observed by a flight of helicopters from the 174th Aviation Company, who, at the time, were involved in a combat assault in the area. Batman's slick was observed in straight and level flight for approximately one minute. Two minutes had elapsed from the time he had first reported the loss of transmission oil pressure to Lead.

Suddenly, he started shouting, *"Mayday! Mayday! Mayday! We are going down!"* Batman transmitted almost continuously until nearing impact with the ground. Over the radio, Lead could hear screaming in the background as the helicopter entered a gradual right turn and began to increase into a rapid rate of turn and then a fast spin. The main rotor blades were observed to slow down, and at seven hundred feet above ground they stopped perpendicular to the fuselage. The slick entered a very fast flat spin during which all of the passengers sitting in the cargo bay area were thrown out of the helicopter. The Huey impacted the ground slightly nose low. The impact completely flattened the helicopter and drove parts of it into the ground. The fuel tank ruptured, and fuel sprayed everywhere igniting the wreckage.

An attempt was made by two of the 174th aircraft to land troops close enough to the wreckage to make a rescue attempt but exploding ammo and grenades made the rescue impossible. The time of impact was 1110 hours--information that was obtained from several of the victims' watches.

According to the official accident report, the copilot, 1st Lt. Richardson, had overruled a Red X on the daily flight maintenance log which meant the helicopter should not have been flown until the noted main rotor transmission malfunction was repaired and corrected. He failed to tell Batman or the crew chief about the critically needed repair. The subsequent crash and the loss of everyone on board the helicopter was solely his fault.

W01 James Terrence Bateman a.k.a. Batman, 1st Lt. Richardson, SP4 Drye, and SP4 Mitchell died instantly from the impact. Their bodies were burned beyond recognition by the ensuing massive fire from the jet fuel. The seven Animals on board were thrown out of the aircraft at an altitude of approximately seven hundred feet, as it began to spin rapidly, and they died upon impacting the ground. (SFC Gordon was the soldier who loaned me his field jacket after I crashed into the river.)

Later that night at the officers' club, Captain Gordy Hines, who was Lead, said that just before the helicopter impacted the ground, he heard Batman say in a very calm clear voice, "Tell my wife, Linda — I love her and the babies!" (As I'm finishing this chapter, tears are pouring down my cheeks and I can't write about Batman anymore! Enough said.)

I was devastated by the accident and the loss of my friends. Two days later, and still very hung over, I boarded a TWA flight back to the "World," i.e., the United States of America. We landed at LAX airport in Los Angeles, and I took a Delta Airlines flight to Dallas Love Field, where my sister Penny met me at the gate. At first she didn't recognize me because I had gained thirty pounds in the past year and a half. Later, as she was driving me down to Waco, Texas, where my mom and dad lived, she asked, "What's wrong with your eyes?" I said, "What do you mean?" She replied, "They are so glassy they look like they've been burned." I said, "I don't know what you're talking about." But in reality I did. It was called the "thousand yard stare." It happened to a lot of combat veterans that were exposed to extreme stress over a long period. Eventually, it went away.

I was finally home, but not for long because I had orders to report to Schweinfurt, Germany, in thirty days.

CHAPTER 29

GARRY OWENS

On April 1, 1970, as I walked up the sidewalk to the headquarters of 3rd Brigade, 7th Cavalry, 3rd Infantry Division, two sergeants passed me, said, "Garry Owens, sir," and saluted. I returned their salute and thought, *Why in the world would they say "Carry on, sir."?* I had arrived in Schweinfurt, Germany, two days earlier and was staying at a beautiful downtown hotel. A taxi brought me to the main gate of Ledward Barracks where A, B, and C Troops as well as Headquarters and Headquarters Company (HHC) of the 7th Cavalry were based. Instead of calling it a "Fort" it was called a "kaserne."

I walked up the steps to the entrance of the main building and entered a very large foyer. The sergeant sitting at a desk asked me if he could help. I said, "I am reporting to Colonel Bills, the squadron commander, and have been assigned to "D" troop out at the airfield." The sergeant got up and said "Follow me, sir, and I'll take you to his office."

Along the walls of the foyer were two huge glass display cases containing three full-sized, very lifelike American Indian mannequins wearing feathered headdresses and authentic looking clothing. Each was armed with an 1873 Winchester 44-40 repeating rifle. Next to their display cases were three more containing six full-sized male mannequins wearing authentic U.S. Army cavalry uniforms from the 1870s. The mannequins were holding Springfield 1873 "trap door" .45-caliber, single-shot carbines.

Several other display cases contained Colt Single Action Army .45-caliber revolvers, sabers, long knives, bayonets, and miscellaneous other old cavalry items. One tall, narrow display case contained a scarred wooden flagpole with dirty streamers of various colors hanging down from the top. It was the actual "colors" (flags) that Brevet General George Armstrong Custer had with him when he (and 211 soldiers) fell at Little Big Horn on June 25, 1876.

I asked the sergeant about the display cases and he told me the 7th Cavalry Squadron in Schweinfurt was the last remaining active duty 7th Cav unit in existence, and therefore was entitled to display the memorabilia. I have to say it was strange finding it in Bavaria, Germany, and something that I never expected to see.

Although the 7th Cavalry is best known for the fight at the Little Big Horn, it also participated in smaller Indian battles, such as the capture of Chief Joseph's Nez Perce at the Battle of Bear Paw in 1877. The regiment was also attempting to disarm the Lakotas, which turned into the Wounded Knee Massacre on December 29, 1890, signaling the end of the American Indian wars. From 1895 until 1899, the regiment served in New Mexico and Oklahoma, then overseas in Cuba from 1899 to 1902. Edgar Rice Burroughs who wrote the *Tarzan* book series was an enlisted trooper with the 7th Cavalry, "B" Company at Fort Grant Arizona territory from May, 1896, until March, 1897.

The regiment served in the Philippines during the Philippine-American War from 1904 through 1907. Although the 7th Cavalry was assigned to the 1st Cavalry Division during World

War I, there was no significant role for horse-mounted troops on the Western Front during the nineteen months between the entry of the United States into the war and the armistice of November 11, 1918. The 7th Cavalry Regiment was dismounted (meaning no more horses ridden) during World War II and served in the Leyte Campaign, and the Luzon, Philippines Campaign.

After World War II, the 7th Cavalry stayed in Japan as part of the occupying force. Coincidentally, one of its officers during this period was Lt. Colonel Brice C. W. Custer, the great-nephew of former commander George Armstrong Custer! The 7th Cavalry fought in the Korean War's bloodiest battles and was awarded three presidential unit citations which were added to the colors. During the Vietnam War, the 7th Cavalry became the 3rd brigade of the 1st Cavalry Division.

The sergeant escorted me to Colonel Bill's office and turned me over to the clerk seated there. In a few minutes, the Colonel and Major George Kyle came out to greet me. I stood up, saluted, and then shook their hands. Maj. Kyle was my new Commanding Officer. After visiting for a few minutes, he said, "We received word from the Department of Army that you were coming and that your application for direct commission has been approved. Welcome aboard, First Lieutenant Corvin." I was flabbergasted to say the least and thought that it might be an April fool's joke, but it wasn't. Frankly, I'd forgotten about the request I'd made nineteen months earlier. "If you sign the promotion documents, we will make it official immediately," Major Kyle said. I readily agreed. He had me stand at attention, removed my chief warrant officer bars, and pinned my silver 1st lieutenant bars on my uniform.

I was now an RLO (Real Live Officer) with command authority. One reason I was thrilled with the promotion was that

I would automatically make captain one year later on April 1, 1971.

After visiting for a while in Colonel Bill's office, Major Kyle took me to the officers' club at Conn Barracks, which was located a few miles away at the airfield. We had lunch; then he drove me to the operations center and headquarters of my new unit, "D" Troop, 3rd Brigade, 7th Cavalry, 3rd Infantry Division. On the way to the unit, I asked Maj. Kyle about the two sergeants saying, "Carry on, sir." He laughed and said, "They were not saying carry on, sir, but rather Garry Owen, sir!" He then explained to me that the nickname of the 7th Cavalry was from an Irish regimental march entitled *Garry Owen*. Instead of saying "Good morning, sir," "Garry Owen, sir" was used. It built the *esprit de corps* for the troops.

Schweinfurt ("Pig Crossing" in German) is a beautiful old city founded in the year 790. It is located in the southern German state of Bavaria in the lower Franconia region; rich with history, culture, and a long relationship and partnership with the American military after World War II.

Until September 2014, the U.S. Army garrison in Schweinfurt was home to roughly six thousand people including about two thousand soldiers, family members, Department of Defense civilian employees, and their dependents.

The garrison was closed due to an ongoing effort to concentrate the U.S. military's footprint in Germany to fewer communities. The city is located along the banks of the Main River and is about eighty miles east of Frankfurt, Germany.

During World War II, both Ledward and Conn Barracks were military installations built and occupied by the Nazis. The airfield three miles to the east of the downtown was built as a secret Luftwaffe fighter base from which Messerschmitt Bf-

109's were flown. Eight large hangers were built with hydraulic elevator floors so the aircraft could be safely stored underground. Near the end of World War II, American forces captured the base and destroyed all of the Nazi aircraft by flooding the underground areas and welding all access doors shut. Rumor had it the aircraft still contained machine guns and aerial bombs.

Schweinfurt is perhaps best known for a World War II bombing raid that took place on October 14, 1943, by the Eighth Air Force; a day that would go down in U.S. aviation history as "Black Thursday." Of 291 American B-17's which left England, 229 bombed the city, and sixty bombers were shot down resulting in 639 men being killed. The target was too deep into enemy territory for American and British fighter planes to escort them.

So the unescorted bombers had to contend with the German fighters stationed at the nearby airfield (at which I was stationed in 1970). The bombing raid was carried out primarily to destroy three large ball-bearing factories (SKF, FAG, and Kugelfisher) located in the middle of the city. Allied forces determined that without ball-bearing production, the German war effort would be severely crippled. Ball bearings are used in virtually every mechanical device from aircraft engines and fuselages to machine guns.

In 1970, the American officers' club was located at the airfield that had been built by the Nazis in early 1938. It was a large two-story Gothic-styled building that was very ornate and beautifully appointed inside. When it was originally built, an underground tram was also constructed that went to a military housing area located on the outskirts of Schweinfurt, where German Luftwaffe pilots and crew lived.

Within a few days of arriving at "D" Troop, I was assigned a furnished apartment in the officers' section of the American military housing compound. It was the one built by the Nazis. Knowing that I lived and flew from a former Third Reich military installation was strange.

To solve my immediate transportation need, I bought a used 1959 VW "bug" from a departing pilot for $200. He had paid the same for it from a departing pilot who paid the same for it from a departing pilot, etc. It didn't look like much but worked fine while I waited for my newly-ordered Mercedes Benz to arrive. Three months later, when my 1970 Mercedes CE-250 arrived, I sold the VW bug to a newly arrived pilot for $200. I paid $5,000 for the new Mercedes! It was a great automobile—very fast on the Autobahn, where I could cruise all day at 110-120 mph when traveling around Europe.

I was assigned the job of Aero Scout platoon leader and had approximately twelve Warrant Officer pilots under my command. Additionally, I had about thirty crew chiefs and mechanics that reported to me.

At first we flew vintage Korean War helicopters that were the OH-13S models (similar to those flown in the 1970s television series *MASH*). All of them had patched bullet holes from the war. Soon we received OH-58's (Kiowa's) which were known as the Bell Jet Ranger model 206. (It is still a major production aircraft by Bell Helicopter Textron, but now is designated as the 505 and capable of carrying six passengers.) The OH-58's we flew in Germany were four-passenger helicopters powered by an Allison 420-horsepower shaft turbine engine. Its top speed was 138 mph and had a range of 374 nautical miles. It was a very stable aircraft, but not nearly as maneuverable as the Hughes OH-6 LOH I had been flying in Vietnam.

The 7th Cavalry's mission was to defend an area of Germany known as the "Fulda Gap" which was an area between the East

German border (no longer existing) and Frankfurt that contained two corridors of lowlands through which tanks might be driven in a surprise attack by the Soviet Union and their Warsaw Pact allies to seize crossings of the Rhine River. Named for the town of Fulda, the Fulda Gap was strategically important during the Cold War.

It was the route along which Napoleon chose to withdraw his armies after defeat at the Battle of Leipzig. The route was also used by the U.S. XII Corp during World War II to attack the German army.

During the Cold War, the Fulda Gap was one of two known routes for a hypothetical Soviet tank attack upon West Germany from Eastern Europe, especially East Germany. The concept of a major tank battle along the Fulda Gap was a predominant element of NATO war planning during the Cold War, and weapons such as nuclear tube and missile artillery were developed with such an eventuality in mind. The 7th Cavalry's primary job was to repel any Russian or East German attack on Western Europe. (As if we would stand a chance against their huge armies.)

Since there was a shortage of pilots in the unit, I went to the U.S. Army flight training center in Schwabish Hall, Germany, to become qualified as a Cobra pilot in case I was needed if World War III began!

One of the first people that I met at "D" troop was Capt. Robert (Bob) Lifsey. He was from Ann Arbor, Michigan, and had learned to snow ski as a child. We became friends, and he told me about the many wonderful ski areas located in Germany and the Alps. Bob was the "D" troop platoon leader for the Cobra Gunships (AH-1G) which had arrived about the same time as the OH-58's.

Bob and I went on several ski trips to Garmish-Partinkirchen, a U.S. Army garrison located in southern Bavaria near Munich. After World War II, the U.S. military confiscated the ski area and hotel and claimed it as a "War Prize." It is still owned by the United States of America and is a major recreational facility for all U.S. military personnel and families stationed in Europe.

We also skied at Berchtesgaden, which is in the German Bavarian Alps near the border with Austria some eighteen miles south of Salzburg. The Berchtesgaden Hof Hotel, located in the center of the city, was one of the hotels at which we stayed. It was a historically significant hotel where famous WWII visitors stayed, such as Eva Braun, General Erwin Rommel, Joseph Goebbles, and Heinrich Himmler (all Nazis).

Obersalzburg, a nearby mountain village, was where the famous "Eagles Nest" was built as a present for Adolf Hitler's 50th birthday in 1939. Both Herman Goring and Martin Bormann had homes built nearby so they could be close to their *Fuhrer* (German for "The Leader").

After the war, Obersalzburg became a U.S. military zone and most of its buildings were requisitioned by the U.S. Army. The Hotel Platterhof was rebuilt and renamed the General Walker Hotel. It served as an integral part of the U.S. Armed Forces Recreation Centers (AFRC) for the duration of the Cold War. In 1995, fifty years after the end of World War II, Berchtesgaden was turned over to Bavarian authorities to facilitate European military spending reductions mandated by the United States Congress.

The snow skiing at both German locations was phenomenal and the views of the Alps were spectacular. We also skied the tallest mountain in Germany called the Zugspitze which was a giant extinct volcano cul-de-sac.

While attending Texas Tech University, I studied French for

two years. In high school, I had studied Spanish for four years, but Tech would only allow me to take junior and senior level (300-400) Spanish literature classes. So I decided to take French, which was an easy transition because, like Spanish, it was a Romance language and the vocabulary was similar. Speaking both languages was helpful while living in Europe, but I decided to also take German language lessons.

That way I could at least ask "Dónde está el cuarto de baño?" (Spanish), "Où sont les toilettes?" (French), and "Wo ist die toilette? (German). Using all three languages, I could travel all over Europe and make myself understood, except in Italy, although most Italians spoke English too.

Most of my military tour of duty in Germany consisted of planning for war with the Soviet Union and the Warsaw Pact through numerous field training exercises (FTX's). These exercises usually lasted for two weeks at locations in Grafenwoehr and Wildflecken. (There's no "Fleckin" like "Wild Fleckin" was the local joke.) Both were large U.S. Army military installations that had multiple firing ranges for helicopters and Sheridan tanks. Our living accommodations at these facilities consisted of a squad-sized canvas tent with a gasoline-powered stove in the center. We slept in army sleeping bags on the ground.

In the summer, it wasn't too bad because the temperature at night was in the fifty to sixty degree range; however, in the winter temperatures frequently were at or below zero, and it was bitterly cold. Regardless of the weather and climate, we still went on FTX's because when World War III started it probably would occur when NATO forces least expected it. The Russians were notorious and famous for attacking and fighting during the extreme cold of winter and we had to be prepared for that eventuality.

After I had been with the 7th Cav for about eighteen months, I received a telephone call at my apartment one evening. When I answered the phone, a voice I didn't recognize said, "Is this Captain Corvin?" (I had been promoted to Captain on April 1, 1971) "Yes, it is. Who is this?" The person answered saying, "My name is Bill Smith and I'm with the Department of Defense. A colleague of mine, Don Jones, and I would like to meet with you tomorrow evening and offer you a job." I said, "I already have one." Bill said, "We know. I'm holding your official U.S. Army 201 personnel file." I was shocked and said, "How the hell did you get that!" He said, "That's not important. Will you meet with us or not, Captain?"

I hesitated a moment and then replied, "Yes I will, but you guys better have plenty of ID to prove you're with DOD or I'm going to do my best to whip your asses, if this is a hoax." He laughed and said "Let's meet at the Rathskeller bar in downtown Schweinfurt tomorrow at 1900 hours and we will talk further then." He abruptly hung up. I sat there a moment wondering what was going on.

Then I recalled an intelligence briefing I attended a couple of months earlier warning us of Soviet and East German spies pretending to be American intelligence officers to snare GIs into working for them. If that was the case here, I was going to deal with it in the most extreme manner!

The next day I went to the airfield and at 1700 hours left to go back to my apartment and change into civilian clothes. About a year earlier, I had purchased a .45-caliber, semi-automatic Colt Gold Cup National Match from the Schweinfurt gun club. There was a pistol range behind our operations building and the ammo was free, so I frequently shot targets there. I checked to make sure there was a round in the chamber and the magazine was full and then stuck it in my waistband, zipped up my leather jacket, and walked out the door to go to the meeting.

I arrived at the Rathskeller bar at 1815 hours hoping that "Bill and Don" were not there. I walked to a small table near the rear wall and sat down facing the front door. The waitress came over and said "Guten Abend! Was wollen Sie? I replied, "Ein Bier, bitte." She left and returned with my beer. I said, "Danke schon," paid her "Zwei Deutschmarks" ($.50), and sat there slowly sipping my beer waiting to see if any Americans came through the front door.

It was very dark in the bar, which was underground, with an outside door leading to stairs going up to the street. Shortly before 1900 hours, two men walked in and stood at the door looking around the room. One of them was holding a briefcase. He saw me sitting at the back wall, said something to the other man, and then they walked over to my table. "Are you Captain Corvin? he asked. "If you really have my 201 file then you ought to know if I am or not!" I replied. He chuckled and said, "I guess you're right. May we sit down?" I said, "Sure, have a seat." I adjusted my jacket because my .45 was uncomfortable in my waistband. Bill and Don introduced themselves and we shook hands. Bill said, "You really didn't have to bring that." I said, "Bring what?" He said, "Relax, Captain, we're on your side." I put my hand on the gun inside my jacket and replied, "You better prove it, right now!"

They looked at each other, then Bill opened up the briefcase so I could see inside and pulled out my U.S. Army 201 personnel file. He shoved it over to me and said, "Tell me if you think it's real." I thumbed through it for a while and saw handwritten notes from various military command officials that appeared to be authentic.

"If you guys are spooks, then you know that any document can be copied in such a way as to make it look like originals," I said. Don spoke up for the first time and gruffly said, "Keep your voice down, Stan." I shrugged and then asked them for their IDs. They both produced official-looking CIA identity cards. The names on the IDs were "Bill Smith" and "Don Jones" which I was pretty sure were not their real names. "Let's cut out the BS and get to the point," I said. "Okay, how would you like to go back to Danang and fly classified missions for us?" Bill said. "I'd rather be dragged by a horse through a cactus patch." I replied. "You're not back in Texas, Stan," Don laughingly said. "Seriously, what do you guys want?" I asked.

They spent the next hour explaining they were recruiting pilots to fly special classified missions out of the old 5th Special Forces' compound at Marble Mountain located near Danang airfield in Vietnam. They wanted me to join their team because I was familiar with I Corp. and I had been recommended to them by someone. (They refused to tell me who it was; however, I learned later that it was Sergeant Major Vidrine.) If I agreed, they offered to have the Department of the Army send me to Fort Rucker, Alabama, to get qualified in CH-47 Chinooks and UH-1N twin-engine Hueys.

I really wanted to learn how to fly twin-engine helicopters so that I would have that training if I ever decided to leave the U.S. Army. "Let me think about this for a few days and then we'll talk," I told them. "I'll call you the day after tomorrow," Bill said. They got up from the table and we shook hands, then they walked out of the bar. I sat there for a few minutes wondering what was going on.

Two days later at 2000 hours, the telephone rang at my apartment. I answered it, and Bill said, "What have you decided,

Captain Corvin?" I replied, "We've got a deal; *if* I can get the Chinook and UH-1N training you offered." He answered, "You will have those orders within the next ten days and report to Fort Rucker fourteen days later." I said, "Then let's do it!" He replied, "I'll get to work on it tomorrow, but under no circumstances are you to tell anyone about this conversation or our meeting the other night. Agreed?" I said, "Agreed!" He then hung up. With that conversation I decided to return back to Vietnam for my second tour.

The next day I went to the airfield and started to walk into my COs office when I remembered what "Bill" had said about talking to anyone. I turned around and went to my desk in the operations building and decided not to tell anyone, including my friends, what I'd done.

In about a week, Maj. Kyle came to me one morning with paperwork in his hand and asked me why I was being transferred to Fort Rucker and then back to Danang. I feigned shock and dismay at being sent back to Vietnam, and told him I didn't know anything about it. Several pilots from our unit had recently received orders to go back to Vietnam on a second tour, so my CO wasn't particularly surprised. Secretly, I was elated to get the training in twin-engine helicopters, even if it meant flying classified missions out of Danang for the CIA.

Three weeks later I departed from Ramstein Air Force Base, Germany, and flew to McGuire Air Force Base in New Hanover, New Jersey. From there I flew to Dallas, Texas, and called my dad in Waco. He was surprised to hear from me and said that he would come pick me up at Love Field in about two hours. I went to the airport bar and waited for him to arrive. When he got there, my mother was not with him because he said she was teaching school. He asked me what was going on and I explained that I was to report to Fort Rucker, Alabama, in a few days to learn how to fly Chinooks and twin-engine Hueys. Then I explained that after the training I was being reassigned back to Vietnam.

He was absolutely stunned and said, "Well, I'll be damned. Your mother is not going to like this, that's for sure!" I replied, "Dad, I'm really sorry, but I have my orders from Department of the Army." Actually, while at Ft. Rucker, I received orders assigning me to the United States Agency for International Development (USAID) who had taken over the 5th Special Forces' compound near Marble Mountain in Danang, Vietnam.

We arrived in Waco at my parents' house late in the afternoon. My mother was there and thrilled to see me. We sat down at the dining room table and I explained that I was going to Fort Rucker for some helicopter training and then back to Danang. I will never forget the look of fear and anguish on my mother's face when she realized I was going back to Vietnam for a second time. She started trembling and crying! I quickly told her that it was going to be okay because I would be flying VIPs who only went into very safe areas. (It was a lie, but I didn't want to tell her the truth.) She said, "Stan, Jr., I know that you are not telling us everything, but frankly I'm so angry and sad that I don't want to know anymore." She got up from the table, went back to the bedroom and slammed the door.

My dad and I stayed up late that night drinking and talking. The next morning, my mother and I had coffee before she left to teach fifth grade at her elementary school. She apologized for leaving me the night before, and said that she wanted us to go to dinner that night. She asked my dad to call my sister, Penny, who was in nursing school in Dallas, to come down and join us. As she got up to leave, I went over and gave her a hug, then she broke down again and started to cry. She pushed me away, walked out to the garage, got in her car, and drove off. My heart was heavy, and I was sad about hurting my mother. Later that afternoon my dad drove me to the local Chevrolet dealership where I bought a two-year-old pickup. I asked him to keep it for me after I finished my training at Fort Rucker and until I got back from Vietnam.

I spent a few days with my family then loaded my truck and drove to the base in Alabama. While driving there, I crested a hill just in time to see several cars being pulled over by the Mississippi Highway Patrol. They motioned for me to pull in behind several parked automobiles. When I did, a patrolman came from the front of the line and walked to my window. He asked me, "Do you have any idea how fast you were going?" I said, "No, sir."

"Well," he said, "I've never clocked a pickup on my radar going as fast as you were at 110 mph." I grimaced and said, "I'm sorry officer, but I've been living in Europe where there are no speed limits and didn't realize I was going that fast." He asked if I was in the military and I told him I was in the U.S. Army getting ready to go back to Vietnam on my second tour.

I showed him my military ID and my International Driver's License that I had obtained in Germany. He wrote me out a ticket and said that because I was in the military, I could write the county judge in a few days and find out what the fine was going to be. I thanked him and then slowly drove away.

Once at my training unit at Fort Rucker, I wrote a letter to the judge telling her what I had told the patrolman about driving in Europe. I added that I was a helicopter pilot going back to Vietnam on my second tour and probably would not live very long. (It was the best sob story I could muster!) Two weeks later I received a letter from County Judge Emma Frickertt thanking me for my service and telling me that the fine would be $18.50 for court costs only! She said that I must also agree not to drive in Mississippi for a year after I left for Vietnam.

I sent a letter back to her that day with an $18.50 postal money order and a promise not to drive in her state for one year. I never heard from her or the Mississippi Highway Patrol again.

The training went well at Fort Rucker, and I actually had fun learning to fly the CH-47 Chinook and the twin engine UH-1N Huey. After the training, I went back to Texas and visited with my family for about a week. My mother was still upset and angry about me returning to a combat zone. But she had been with my dad for twenty-five years while he was in the Air Force, and understood the way things worked. I flew from Dallas Love Field to McCord Air Force Base and then on to Danang, Vietnam.

CHAPTER 30

ASSIGNED TO USAID

Arriving at Danang airfield, I gathered my luggage and flight gear, and went to the check-in desk located in the terminal. I told the sergeant that I needed a ride to the old 5th Special Forces compound near Marble Mountain. He asked me for my military identification card which I gave him. After looking at it and checking a list on a clipboard, he told me, "Sir, my instructions are to have a driver take you to the USAID complex located there." "That's great sergeant. Do you have a jeep outside?" I said. "No, sir. We have an air-conditioned car that will take you," he replied. *I think I'm going to like it here. USAID certainly has better amenities than the Army*, I thought. A young private came over to me and carried my bags outside to a grey four-door Chevy sedan with no markings. We got in the car and the driver turned on the A/C full blast. Within minutes the interior was cold. It was first time I had ever driven in Vietnam in a vehicle with air-conditioning.

While driving through downtown Danang and to the Marble Mountain airfield, I was surprised to see no American military vehicles or personnel on the streets. There were plenty of military vehicles, but they all belonged to the Vietnamese Army.

On my first tour in 1968, there were 536,100 Americans in Vietnam. That number had dropped to 475,200 in 1969, and

334,600 in 1970. When I arrived back in 1971, at the beginning of the year, there were only 156,800 in the entire country, and by the end of the year that was down to 24,200. Four months later, on April 29, 1972, total American troops in Vietnam were only 600 and I was one of them! Clearly the war was winding down and I wasn't sure what my role was going to be flying for the civilian organization, USAID.

As we neared the complex, I noticed there were no helicopters or airplanes flying from Danang Air Force Base or Marble Mountain air strip. The sky was completely empty of aircraft. Two years earlier, it had been filled with all types of aircraft taking off and landing. It was eerily quiet and strange not seeing any this time. I began to have an ominous feeling about my new assignment.

We arrived at the main gate of the China Beach complex and were met by a Vietnamese MP guard. He recognized the driver and asked for my identification, which I gave him. He took it into the guard shack, made a telephone call and came back saying, "Here's your ID, sir. They are expecting you at headquarters." I thanked him and the driver took me to the old 5th Special Forces' headquarters building where I had frequently met with Sergeant Major Vidrine two years earlier. I noticed that all signs of their occupation of the complex since 1967 were gone! There also were no indications whatsoever that it was occupied by any American organization.

When we arrived, the driver got out and opened the door for me! Again I thought, *Wow, this is totally different than my Army experience.* I walked into the building and the driver followed me with my luggage. A civilian clerk motioned me over and asked me for my military ID. I gave it to him and he logged me into a large ledger book. He handed it back to me and told me to take a seat. "Who am I waiting for now?" I asked. "Somebody will be with you in a few minutes," he answered.

I went over to a leather couch and sat down listening to the quiet hum of the air-conditioning system. In a few minutes I heard a door open and someone walk down the corridor in my direction. I looked up and saw a forty-three-year-old man wearing a white short-sleeved shirt and a tie. I stood up as he came over to me, shook my hand, and said, "Glad you made it here okay, Captain Corvin. How was the flight?" I said, "It was long, cramped and tiring. Who are you?"

He laughed and said, "My name is James Wesson, and I've already heard that you are very direct and abrupt. But that's okay with me. I'm a no-nonsense guy too." We walked back to his office and sat down at a conference table. Then he said, "You will receive all your flying assignments from me and report only to me afterward. Do you understand?" I replied, "Absolutely, sir!" He chuckled and said, "Stan, we are very informal around here so you can forget about any military bearing issues. Most of us are civilians working for the U.S. government." I asked, "Just out of curiosity, who's the boss?" He smiled and said, "I am!"

We talked for about two hours with James explaining what the USAID mission was all about and its affiliation with the CIA. He also said that no one ever used last names and not to expect it when being introduced to someone new. I told him that was going to be fine with me. He got up and said, "Let's get you settled into your new quarters. How about that?" I started to say "Yes, sir," but changed it to "Sounds good, James." He grinned and clapped me on the shoulder and said, "That's more like it."

We went to the front entrance and he told the clerk to have someone pick me up and take me to building "A," room 3. We shook hands again and he said, "Let's have dinner in the cafeteria this evening around 7:00 p.m. and I'll introduce you to two other pilots that fly for us." I told him, "I look forward to it."

A jeep pulled up in front of the door and I loaded my two bags in the back and got in the front passenger seat. The driver was Vietnamese. He took me to a nearby single-story building with a large "A" painted on the front next to the door. He said "Dai Uy, your room is number three on the left side of the hall." (Dai Uy is pronounced "Die Wee" and is "Captain" in Vietnamese) He handed me two keys and I unloaded my bags from the jeep.

I went to the front door and opened it. Cold air engulfed me as I walked into the hall. I thought, *We're not in Kansas anymore, Dai Uy!* and approached the second door to the left with a number three on it. I unlocked the door and went into the air-conditioned room that was to be my home for a while.

The room was ten feet by twelve feet with a single bed in one corner made up with pillows, sheets, and a bedspread. Next to it was a nightstand with a lamp, and beside that was a small desk with a telephone and lamp. There was a built-in closet next to which was an attached sink, a mirror, and a small refrigerator. I was amazed! I had all the comforts of home. It basically was a modestly-furnished hotel room; not at all like the sweltering hot, unfinished wood framed hooch I'd lived in for sixteen months at the Warlords in Chu Lai. I had definitely come up in the world; or so I thought at the time.

I unpacked and walked into the hall looking for the bathroom. It was at the end, so I went down there to check it out. Inside there were a half-dozen shower stalls with curtains and six commodes, each in its own private enclosure. Along one wall were six sinks with mirrors above each. There were two large open shelving units with folded white towels and wash cloths. This was definitely better than any accommodations I had experienced in the Army. I walked back to my room, unpacked, laid down on the bed, and immediately fell asleep. I'd been up for nearly forty-eight hours.

The twenty-three hour flight from McCord Air Force Base in Washington State to Danang had been on a Military Air Transport Service (MATS) C-141 troop carrier. It had a limited number of passenger seats that were jammed together so there wasn't much legroom. Box lunches with sandwiches inside were served enroute by the male Air Force crew. (No cute female stewardesses!) Our flight path included a stop at Elmendorf Air Force Base in Alaska, then nonstop to Tokyo, Japan, for refueling. From there we flew directly to Danang Air Force Base.

I was awakened by the telephone ringing. I answered it and James said, "I probably woke you up, but wanted to make sure your accommodations were okay." I mumbled hoarsely, "They're much better than okay." He laughed and said, "I'll meet you in the cafeteria in about an hour for dinner." I asked, "Where is it located?" He said "Do you remember where the steam bath and private massage rooms were located when Special Forces were here?"

I said, "Of course. I was here when Sergeant Major Vidrine had them built and stocked with fifteen Chinese prostitutes." He said, "Well, that's all been torn down and a modular cafeteria, bar, and recreation room has replaced it." I said, "I'll meet you there in one hour." He replied, "See you then." and hung up.

I got up, showered, and dressed in civvies. I walked to the cafeteria and entered the front door. The inside was brightly lit and cool from the air conditioning. There were a couple of guys sitting at a table eating dinner, but no one else in the room. I walked over to the bar, sat down, and a Vietnamese bartender asked me what I wanted to drink. I told him a beer, and suddenly I had a strange feeling like I had come home! I quietly murmured to myself, *This is where I belong.*

The Danang 5th Special Forces compound was an interesting place. Opened in November 1967, it was designated Forward Operational Base #4 (FOB#4). Located on China Beach, adjacent to Marble Mountain Airfield, the base was responsible for clandestine reconnaissance operations into Laos, the DMZ (Demilitarized Zone), and North Vietnam.

One year later, in October 1968, FOB #4 was designated as Command-and-Control North (CCN) responsible for all covert operations north of Danang. In early 1971, 5th Special Forces Group was withdrawn from Vietnam, and the site was transferred to American civilian intelligence personnel, i.e., USAID and the CIA.

I turned around on the barstool when I heard the front door open. James walked in, came over, and sat down next to me. He ordered a beer and said, "How do you like the accommodations?" I replied, "They're better than I expected." He said, "Well, our appropriations funding allows us to live a little better than the military units." There was a pause in the conversation and then he said, "Let's move to a table and talk about what you'll be doing."

We sat down at a corner table and I moved around so that my back was against the wall. "Are you always hyper-alert and on edge?" he asked. "Only when I'm in Vietnam," I replied. "My guys in Germany said that you were carrying a .45 automatic when you met them in the bar in Schweinfurt," he said. I looked surprised. "We are a close-knit organization that stays in touch with each other when we are arranging for new people to come into our fold," he said. "I wasn't sure what to expect when I met them, so I decided to be cautious," I told him. He smiled,

"*Caution and secrecy* is our unofficial motto! I'm hungry, let's get something to eat."

We went to the cafeteria line where there was a selection of steak, chicken, salad, and dessert. (The food was much better than anything served in the Army, except of course in the Generals' mess.)

After eating and talking about football and the anti-war situation back in the USA, James asked me, "Have you ever heard of the Phuong Hoang civic action campaign?" I said, "I don't think so." Then he asked, "How about the Phoenix Program?" I leaned back in my chair with a surprised look on my face and replied, "Is that what this is all about?" He said, "Yes, it is, and we need a few reliable military pilots to transport civilian operatives around Northern I Corp and other locations outside of Vietnam."

"So what you're telling me is that I will be flying "spooks" on covert operations?" I asked. He slowly leaned forward, put his arms on the table and said to me, "Don't ever use that term again! The people you will be flying are dedicated patriots who are performing an essential service to the national security of the United States of America. We prefer to call them "operators" and their jobs are extraordinarily dangerous. They work in small groups, or alone many times, in isolated areas with absolutely no help available if they get into trouble." I apologized for my flippant comment and James leaned back in his chair, took a sip of his beer and glared at me.

The Phoenix Program was a rural hamlet security initiative run by the Central Intelligence Agency. It relied on centralized intelligence gathering to identify and eliminate the Viet Cong infrastructure which was made up of the upper echelon of the National Liberation Front (Communist) political cadres and party members. This program was one of the most controversial of all operations undertaken by United States personnel in South Vietnam. American-led South Vietnamese "hit teams" arrested, tortured, and killed many suspected communist leaders. After the war, the program was acknowledged by top-level U.S. government officials, as well as Viet Cong and North Vietnamese leaders, to have been very effective in reducing the power of the local communist cadres in the South Vietnamese villages, hamlets, and countryside. From 1968 to 1972, the Phoenix program resulted in the deaths of approximately 84,000 communist officials.

Finally, after an awkward silence, James quietly said, "We have recently lost a lot of good people and I'm sensitive to any offhand remarks about them." I apologized again and vowed to myself to be more careful in what I said. James then went on to explain that I would be flying the UH-1N Huey to pick up and deliver the American operators to various villages in remote locations of the I Corp area of operations (AO). "You and the copilot will be flying alone, mostly at night, with no backup available at all. You've probably noticed that there are virtually no aircraft flying around here now. Which also means there is no help if you get into trouble, so you'll be flying the twin engine Huey because of its redundancy and reliability," he said.

He continued to explain that occasionally I would be asked to fly missions thirty to forty miles out over the South China Sea to dispose of body bags. "Will you have a problem with that?" he asked. "Are they all communists?" I asked in turn. "Absolutely!" he said. "Then it will be my pleasure to rid the world of the Commie pinko fag bastards," I said with a smile.

He laughed out loud at that. "Stan, my friend, you are going to fit in well around here." For a moment I flashed back to the day, on my first tour, when I found the murdered Ruff Puffs, innocent villagers, raped women, and children burned alive. I smiled to myself and thought, *I am once more the Avenger ready to administer my righteous wrath!*

James stood up and said, "The other pilots will arrive over the next two days, so go ahead and get settled in to your quarters. You'll begin flying a few days after they get here." I asked, "Are you going to introduce me to the two pilots that are already here?" He replied, "They are with the commo section at Marble Mountain trying to get the old KY-28 encryption machines to work in the new Hueys. They probably won't be back before midnight." I said, "I'll try to meet them tomorrow. By the way I need to go to the PX and stock up on a few things." He said, "Come by the office tomorrow morning and you can take a jeep there."

I thanked him and we both walked out into the stifling hot, humid night. I was really glad that I had an air-conditioned room in which to sleep. He went back to his office and I went back to my room. The next morning I picked up a jeep at the main office and drove to the Danang PX still located on China Beach.

The PX had been significantly reduced in size as American troop withdrawals took place. I bought some toiletries, a fan, a clock radio, three thick spiral-bound notebooks, and two bottles of scotch, then drove back to the compound where I unloaded everything in my room.

I slept late the next morning and awoke around 9:00 a.m. when I heard noise in the hallway. I got out of bed, opened the door, and saw two guys in OD green T-shirts and skivvies walking down to the bathroom. They apparently heard my door open, because they stopped walking, turned and looked at me standing in the doorway. I yawned and said, "Good morning!"

They walked back to me and one said, "You must be the FNG."
I laughed and said, "Now I really feel like I'm back in Vietnam."
We shook hands and I introduced myself. Their names were Bill
Swofford and Darrell Yates. Both were army CW-2's who had
arrived back in Danang a week earlier on their second tour in
country. We talked for a few minutes then they invited me to eat
breakfast with them at the cafeteria. I went back in my room to
get my shaving kit and walked down the hall to the communal
bathroom.

While shaving, I saw that Bill, at the sink next to mine, had
several small indentations on the top and back of his closely
shaved head. When we had met in the hall, Darrell did all the
talking and Bill didn't say a word. "So, Bill, how did you get the
dents in your head?" I asked.

"When I was a kid living in Arkansas, my mom had a really
vicious boyfriend who once beat me with a ball peen hammer
when he got drunk," he replied quietly.

"That's too bad," I said.

"No problem, the next night when he passed out on the sofa,
I took my baseball bat and hit him as hard as I could in the face
while he was asleep. When he got out of the hospital a week later,
he packed up and left."

"How old were you?" I asked.

"Twelve years old, and I don't want to talk about it anymore,
okay?"

"Sure." I said.

Over the next four months, Bill flew with me on our nightly
missions, and I got to know him well enough to believe that he
was a deeply troubled sociopath. He was introverted and a loner
who stayed by himself most of the time. I decided that I would be
very cautious around him.

CHAPTER 31

"SPOOKY" FLYING

At 1900 hours, Bill and I pre-flighted the UH-1N (Iroquois) twin Huey sitting in a heavily guarded revetment at Marble Mountain airfield. While at Fort Rucker, Alabama, after learning to fly the enormous twin engine and rotor Boeing CH-47 "Chinook" heavy cargo helicopter, I spent two weeks transitioning into the streamlined Bell 212 helicopter.

Several days were spent in ground school learning about the twin engine power plants, beefed-up rotor systems, and dual hydraulics. The 212 was very similar to the single engine Hueys which I'd flown before; however, it was slightly bigger, longer, and heavier. The aircraft had a fifteen-seat configuration with two pilots and up to thirteen passengers. It was powered by two Pratt & Whitney turbine jet engines driving a single output shaft to the main rotor system. The engines were capable of producing a combined 1800 shaft horsepower. Should one engine fail, the remaining engine delivered 900 shaft horsepower enabling the helicopter to maintain cruise performance at maximum weight. USAID had six of these aircraft in Danang.

They were modified with an added Stability Control Augmentation System (SCAS) which provided rudimentary computerized servo inputs to the rotor head to help stabilize the aircraft during instrument flight conditions. This modification allowed the removal of the gyroscopic "stabilization bar" on top of the main rotor head, relying instead on the computer system for stability.

Complementing the usual helicopter radios, consisting of an FM, VHF, and UHF transmitters/receivers; the UH-1N's were equipped with a specialized voice encryption device based upon an analog transistor circuitry called a KY-28. In 1968, the encrypted equipment was put into service because the North Vietnamese were intercepting plain text radio transmissions and exploiting the resulting gathered intelligence against American forces.

The KY-28 was fitted with an internal shock sensor. If the helicopter crashed, the resulting "G" forces would trip this sensor thus resetting the crypto key and rendering the radio useless to the enemy. The pilot's microphone was plugged into the KY-28 control assembly mounted on the helicopter center console. This in turn was wired directly into the audio control inputs of the other transmitter/receivers. Voice quality and recognition using this crypto device was *terrible.*

Even under optimal conditions, everyone sounded like *Donald Duck.* The system was used only in FM voice communications, which primarily occurred between the aircraft and someone on the ground. Transmission and reception had a one second initialization delay which made the system impractical when a helicopter was being fired upon and immediate communication with a ground unit was needed.

The UH-1N's had the normal aircraft navigation aids of ADF, VOR, and ILS with glide slope receivers. USAID had the helicopters additionally equipped with both TACAN and DECCA receivers which were highly sophisticated and precise navigation units capable of pinpointing a specific location on the ground to within thirty feet. The DECCA unit had a moving map display that constantly showed the helicopter's position in relation to the terrain over which it was flying.

Both these units were critical to me, because many times I had to land at night with only a grid coordinate on a map and no visual or recognizable terrain features nearby. Most of the landing sites were on rural dirt roads with no cities, towns, hamlets, or villages nearby.

Thankfully, Vietnam at that time was sparsely populated in the rural areas, so there were no power lines or telephone wires alongside the roads with which to contend. Wire strikes with power lines were a common cause of helicopter crashes near populated areas.

For three days, Bill and I flew with a civilian technician who taught us how to use the TACAN and DECCA navigational aids. It was very important instruction because our lives depended upon our ability to land at an exact location amongst "friendlies." Failure to do so would mean capture, along with horrible, unimaginable torture, and execution by the NVA and VC who hated the USAID and CIA. We were highly motivated to be very proficient in the equipment's use.

Prior to our first flight I went to the armorer, where I learned that he had several new Carl Gustav model 45 submachine guns in 9mm parabellum. It was commonly called the "Swedish K" because it was manufactured in Sweden. He gave me one after I explained that I had a thirteen-round 9mm Browning High Standard semi-automatic pistol as my personal side arm. It made sense to carry two weapons that used the same ammunition.

The Swedish K was a fully-automatic compact sub-machine gun with an overall length of twenty-one inches when the wire stock was folded. It had a straight blow back action that was capable of a cyclic rate of fire of six hundred rounds per minute and an effective range of about two hundred yards. Its magazine held thirty-six rounds. The armorer gave me a small soft-sided case and four extra magazines for the gun.

He also gave me five hundred rounds of 9mm parabellum ammo for both weapons. I had three extra thirteen-round magazines for my Browning pistol. Combined, I had a total of 232 rounds of ammunition with which to defend myself, if needed. (Ultimately I would need it in the final fight for my life on April 29, 1972! But that's another story and chapter in this book.)

We finished pre-flighting the aircraft, and I climbed in the left seat while Bill sat down in the right. The crew chief and A&P mechanic got in back on the right and left sides. As we buckled our harnesses, I said, "I've got the aircraft." I started both engines and checked to make sure the gauges were in the green. Then I finished the checklist items as Bill turned on all the navigation aids and radios and initialized the KY-28 encryption device.

Soon everything was ready. I picked the helicopter up to a three-foot hover and slowly backed it away from the revetment. As I turned onto the taxiway leading to the runway, I called Marble Mountain tower and said, "Tower, Helicopter Uniform Sierra 01 ready for takeoff on 36, over." The tower answered and said, "01, you are cleared for takeoff on 36." I replied, "Roger," taxied to the center of the runway, and took off north on our first night mission.

After ten minutes we crossed the Hai Van Pass, which is a seventeen hundred feet saddleback passageway located at the end of the Annamite mountain range on the South China Sea. It is near the Ai Van Son mountain peak which is 3,845 feet in altitude. The area is very beautiful and scenic.

Bill entered the coordinates of the rendezvous spot on both the Decca and TACAN navigational instruments. This allowed us the ability to fly in a straight line to our pickup point. Our mission for the evening was to pick up a lone American intelligence operative, along with three Vietnamese police officials, and deliver them to another rural road intersection thirty miles northwest of Hue. From that drop off point, we were to go to map coordinates twenty miles further south and pick up two American civilians and take them back to Hue.

The NAVAIDS worked perfectly and we were able to pinpoint both locations with no difficulty whatsoever. After the final departure of our passengers at Hue we returned back to Danang and Marble Mountain airfield. There we refueled the aircraft and parked it in the secure revetment. Our total flight time was approximately three hours. I thought, *Man, this going to be a piece of cake flying only a few hours each night.*

The next night we repeated a similar flight plan only this time instead of returning back to Danang, we flew to Quang Tri which is north of Hue, refueled and picked up and delivered different American personnel and Vietnamese police officials. When we finished our final flight, the sun was rising over the South China Sea. We returned back to Marble Mountain Airfield (MMAF), refueled and parked the helicopter in its revetment. Our total flying time had been approximately eight hours.

We fell into a routine of flying most of the night, returning to MMAF, sleeping during the day, and then repeating everything the next night. For the most part, all of our pickups and drop-offs were with different Americans and Vietnamese officials.

Then one evening, as I landed at a remote rendezvous dirt road location, a three-quarter ton South Vietnamese Army pickup backed up to the helicopter and some guys loaded four body bags in the helicopter cargo bay. A young American civilian intelligence operator with a crew cut climbed aboard, put on a headset and said to me, "On the way back to Danang make a detour out over the sea so that we can discard these body bags." I said, "Sure, how far offshore?" He replied, "About fifteen minutes."

We took off. I climbed to three thousand feet and headed southeast. As I approached the beach, I turned ninety degrees perpendicular to the shoreline and flew out over the South China Sea. After fifteen minutes, the operator got on the intercom and said, "This will do fine. Please slow the aircraft down to sixty knots and I'll throw these four bags overboard." I asked, "Shouldn't I descend down to a lower altitude?" He answered, "No, that's not necessary." When I slowed the helicopter down, he stood up and dragged each of the body bags to the door and threw them out. Then he said, "Let's head back to Danang."

We returned to Marble Mountain Airfield and I shut the aircraft down. When I got out, the operator came over to me. "Can I hitch a ride with you guys?" "Sure, but I have a question," I said. "Were the people in the body bags dead? I thought I saw movement when you threw them out?" "They are now and that's all you need to know," he smugly replied. "You asshole. What an idiotic thing to say!" I snarled as I stuck my face close to his. He shrugged his shoulders, walked away and over his shoulder said, "I'll find somebody else to hitch a ride with." I didn't like what we had just done; however, I knew it was part of what I was expected to do, so I just shut up. Fortunately, that was the only night flight out over the sea that I was asked to make. There were no more.

We continued to fly nightly missions over the next four months. It wasn't particularly exhausting, but it was stressful never knowing who was going to be at the rendezvous point and if they were going to shoot when we landed. Every fifth day, we were given a day off and time to go to the beach or hang out in our rooms. Bill Swofford never went outside his room, never went to the beach, and never played cards or socialized with anyone in the recreation room. He was completely reclusive.

Once, when I walked by his room, the door was open, and I saw a bayonet stuck in the wall just above his bed pillow. Laughingly I asked him what that was for and he said, "To gut anyone that comes near me while I'm asleep." He didn't smile or make any effort to explain it at all. I concluded that he was dangerous, mentally unstable, and not to be kidded about anything. I also decided that wild horses could never make me go into his room while he was sleeping.

One morning, after refueling from a nightly mission, James Wesson saw me as I returned to my quarters. He waved and walked over asking me if I would take Bill and go to Vung Tau the next day to pick up new NAVAIDS and KY-28 radios. "Sure, it will be a nice break," I said. "I'll arrange everything and you guys can leave tomorrow at noon. It's about a five-hour flight along the coast, if you refuel at Nha Trang on the way. You should get there before dark," he said. "Thanks, I look forward to it," I replied and went to my room to sleep.

Later that evening, I walked down the hall and knocked on Bill's door. He opened it and I told him about the trip to Vung Tau. "I've been there once. An Aussie helicopter company is stationed at the base. They're a bunch of loud, profane, bearded assholes that I don't like at all," he said. "Well, I doubt that we will have any dealings with them—just the American commo section," I said. But I was wrong—very, very wrong!

CHAPTER 32

THE FROG STORY

Vung Tau is a seaside resort city in southern Vietnam sixty miles northeast of Saigon (now Ho Chi Minh City). It has several beautiful beaches with emerald green water, perfect for snorkeling and scuba diving. During the French colonial period, when the country was known as Indochina, the president of France, Paul Doumer, built a large mansion there which is still a prominent landmark.

During the Vietnam War, the resort was used by both the Americans and Vietcong as an R&R site. Of course you couldn't tell who the VC were because they looked like all of the other indigenous Vietnamese tourists. But they were there!

I took off with Bill at 1100 hours and headed south along the beach climbing to eight thousand feet. The trip was approximately five hundred miles, so I planned to refuel at Nha Trang Air Force Base, which was about half way. The weather was perfect and, in pilots' terminology, was known as "CAVU" (Ceiling and Visibility Unlimited).

After about two and a half hours, the DME (distance measuring equipment) indicated the base was twenty miles in front of us. I called the tower and told them we were coming from the north to land and refuel. They cleared me and we approached the base where we landed and refueled. During the entire two and a half hour flight, Bill had not said a word, but then again, rarely did he ever talk when we flew our nightly missions. After refueling and stretching our legs we took off and climbed back up to eight thousand feet.

After a while, I asked Bill if everything was okay. He responded, "I guess so." I could tell that something was bothering him, so I turned off the intercom to the crew chief and mechanic sitting in the back and said to Bill, "What's going on, buddy?" He hesitated a moment and then answered, "The one time I was here before, I was sunning on the beach and got into a fight with three Aussies who were making fun of me because of the dents in my head." I asked, "When was that?" He replied, "Three years ago when I first arrived in country, on my first tour." I said, "Things have probably changed, so I doubt that there will be any problems." He said, "You're probably right, Stan. Let's just drop it." I said, "Okay. Don't worry, we are only going to be here overnight. By the way, out of curiosity, who won the fight?"

He answered, "I didn't have a scratch on me and I put all three of them in the hospital after a three-minute altercation. They were very drunk and I wasn't at all. The coke bottle I was drinking from worked really well as a weapon. But that's enough about it!" From that point on Bill didn't speak.

We approached Vung Tau from the north and got clearance to land. After refueling at the POL site, I taxied over to a hanger that had a large sign with COMMO/AVIONICS painted on the front. I told the crew chief to go inside and find out if we could pick up the NAVAIDS and KY-28's there. After a few minutes, he came back and said everything would be loaded into the helicopter the next morning before we took off because all the items were classified instruments and I had to personally sign a hand receipt for them. At the time, my security clearance was

"Crypto Top-Secret" because of the encoding capability of the KY-28 and the classified missions I flew.

We taxied back to an area where there were multiple revetments built for helicopters. The tower said that I could park in any of the empty ones, and a security detachment would be assigned to watch over it until we left the next morning. The tower operator said, "Who are you guys? We received information this morning you were coming in and to provide twenty-four-hour security for the aircraft." "We fly for a federal government agency and have some special agriculture and farming detection equipment on board that needs to be protected. It's no big deal!" I laughingly said. The tower said nothing more and I didn't either. I don't think they believed me either.

While shutting the helicopter engines down, an Army staff sergeant drove up in a jeep. The driver came over to me and said that he was from HHC 135th Assault Helicopter Company and he would take us to living quarters they kept for visitors.

The 135th Assault Helicopter Company and the Royal Australian Navy Helicopter Company had been formed two years earlier and was designated an "Experimental Military Unit" or EMU for short. The unit's role in Vietnam was to support the Royal Australian task force (ground infantry) and other free-world units (South Koreans and British) working in III and IV Corp. They were the only US/ Australian helicopter unit in existence. Their motto was *GET THE BLOODY JOB DONE*. The joke about their short name was the fact that emus can't fly!

With the two crewmembers, Bill and I got in the jeep and were driven a couple blocks away to an air-conditioned Quonset hut. The sergeant said the two enlisted men could stay in his hooch, and Bill and I were to share a room in the Quonset hut.

I asked him where the mess hall and officers' club was located. "They are just behind you," he answered.

They were both nice air-conditioned facilities close to where we were staying overnight. He told me that dinner was being served and if we hurried we could beat the crowd because all the pilots and crew were returning from Tay Nihn where they had been flying on a combat helicopter assault mission.

The two enlisted crewmembers went into a hooch with the sergeant. Bill and I went into the air-conditioned hooch containing four metal Army beds. I was a little worried about sleeping in the same room with Bill, but didn't say anything. We left our small RON (remain overnight) bags on the beds, but because the room was not secured, Bill took his Car-15 and I took my Swedish K with me. We ate excellent steak and lobster in the mess hall. The cooks told us the Australian Navy provided the lobsters twice a week to be served to all the pilots and crewmembers. It was all very civilized.

After eating, Bill and I went to the officers' club which was a large temporary structure being used while a new club was being built. It had a dozen tables and a long plywood bar. We walked to the bar and I sat at the end with Bill to the left of me. We ordered two beers—the bartender came back and set them down in front of us. I gave him $2 MPC and told him to keep the change. (Beers still cost 10 cents each.)

While sitting there, I noticed that Bill had his bayonet stuck in his right boot. I thought that was amusing because I used to do the same thing until I lost mine in a river. We sat there not talking and drank our beers. Off in the distance, I heard a large group of helicopters approaching. We were only a hundred yards away from the flight line, so in a few minutes the sound of the rotors and engines rattled the bottles behind the bar—the noise was deafening. (Not that Bill and I were heavily engaged in a conversation.)

Soon everything was quiet as the helicopters were shut down. We could hear boisterous, loud, raucous laughter and yelling from the crews. Suddenly, the front door opened with a bang and approximately twenty Australian pilots and crew members rushed in. The group saw us sitting at the end of the bar and stopped talking.

An Australian Navy Lieutenant came over to me and introduced himself. I explained that we were staying in their visitor's quarters and were leaving the next morning for Danang. He was the XO and seemed to be a pretty good guy. He said to let him know if there was anything we needed, then he went to the other end of the bar where everybody had spread out.

Several of their helicopters had been hit by AK-47 ground fire but no one was injured, so they were very excited about what had taken place on the mission. Soon the noise level increased as everybody relaxed and had several beers under their belt. The conversation was primarily about their mission that day; however, several Aussies kept saying that they wished they had "Matilda" along for the ride.

Several of the Australians left and in a few minutes returned with three cooks carrying large trays of steak and lobster tails with all the trimmings. Everyone sat down at the tables and the cooks started serving the food, which I learned was a tradition that the EMUs celebrated whenever the unit came under heavy fire while on a mission. Once everyone had eaten and the dishes cleaned away the serious drinking and singing began.

For a couple of hours this went on as people came and left, then somebody said, "Let's bring Matilda out and show her to our guests." I thought that maybe Matilda was a Vietnamese barmaid, but I was wrong. The door opened and a large Aussie sporting a red handlebar mustache and bushy beard walked in carrying a big wire cage. He strolled over to the bar, set it down, and opened its door. In a few seconds, the biggest, ugliest, and nastiest looking frog I'd ever seen crawled out onto the wooden bar.

They explained that Matilda was a giant cane "toad" and the EMU's mascot. Her body was approximately nine inches long (not counting the length of the legs) and she weighed nearly five pounds. Her breed had been introduced into Australia as a method of agricultural pest control, but was now considered an invasive species which killed many of its native predators because of its highly toxic skin and poison glands.

Her handler took a small saucer and poured some beer into it. Then while wearing Nomex flight gloves, he picked Matilda up and sat her next to the saucer. A few seconds later, she began lapping at the beer. The pilots all thought this was hilarious and started cheering and clapping their hands.

After a few moments, Matilda stopped drinking and started slowly crawling down the bar towards Bill and me. Everyone was quiet, in gleeful anticipation of our reaction, as they watched her move closer to us. When she got in front of Bill, she stopped for a moment.

Bill had been sipping his beer and carefully watching Matilda crawl towards him. I saw him shift on his barstool and move his right shoulder as if to put his elbow on the bar. Suddenly, he reached down and pulled his bayonet from his right boot scabbard and forcefully stabbed Matilda in the back, impaling her large ugly squirming body to the plywood bar.

I sat there in horror wondering what was going to happen next as the EMUs jumped up. Bill never said a word, but grabbed the toad by the back as he pulled the bayonet out. He slowly looked at all the silently standing pilots and then lifted the toad up to eye level with his left hand. Taking the razor-sharp bayonet blade, he sliced opened the toad from her chin to her anus. Matilda's blood and guts flowed down onto the bar as he stuck the bayonet into the wooden top.

Then he took his right hand and scooped out all her remaining entrails onto the ground. As her eyes began to get cloudy and glaze over, and her violent wiggling diminished, Bill again looked at the EMU pilots, then at the toad. He opened his mouth, *very wide*, and took a bite out of her upper and lower lips. He looked around at all the EMUs, with blood and gore dripping down his chin, then after a few seconds, he spit Matilda's lips on the ground as he threw her body against the wall. He reached for his beer, took a big mouthful, rinsed it around his mouth, and spit it out on the wooden floor. Then he did the same thing again. He took the remainder of the beer, poured it over his hands, made a washing movement, then grabbed a bar towel and dried his hands and cleaned his face. All the while, the EMUs stood silently and watched the scene play out, with horror, fascination, and disgust.

I had moved slightly away from Bill, trying to keep from getting splattered with toad blood and guts, while wondering how in the world we were going to get out of this alive. Bill reached over the bar and got a fresh can of beer and began to drink it while looking straight ahead at the liquor bottles on the wall. Then, slowly he grabbed the bayonet and wiped the blade with the beer and blood soaked towel and slipped it into the scabbard inside his right boot. He continued to drink his beer as if nothing had happened.

I sat there and with my right hand moved my loaded Swedish K onto my lap thinking, *It is absolute insanity to get into a firefight with twenty Australians over a dead frog/toad.* But then Vietnam was frequently an insane place and almost anything could happen, so I wasn't sure.

In a few minutes, the Aussie commander stood up and walked over to Bill. "That was a friggin' bloody bad thing you just did. You can get stuffed for all we care!" he said with disgust. Then he turned around and said to the group, "Mates, let's leave these derro DADS to themselves." (DADS is an acronym meaning Dumb As Dog Shit!) After saying that, everyone filed out the door and left us with the bartender. He removed his apron, threw it on the bar, and angrily said, "The club is closed."

I leaned over to Bill, about to tap him on the shoulder, when I remembered that he hated to be touched. "Let's call it a day and go back to our room," I said. We gathered our weapons and walked back to the Quonset hut. He never said a word about what had just taken place. Once inside, we undressed and I started to crawl under the mosquito netting draped over the bed, when it dawned on me that somebody might want to avenge the toad's death.

Since the door could not be locked, I moved a metal army bed over in front of it and put my loaded submachine gun against the wall next to my head. Although I was tired, I had trouble going to sleep, thinking about the evening's events and being in the same room with someone I now considered to be an absolute psychopath! The head of Bill's bed was up against the wall and before he stretched out, he took his bayonet out and stuck it over his head into the plywood. As everything got quiet, I could hear him softly snoring and rats scurrying around the floor looking for something to eat.

Sometime in the middle of the night, I heard a loud thud hit the front door and immediately thought that it might be a grenade. I counted to five, but there was no blast, so I assumed somebody threw a rock at our door just to screw with us for what happened at the officers' club. Bill never made a move or woke up. Eventually, I went to sleep.

Early the next morning, I awoke and saw that it was light outside. I rolled over on my right shoulder and looked at the foot of Bill's bed, which was perpendicular to mine. To wake him up, I said, "Good morning." Then I noticed something wiggle under the mosquito netting. Looking at it more closely, I saw that it was a really big rat trapped between the netting and the mattress.

He was stirring and groggily said, "Morning." Now I clearly could see the rat. "Bill, I hate to tell you this, but there's a big rat trapped inside your mosquito netting up against the mattress," I said. "Bullshit!" was his reply. "I'm not joking, there really is one trapped at the foot of your bed," I said. Bill stretched out his legs and with his foot pushed the mosquito netting away from the mattress, which freed the rat, and then all hell broke loose! The rat hopped up on top of the mattress, ran up between Bill's legs, and into his large, open Army OD green skivvies.

What followed next could only come out of some perversely funny *Three Stooges* movie. Bill grabbed his bayonet and started screaming hysterically, "Get it off me! Get it off me!" While flailing around with the sharp knife, he tore the mosquito netting down from its two "T" shaped hangers and inadvertently wrapped himself, and the rat, inside of it.

I jumped up and ran over beside him shouting, "Bill, be still and stop swinging the bayonet." He was screaming, "It's biting me! It's biting me!" I grabbed his arm with the bayonet and quickly unwrapped the mosquito net from around him. As I did so, the rat sprang out of his underwear, jumped off the mattress, ran across my right foot and scurried away.

Bill quickly stood up, jerked his skivvies down to his knees to assess the damage to his privates. After a few minutes of self-examination, he started to calm down somewhat and said that he thought the rat had been scratching, but not biting him. There were no puncture marks or blood on his genitals, but there were numerous healed cigarette burn scars everywhere! Embarrassed by what I had just seen, I quickly looked away and went over to my bunk to get dressed. It was obvious that he had been horribly tortured and abused as a child. I then understood why he was so reclusive and fearful of being touched or suddenly awakened.

While we were getting dressed, in a barely audible voice, he softly explained, "When I was growing up as little kid, my mother had lots of boyfriends and sometimes while she was working, they hurt me." All I could do was shake my head sympathetically and say, "That must have really been terrible." He replied, "It was, but she died from a heroin overdose when I was thirteen, and I went to live with my grandma after getting out of the Arkansas juvenile delinquent facility. I liked living with my grandma because I finally felt safe for the first time in my life."

We both finished dressing, gathered our things, and I moved the other bed away from the door. Opening the door, I saw the carcass of Matilda impaled there by an old rusty bayonet. Under the dead toad was a piece of paper that said, "You bloody wankers better leave and never come back or you won't survive the next time." The note of course was not signed. That was the "bump" I'd heard in the middle of the night.

We walked a few blocks to the flight line where the crew chief and mechanic had already opened everything up for the preflight inspection. After that was completed, we strapped in and I started the engines. When everything was "in the green," I picked the helicopter up and backed it out of the revetment. I got on the intercom and asked the crew chief and mechanic if there was a security detail at the aircraft when they first got there. They both said, "No." I decided then that we had obviously worn out our welcome.

We taxied over to the COMMO/AVIONICS hanger. The crew chief jumped out and went inside. In a few minutes he came back riding on a "mule," driven by sergeant, with a bunch of boxes loaded on it. The avionics and instruments were unloaded in the cargo bay, and the sergeant driving the "mule" came around to my door and handed me a clipboard itemizing the equipment. He made a signing motion with his right hand. I asked the crew chief if all the boxes were sealed and he said yes, so I signed the "hand receipt." The crew members closed both doors. I called the tower and got clearance to depart Vung Tau to the north. We took off and I climbed up to eight thousand feet and headed back to Nha Trang for refueling and then on to Marble Mountain Airfield. The flight home was uneventful and very quiet. Bill as usual didn't talk, but now I understood him better and it no longer bothered me.

CHAPTER 33

ASHES TO ASHES

When we arrived at MMAF, I hovered over to our commo hanger and shut the aircraft down while the crew members unloaded all the cargo. James Wesson drove up in a jeep and asked me to ride back to headquarters with him. I loaded all my gear into the vehicle and told Bill to park the helicopter in a revetment once it was unloaded.

While we were driving, James soberly said, "I got a call from the commander of the EMUs and he told me what Bill did to their mascot. Did he really gut the frog and eat its lips?" I said, "He certainly did." James started laughing and said, "I wish I had been there to see the look on those Aussie pricks' faces." I looked at him questioningly and he explained, "I've tried to work with them in the past and it's been a royal pain in the ass dealing with their Australian egos. I'm glad that Bill took them down a notch or two." He continued to laugh occasionally as we drove to the headquarters building. I sensed that he wasn't telling me something.

When we arrived, I said, "Is there anything else we need to talk about?" He answered, "Yes, let's go inside and I'll explain what's going on." Once in his office, he shut the door, turned to me and said, "Because of congressional pressure and the fact the war is winding down, our classified operations are being terminated." I grinned and said, "I hope not with extreme prejudice." He laughed and said, "Absolutely not! We have two more weeks before everything is being shut down and I'll need you and Bill to continue flying the classified missions for another week."

I asked, "What happens after everything is shut down?" James replied, "You'll both be reassigned to an I Corp army helicopter unit. Where would you like to go?" I thought about it for a few moments and then said "How about the 62nd CAC across the flight line? He said, "I'll call their CO today and have the orders cut for you to transfer to them. Do you think Bill will want to move there too? I replied, "Probably, but I think you need to tell him what's going on." He said, "I will later this afternoon. Meantime, plan on flying for me starting tomorrow evening." I got up, walked to the door and said, "No problem, I look forward to it." Then I asked, "Where will you be going?" He said, "I hear that Berlin is beautiful in the wintertime. I've never been there." Then he closed the door.

I walked out of the headquarters building and down the street to my living quarters. I was a little sad to be leaving this assignment because of the amenities, but was looking forward to flying for the "Coachmen" which was what the 62nd Combat Aviation Company (CAC) pilots were called.

In 1969, the Coachmen mostly flew VIPs and high-level dignitaries for the 24th Corp. Their passengers had ranged from Miss America 1969 to U. S. Congressman and Senators to Colonel Frank Borman, the famous astronaut.

They also had flown Bob Hope, Martha Ray, Joey Heatherton, and famous rock and roll bands and entertainers, as they performed for the troops in I Corp. The helicopters they flew, were UH1-H single engine Hueys that were very low-hour aircraft and all looked brand-new. The pilots were housed in a new two-story air-conditioned building with two people per room. However, with the war winding down by May of 1971, most of their missions consisted of single-ship flying for American advisors embedded with the Vietnamese army units. (ARVN) There were no more VIPs to fly.

Later that evening there was a knock on my door. I opened it and Bill was standing in the hallway. He asked if he could come in. "Sure," I said. I sat down on the bed indicating for him to sit in the chair. "Did James tell you that the program is ending and we are being reassigned?" he asked as he sat down. "Yes, he did." "I understand we are going to the Coachmen. Is that true?" "Yes, it is, if and when their CO approves the transfer next week," I answered. Then he said hesitatingly, "Stan, when we move into their officers' quarters, I would like to room with you if that's okay." It was the first time he had ever shown any emotion during a conversation with me. "Bill, I would like that," I said.

After our trip to Vung Tau, my attitude towards him had changed completely. I no longer thought he was a sociopath or a psychopath, but only a wounded and damaged young man who had survived a horrible childhood. He stood up and stuck out his hand to shake mine. It was also the first time I had seen him voluntarily touch someone else. We shook hands. "Thanks. I really appreciate how good you've been to me these past few months," he said. The way he said it sounded slightly strange and ominously final.

The next evening I walked over to headquarters and met with James to be briefed on our nightly mission. Afterwards, I went to my room, gathered my flight gear and my guns, and hitched a ride to the helicopter with a passing jeep. Bill and the two crewmembers were already there pre-flighting the aircraft.

After everything was checked, we climbed in and buckled up. I started the engines and waited for all the gauges to indicate green.

While waiting, Bill looked over at me, smiled and gave me a thumbs up with his right hand. I thought, *I'm either getting accustomed to his strange ways or he's becoming more human.* I decided that with our newfound friendship it was probably the latter. I smiled back at him and said, "Let's go."

We took off from Marble Mountain Airfield and headed north to Cam Lo where we were to pick up an American advisor and three Vietnamese officials. Bill set up all of the NAVAID frequencies and did a communications check with the KY-28. When we arrived at the airfield, it was pitch black dark. We picked up our passengers and flew to a grid coordinate about twenty miles northwest across the demilitarized zone. I was very nervous about flying in known enemy territory. (As if the rest of South Vietnam wasn't!)

It was the third time I had ventured into North Vietnam on a nightly mission. The other two times had been without incident and I expected, or at least hoped, this mission would be routine too. As we neared the rendezvous point, I initialized the crypto unit and waited for the beep and green light to indicate that it was ready to transmit. When the light came on, I transmitted in the blind that we were ten minutes out.

A Vietnamese voice speaking English said, "We are ready for you." This was not the usual response from the ground and made me very uneasy. Before I landed, I asked the voice to authenticate his identity with the SOI codebook. He did so correctly and I decided that I was just being nervous because we were flying in North Vietnam. I followed the DECCA unit navaid to the coordinates, slowly descended to a dirt road, and touched down. The four passengers quickly jumped out of the helicopter, and I immediately pulled maximum power and took off, circling back to the south. As I turned, I saw multiple muzzle flashes from several locations around where I had just landed. Then I heard loud machine-gun fire and bright green basketball-sized tracers passed close by the right side of the helicopter. The enemy's .51-caliber machine gun bullets started hitting us.

The aircraft shuddered heavily as the bullets continually impacted the right underbelly. Suddenly, it was as if someone had thrown a bucket of bright red paint all over the inside front windshield, center console, and instrument panel. I felt the warm liquid running down the right side of my face and neck. In the faint glow of the red interior lighting and white gauge lights, I saw an enormous amount of blood and brain matter splashed everywhere.

"Are you guys okay back there?" I yelled on the intercom. The mechanic sitting in the left rear seat answered, "Sir, this is Artie and I'm okay. But I think Don has been hit. I heard him scream!" I turned to the right in my seat and could see the crew chief leaning forward with his bloody face pressed up against the door, not moving.

I looked over at Bill and saw that he was slumped forward against his shoulder harnesses with his head lowered against his chest. A large part of the top left of his SPH-4 flight helmet was blown away and blood was spurting out of his head and neck in long thin streams as his heart continued to beat. Then it stopped!. I asked the mechanic to unbuckle and check on the crew chief. He got up and a few minutes later plugged his helmet into a Y-cord in the back of the helicopter. "Sir, a .51-cal round came up through Don's butt, exited out the left side of his head and he's dead." "Roger that, Artie. I thought he had been hit. Mister Swofford is dead also." I said. I told him to go back to his seat and buckle in while I climbed to ten thousand feet and radioed Quang Tri tower. "Quang Tri tower, this is Uniform Sierra 01, we've been badly shot up and I have two dead crewmembers. I'm going to land at your MASH hospital helipad. Please call them and have somebody meet me when I land," I said with a shaky voice.

The tower immediately answered and said that they would make the call. It took me about forty-five minutes to reach the hospital landing pad during which time I called the USAID staff duty officer (SDO) and told him what had happened. In a few minutes James got on the radio with me.

I told him that we had landed at the correct coordinates and were ambushed by whoever was on the ground. He asked me if I'd heard any more from the passengers I dropped off, and I told him that I thought they were probably dead because of all the gunfire I'd seen on the ground. "I'll be there in about thirty-five minutes. Don't leave or talk to anyone until I see you," he ordered. "Okay, I'll see you in a little bit," I replied.

I had flown over the MASH helicopter landing zone many times in the past and had no trouble finding it in the dark. I landed and hovered to the edge to shut down so that I would be out of the way of any MEDEVAC aircraft that needed to use it. As the blades slowly stopped turning, six medical personnel came running over to the aircraft rolling two gurneys. I unstrapped my harnesses and walked around to the right door.

A doctor came up to me and asked if I had been hit because I was covered in blood and brain matter on the right side of my face, arm, and shoulder. I assured him that I was okay, then he climbed up on the right skid foothold and looked at Bill's face. A second later he looked back at me and shook his head. I went to the rear of the helicopter and saw another doctor and several orderlies removing the crew chief's body from his shoulder harness. Most of the left side of his head and face was gone. They put his body on a gurney and rolled him into the hospital. Bill's body was placed on a gurney too, and rolled into the hospital. A .51-caliber bullet had come through the floor of the helicopter, gone through the ceramic armor plating, hit him in the lower right back, and exited out the top left side of his head. He never knew what hit him. One instant he was alive; the next he was dead.

When I walked into the hospital, two nurses came over to check on me and make sure that I was okay. I removed my blood soaked Nomex shirt, threw it in a trashcan, and they gave me a couple of clean towels and wash cloths. Then they showed me to a large sink where I could wash off all the blood and brains.

I cleaned up as best as I could and stood there with both hands on either side of the sink, slowly shaking my hanging head, watching the bloody water drain out. All I could think about was how tragic and tormented Bill Swofford's life had been from the time he was a terribly abused little boy, living in a filthy trailer in Conway, Arkansas, up until a few minutes ago when he was instantly killed by an enemy bullet.

Standing there, I remembered writing the last line in my poem, *Eagles of the Realm ... our rapidly beating heart is as fragile as newly-formed ice and will soon stop forever.* Then my tears began to flow and mixed with the blood draining in the sink. (I've never forgotten the sight and am still moved to tears today as I'm writing this.)

I stood there awhile then felt someone put their hand on my shoulder. I turned around to find James Wesson standing there. "Let's go get a cup of coffee and talk," he said. "Sure thing," I mumbled. We walked into the MASH break room, got two cups of coffee, and sat down at one of the tables.

James set a small portable tape recorder on the table. "Tell me what happened," he said. Through the swinging doors, I could see two civilian operators standing there holding M-16s at port arms preventing anyone from coming into the break room. I told him what had happened from the time we took off until I landed at the MASH helipad. While I was talking, he was taking notes on a yellow legal pad.

When I finished he turned off the tape recorder, looked at me and said, "Obviously, there was a leak somewhere that allowed the Communists to know when and where you were going to land. I'll have my people check it out, but I can tell you now that we will never find out who leaked the information before our whole operation is shutdown next week. Stan, you cannot, under any circumstances, ever discuss this situation or your mission with anyone. Do you understand that?" I said, "Yes, absolutely. I won't say anything to anyone."

I thought about that for a minute and then said, "What should I do about my helicopter and Artie the mechanic?" James said, "I'll arrange to have it picked up by a Chinook sling load tomorrow and brought back to MMAF. You and the mechanic will fly back with me."

I walked outside the MASH hospital wearing my bloody T-shirt, got my flight gear and weapons from my shot-up helicopter, and got into James's. Artie was already sitting in the rear cargo area crying with tears running down his cheeks. "Are you sure you are okay?" I asked him. "I'm alright, but Don was my best friend and hoochmate," he cried. "I know," I gently said to him, "It's hard to lose a good friend. That's why it's better not to ever become close to anyone over here." He nodded his head in agreement, but didn't say anything more.

When we landed at MMAF, I went to my room, cleaned Bill's blood off my helmet, showered, and went to bed. I had trouble sleeping that night, thinking about what I'd told Artie. When you're so far away from home and family, it's hard not to seek out and find someone to at least share your misery. Bill and I were not close friends; but I empathized with him after learning about his horrific childhood.

The body count of American crew members who were killed while flying with me was now up to three and I was still alive. "Dear God, why am I still alive?" I asked myself for the first time. But I had no answer. Soon, the number of dead would increase, but I would live.

My nightly flying of classified missions for the CIA and the Phoenix program was over. James decided not to schedule any more night missions for fear of losing more crewmembers in the last week the program was in effect and operational. Because the Paris peace negotiations to end the war and obtain the release of the American POW's were ongoing between Henry Kissinger and the North Vietnamese emissaries, my incursions north of the DMZ needed to be kept a secret, *and they have been until now*.

Finally, Bill Swofford's body was returned to the U.S., but all of his family was dead, so I'm not sure where it went. What a sad, pathetic, and short life he had led. He was only twenty-two years old! By comparison, at twenty-six, I felt like an old man. The unrelenting stress of the intense combat flying I had experienced was rapidly aging me mentally and wearing me out emotionally.

But, Bill will always be the young, unpredictable, and fearless protagonist in my *Frog Story* and thus will live on forever, or at least as long as this book exists.

Mary Elizabeth Frye wrote the following poem in 1932 that

exemplifies my attitude *(then and now)* about death, dying, and the loss of so many of my band of brothers:

Do not stand at my grave and weep.
I am not there. I do not sleep.
I am a thousand winds that blow.
I am the diamond glints on snow.
I am the sunlight on ripened grain.
I am the gentle autumn rain.
When you awaken in the morning's hush
I am the swift uplifting rush
Of quiet birds in circled flight.
I am the soft stars that shine at night.
Do not stand at my grave and cry;
I am not there. I did not die.[4]

BILL, REST IN PEACE, MY FRIEND

- STAN

CHAPTER 34

62ND CAC
"THE COACHMEN"

Two days after returning back to the Marble Mountain Airfield USAID complex, I borrowed a jeep and drove over to the Coachmen headquarters and met Major Charles Dodd, their commanding officer. He was friendly and said that they were very shorthanded and needed experienced pilots, especially ones that were instrument-rated, because they were the last operational aviation unit in all of I Corp. As the war was ending, the other American helicopter companies had left for the United States or Germany. He was also interested in having me fly for the Coachmen because I was very familiar with their AO, which went from Danang north to the DMZ. "Stan, we've got an air-conditioned double room that is yours if you don't mind sharing it with a second lieutenant," he told me. "That's not a problem for me, but is he a pilot?" I asked. "Yes, he is, but he'll be promoted to first lieutenant in about thirty days," Major Dodd answered. "Sounds good to me, sir. I look forward to meeting him and moving over here," I said. "Go ahead and plan on moving in this afternoon and you can start flying missions in a couple of days," he said as we stood up and I saluted him.

I was back in the "real" Army now and needed to remember

my military bearing and manners. It actually felt good to be back in a military unit even if the "perks" weren't as good as USAID's.

I left and drove back to the USAID complex that afternoon and packed up my belongings in the jeep. I went up to HQ and said goodbye to James Wesson. "Stan, thanks for signing on and helping us out. I'm sorry that things ended so badly," he said. "Maybe I'll see you again," I said. "I wouldn't count on it. Spooks are rarely seen or heard," he said as he winked and laughed. We shook hands and James told one of the clerks to drive me over to the Coachmen headquarters across the airstrip. When we arrived, one of their clerks hopped in the back of the jeep and showed me where my room was located. Arriving there, the driver and the clerk helped carry everything to a room that I would share with 2nd Lieutenant David Roberts.

I knocked on the door and a tall, lanky, smiling redheaded guy opened it. "I'm Captain Corvin, your new roommate," I said. "Welcome, sir. Major Dodd told me at lunch that I was getting a new roommate who has lots of experience flying in our AO and is on a second tour in country. May I call you by your first name?" he asked. "No, Lieutenant you may not!" I answered and walked into the room. He stiffened and stopped smiling when I said that. "When you make 1st Lieutenant, you may call me Stan. Until then, "Sir" will be just fine," I said with a smile. We shook hands and he enthusiastically said, "Yes, sir!"

David had graduated from one of the last helicopter flight school classes and was on his first tour in Vietnam. He had been flying for about a month with the Coachmen and was a peter pilot who flew in the right seat of the UH-1H Hueys. He had a total of three hundred hours flight time including two hundred hours of flight school training. I had over thirty-five hundred hours flying time (not including flight school) and was a Senior Aircraft

Commander, so in all likelihood he and I would be flying together some.

There were two Army bunks placed end to end against the back wall with a partition separating the two. All my clothes and gear had been placed on the empty bunk and the desk sitting next to it. After the driver and clerk left, I unpacked my clothes and put them in the two footlockers under the bed, took off my shoulder holster and laid it and my Swedish K in its soft case on the desktop. "Lieutenant, I'm going to take a nap. Do you have any objections to that? I asked. "No, sir. I do a lot of reading and writing letters home to my girlfriend so I'll be quiet," he answered from his bunk. I thought, *Hmm. This may be okay after all.*

I had not slept well since the night Bill was killed and was tired, so I stretched out on the bed and rested for a while. A couple of hours later, David said to me, "Sir, dinner is about to be served at the officers' club. Would you like me to show you where it is and introduce you to some of the other pilots." I groggily said, "Sure, Lieutenant. I'll be ready in a minute."

The officers' club was about a block away from the two-story barracks that was designated for officers. Lieutenant Roberts told me that he was from a little town in northern Michigan called Grayling, and that his parents owned a small hardware store there. He had graduated from Michigan State University with a degree in business, and was a distinguished military graduate of their ROTC program. While growing up near Grayling Army Airfield, he frequently would see helicopters flying in and out of the Michigan National Guard Military Reservation. He decided that he wanted to be a pilot, so that's what prompted him to join the ROTC.

After graduating from college and becoming a second

lieutenant in the U.S. Army, he was accepted to primary helicopter training at Fort Wolters, Texas. From there he went to Fort Rucker, Alabama, and then on to Danang, Vietnam. Normally the Army would not send a second lieutenant to Vietnam; however, the war was winding down and there was a shortage of pilots, so he was assigned in country after flight school.

After walking into the 62nd CAC officers' club, I had the feeling that I'd been there before. Then I remembered that I had eaten dinner there once while flying for USAID. The Army intelligence officer, a Lieutenant Colonel I was to fly that night, was staying with their unit and did not want to depart until around 2200 hours. So, I spent the evening sitting with him at a table drinking cokes while he nervously fidgeted with a deck of cards playing solitaire. He was sweating profusely even though the Club was air-conditioned and his hands were shaking badly. *This guy's in the wrong line of work if he is so nervous about the mission,* I thought. Then he jumped up and ran out the front door. He came back shortly wiping his mouth with his handkerchief and smelling of vomit.

"Sir, if you are ill then we can scrub the mission and you can go another time," I said. "No, Captain, I must go tonight," he responded. Later on we took off, and I dropped him off at a rendezvous point west of the DMZ and never heard any more about him.

David and I went over to the serving line to get our food. It was basic U.S. Army chow but very good tasting. Major Dodd came over to me as I was standing in the line. "Did you get all settled in, Captain Corvin?" he asked. "Yes, sir. Everything's going to be fine," I answered. "Good. Why don't you come to operations tomorrow morning and the OIC will brief you on the types of missions we fly for the American advisers. Afterwards, he'll probably assign you a mission for the next day," he said. "That sounds good, sir. I look forward to flying with you guys," I responded. Lieutenant Roberts then said, "Sir, is it okay if I go with Captain Corvin to the briefing and then fly as his peter pilot?" Major Dodd looked at me and asked, "Is that all right with you?" I replied, "Yes, sir, it is."

The next morning Lieutenant Roberts and I walked over to the operation building that was next to the flight line. Parked in front were approximately fifteen immaculately clean UH-1H Hueys. They were single engine helicopters that had been primarily used for flying VIPs around I Corp. Since there no longer were VIPs in the AO, they were used to take American advisors to field locations in support of ARVN soldiers and units.

We walked inside operations and I met Captain Joe Ingram, the OIC. He spent about an hour explaining what their primary mission was all about and then asked me if I was familiar with the I Corp AO and all the fire support base locations. I told him I had over two years of flying in the northern segment of South Vietnam. "Stan, we don't have anybody that has flown in this area as much as you have," he told me. "That's great, Joe, but I also have my helicopter and airplane instrument rating, so I'll be happy to fly any of the missions that need to be done during IFR conditions (low visibility, heavy clouds and rain). Danang Air Force Base has several really good instrument approaches that I can use if the weather gets bad," I said. Joe looked at me and said, "Outstanding! We only have one other pilot that is instrument-rated." Then he turned to David and said, "Lieutenant, you will be Captain Corvin's peter pilot for the next several months beginning tomorrow morning at 0800 hours. You can learn an awful lot from him if you pay attention and can keep your head out of your butt."

David smiled and said, "I plan on being the best peter pilot in the unit and am looking forward to flying with Captain Corvin and learning from him." We got our instructions for the next day's mission and Captain Ingram handed me a small thin booklet with a dog tag chain going through a hole in a corner. He said, "Stan, this is the new SOI codebook which you can use to authenticate the identity of military personnel. You will need to sign a hand receipt for it." I signed for it saying, "Joe, if Coachmen 22 is available, I'd like to use that call sign." He said, "No problem, Coachmen 22 it is then," as he wrote it on the scheduling board for the next morning's mission. David and I walked out of the operations building.

The SOI (Signal Operating Instructions) codebook is a set of printed code words and radio frequencies for each day that can be used by pilots to identify and communicate with "friendly" military personnel on the ground or in the air; i.e., they must give the proper response when asked to authenticate. If they don't, they are the enemy. The SOI's were closely controlled and monitored upon their daily issuance. If one was missing, the assumption was all were compromised, no longer useful, and must be destroyed; therefore, they all had to be replaced.

On the way back to our quarters, David was very talkative and excited about flying with me. After a lull in the conversation, I said, "You may not be so excited when I tell you that three of my crew members have been killed flying with me." That sobered his attitude and he looked at me saying, "Sir, I'll try not to be the fourth."

We got back to our room and I spent the next several hours going through the flight checklist for the UH1-H helicopter that I would fly the next day. Afterwards, I went down to the flight line, which was only about a half a block from my room, and spent a couple of hours familiarizing myself with the layout of the single engine helicopter I would be flying.

Over the next several months, David and I flew routine missions delivering American advisors to various locations where they were embedded with Vietnamese Army units. All of the missions were flown during the day and as I flew around the I Corp AO rarely did I see or hear any other helicopters or airplanes. On my first tour, three years earlier, there always were dozens of aircraft flying around. It was somewhat disconcerting to be so alone in some of the remote areas I flew, especially in the mountains to the west near the Ho Chi Minh Trail.

One morning, we picked up a couple of advisors and headed west to a newly built fire support base on top of a five thousand foot mountain. When we arrived, I saw that a small dirt landing pad had been built with a deep trench dug along two sides. Six feet away from the trenches was a four-thousand-foot cliff. As I approached the pad, the helicopter was difficult to control because of the forty to fifty mile-per-hour wind gusts at the mountain top LZ. I managed to roughly set it down when suddenly the dirt next to the trench collapsed causing the helicopter to roll to the right about forty-five degrees and hang there. The main rotor blades were spinning ten feet over the edge of the cliff. I was able to hold the aircraft in place using full left stick, but there was severe mast bumping from the extreme angle at which the aircraft sat and was stuck. I tried repeatedly to lift to a hover but the right skid was lodged deep in the trench. The two advisors, sitting in the cargo bay, were holding on to their seats trying to keep from sliding out the cargo bay door and falling down the cliff. The crew chief, who sat in the right rear, was holding on to the M-60 machine-gun pintel mount to also keep from falling out.

I got on the intercom and said, "I can't pick up to a hover

so I'm going to roll the aircraft to the right over the edge of the cliff. I want everybody to quickly unbuckle your harnesses and climb out the left door and move away from the helicopter. That includes you too, David." He protested saying, "Sir, I want to stay with you." I said "Lieutenant, get out now. That's an order!" He and the others unstrapped and carefully crawled out the left cargo door and fell onto the dirt landing pad. I thought with five less people in the helicopter I might be able to pick it up to a hover; however, when I tried, it was still stuck. With the severe mast bumping occurring, it was only a matter of time before the main rotor shaft broke and the fuselage, with me strapped in, fell down the four-thousand-foot sheer cliff.

After several more unsuccessful attempts to hover and free the stuck skid, I realized that I was in real trouble and had to roll the helicopter to the right and allow it to fall down the side of the cliff. Hopefully, there was enough altitude that I could gain control of the aircraft before it hit the sides of the cliff or the ground at the bottom. I was glad there were no other people with me because I was certain that I was about to die and I didn't want any more of my crewmembers to be killed.

I applied full power with the collective and moved the cyclic stick to the center neutral position which stopped the mast bumping, but no longer held the right helicopter skid in the trench. Immediately, the aircraft rolled over to the right another forty-five degrees and began to fall down the face of the cliff. As it picked up speed, I realized I was looking straight down at the ground as it rushed up to me.

With the rapid acceleration of the fall, I was able to fly away from the cliff and finally stop the descent and bring the aircraft to level flight approximately twenty feet above the ground at the base of the cliff. I reached a speed of over one hundred and eighty knots, which severely exceeded the VNE (Velocity Never Exceed) of one hundred and twenty-five knots.

Checking my gauges, I saw that everything was in the "green" but my fuel level was at the twenty-minute fuel remaining empty mark. I didn't have enough fuel to again land on the dirt helipad, pick up my crew, and make it back to the nearest refueling site before the engine quit. I called the fire support base (FSB) and told them that I would return to pick up my crew after I had refueled. Turning east, I headed to Dong Ha which was thirty miles away. Within a minute, the low fuel warning buzzer started beeping loudly. Alone, I continued flying low level straight to the airfield, prepared to quickly auto rotate to the ground if the engine quit. I made it to the POL refueling area without further incident and was able to fill up with JP-4. The right skid was slightly bent, but the aircraft was sitting nearly level.

Hueys are tough birds and I had put this one through some very extreme maneuvers. I shut it down and climbed up top to see if there was any damage to the main rotor driveshaft, the rotor hub and the "Jesus" nut, but they looked okay. (The Jesus nut is a large retaining nut that holds the main rotor system in place. If it comes loose, the helicopter falls out of the sky and all the pilot can say is "Oh, Jesus!" And crash!)

Taking off, I headed back west, climbed to six thousand feet and called the radio operator at the FSB and told him to have my crew and the advisors ready to get on board the helicopter when I arrived. Arriving thirty minutes later, I slowly approached the dirt helipad and saw David, the crew chief, the door gunner, and the two advisors squatting beside it. I touched down, but kept power applied so there was no weight on the skids. All three of my crew climbed aboard along with the two advisors. After strapping in and putting on their flight helmets, both the crew chief and David started talking at once. Each said they thought I was going to crash because the helicopter was almost inverted when it rolled off the dirt landing pad at the edge of the cliff. They said they ran to the edge and watched me recover from the fall just above the ground.

"If the cliff had been twenty feet shorter, I would not have been able to level out and would've hit the ground in a dive at over 180 mph," I told them. Everyone was amazed that I had survived! We flew back to Danang and dropped off the two advisors.

Arriving back at my flight line, I "Red X'd" the helicopter so the maintenance section could check out the main rotor hub and driveshaft for damage and also see if exceeding the VNE had overstressed the fuselage and blades. The damaged right skid was the only thing that needed to be replaced.

David and I took our gear back to our room and then went to the officers' club for dinner. He excitedly told everyone about what happened and said that it was an amazing display of unselfish courage and flying. Several pilots came over and congratulated me for getting out of a bad situation. I thought, *I had no choice but to do what was necessary to stay alive.* Later that night, as I lay in bed, I thought about the extremely dangerous and potentially catastrophic events of the day and, for the first time, thanked God for allowing me to live through it all. But it wasn't the last time I thanked Him.

For several months, I continued to fly routine missions with David and had no other mishaps. Then one night, about 0300 hours, I was awakened by the loud explosions of multiple incoming NVA 122mm Katyusha enemy rockets hitting the flight line. Each rocket was ten feet long, four and three-quarters inches in diameter, weighed 147 pounds and had a warhead weight of 46 pounds. When impacting the ground, they created a crater twelve feet in diameter and three feet deep. As the explosions neared the officers' quarters, I jumped out of bed and ran to a half-buried bunker seventy-five feet away from my front door. The bunker was made from a six-foot-diameter section of corrugated culvert pipe twenty feet long that was buried halfway on its side in the ground with sandbags piled on top. The ends had been cut with a welding torch and were ragged and sharp.

I dived in the front opening and landed in the sand at the bottom. Behind me, I could hear David running to the bunker too. When he dived in, there was a loud sickening "THUD" at the opening, and he collapsed unconscious on top of me. As we lay there in the pitch black, I could not see anything, and David was not moving at all. Soon I began to feel warm liquid running over my arms as I was holding his head.

Another pilot jumped in the other end of the bunker and had a flashlight with him. I asked him to shine it on David to see what was wrong. Apparently when he dived into the bunker he missed the opening by a couple of inches and the sharp metal edges hit his head at the hairline and scalped him all the way back down the skull to nearly his neck. The scalp, with the hair attached, was laying down his back and he was out cold. Blood was pouring out of the wound and all over my arms and t-shirt.

A few minutes later, the all clear siren was sounded and we were able to carry David out of the bunker and take him to my quarters. I wrapped a clean towel around his head as he slowly started to wake up and moan. The other pilot ran to HQ and got a jeep. We drove him to the 95th MASH hospital across the runway and they put him on a gurney. In a few minutes, the doctor came out and said that he would be okay, but would need the wound cleaned and many stitches to attach the scalp back on his head. I was covered in David's blood and the doctor asked me if I was okay. "I'm fine. It's all his blood," I said. I started laughing at the image of seeing my peter pilot scalp himself as he dived in the bunker. (Black humor was often used to mitigate the effects of horrific images and seeing David's bloody bare skull certainly fit the criteria for its use!)

After two days, David came back to our unit with a huge white gauze turban wrapped around his head. He was unable to fly until the wound healed because he could not wear a flight helmet, so that ended his time flying with me as my peter pilot. For the next several weeks he had to go to the infirmary daily to have his stitches checked and determine if any infection was present.

The heat and humidity of Vietnam was not conducive to healing a wound as large as his, so the doctors and our CO decided to send him back to the United States where he was assigned to an aviation unit at Fort Huachuca, Arizona—the driest place in the USA! Three months later he was awarded a Purple Heart for the head wound he received while diving into the bunker, which had to be one of the strangest reasons ever to receive the medal. (One scalp. One purple heart!)

CHAPTER 35

SHOT DOWN TWICE

Be strong and courageous;
do not be frightened or dismayed, for the Lord your
God is with you wherever you go. (NLT)

Joshua 1:9

"**M**AYDAY! ... MAYDAY! ... MAYDAY! This is King 18! Any helicopter in the Danang area, please come up uniform guard, over!" (There was no answer!)

"MAYDAY! ... MAYDAY! ... MAYDAY! This is King 18! Any helicopter in the Danang area, please come up uniform guard, over!" (There was no answer!)

"MAYDAY!... MAYDAY! ... MAYDAY! This is King 18! Any helicopter in the Danang area, please come up uniform guard, over!" (There was no answer!)

After an early morning flight, ending at 0700 hours, my new co-pilot, Captain Van Cunningham, and the crew chief were hot refueling our helicopter at the Danang POL (petroleum, oil, lubricants) site when I heard the above emergency call come in on the Guard channel (243.0 MHZ) of my UHF radio. King 18 was an Air Force Command and Control (C&C) officer in a C-130 four engine turboprop that coordinated search and rescue (SAR) missions for pilots shot down in North and South Vietnam.

SARs had long-range radios which could communicate with any military aircraft and also the survival radios carried by all pilots. With multiple C-130s available in their squadron, they flew twenty-four hours a day, three hundred sixty-five days a year waiting for an emergency call from a downed pilot regardless of the branch of service. King 18 repeated the emergency call again, but there was no response from any helicopters or other aircraft.

On April 29, 1972, there were fewer than six hundred American military personnel left in ALL of Vietnam as the war was drawing to a close. Frequently, I flew all day and never saw or heard another helicopter nor or any other aircraft for that matter.

"This is King 18. We have an American fighter pilot shot down near the DMZ and need assistance in rescuing him before he is captured by NVA soldiers. Any helicopter in the Danang area, please come up uniform guard if you can assist, over!"

After that second desperate plea for help, I decided that I would try to find and rescue the pilot, primarily because I was very familiar with the western DMZ AO where he was located.

Once the fuel tanks were topped off, Capt. Cunningham and the crew chief climbed aboard and strapped into their seats, I got on the intercom and told them what I had just heard on the UHF guard frequency.

Then I said, "Van, I want you, the crew chief, and door gunner to get out of the aircraft and stay here while I try to find and pick up the downed pilot." Immediately their collective response was, "Absolutely not! We are not going to stay here while you go look for him by yourself!" I said, "Listen up guys, I am the Aircraft Commander and outrank you, Capt. Cunningham, so everybody get out now! That's a direct order!" They all three sat staring at me, then Van said, "Capt. Corvin, we are not going to un-ass this helicopter no matter what order you give us. So let's go find this guy and bring him home."

I said, "Look, our chances of success are not very good. With the North Vietnamese Easter Offensive going on, we will most certainly be killed or captured by the NVA if we fail in our attempt to rescue the pilot! Are you guys still willing to go with me, knowing our odds of success are very bad?" They all responded emphatically, "Yes. Absolutely!" After a moment I said, "Okay then. Let's do it."

Taking off and headed northwest, I tuned the UHF radio to the guard frequency and transmitted saying. "King 18, this is Coachman 22. I have just refueled at Danang Air Force Base and will attempt the rescue of the downed pilot. I'm flying a UH-1H Huey with four souls on board. What are your instructions, over?" King 18 answered my call immediately, "Coachmen 22, please authenticate your identity from the current SOI and tune your UHF radio to the published frequency, over." I gave the codebook, hanging from the dog tag chain around my neck, to Van and had him verify our identity and change from the guard radio frequency to the SOI one. "Coachmen 22, you are authenticated can you hear me okay, over?" King 18 asked. "That's affirmative, over," I answered. "The coordinates for the downed pilot are near X-Ray Delta 825475, which is approximately 110 nautical miles northwest of Danang. How quickly can you get there, over?" King 18 asked. I did a fast mental mathematical calculation and answered, "It will take me approximately fifty minutes to reach him and still leave me one and a half hours until *Bingo* fuel, over."

King 18 said, "Roger that, Coachman 22. Please hurry because the pilot says he is hidden in tall grass but is surrounded by approximately one hundred enemy troops that are searching for him, over."

"Does he have a survival radio and are you talking to him on it, over?" I asked. "That's affirmative on both questions. Once you get close to his position you should be able to talk directly to him, over," King 18 answered. Thus began the most deadly and dangerous mission of my military flying and the most arduous physically and mentally. It also was the last time I ever flew as a U.S. Army helicopter pilot.

For three weeks, since March 30th, in our daily briefings at the TOC, we had been updated about the massive North Vietnamese ground and artillery offensive and were ordered not to fly north of Danang beyond five nautical miles. But now I was flying to coordinates one hundred five nautical miles northeast of where my standing orders required me to stop—all behind enemy lines!

I didn't hesitate in making my decision to go, nor did I call my HQ or TOC to ask permission. If I succeeded in finding the pilot and brought him home, I would be exonerated and the U.S. Army would forgive my disobedience. If I failed, my crew and I probably would be killed and it wouldn't matter that I had disobeyed a standing order. Regardless of the outcome, I was determined to try and save the downed American pilot.

The Easter Offensive of 1972, was a military campaign conducted by North Vietnams communist People's Army of Vietnam (PAVN also known as NVA) against the Army of the Republic of Vietnam (ARVN), the regular Army of South Vietnam and the United States military. This conventional ground invasion was a radical departure from previous North Vietnamese attacks. The offensive was not designed to win the war outright, but to gain as much territory and destroy as many units of the

ARVN as possible to improve the North's negotiating position as the Paris Peace Accords drew towards a conclusion.[5]

At noon on March 30, 1972, two NVA divisions (thirty thousand troops) supported by more than one hundred fifty T-54 Russian and Chinese tanks rolled south over the demilitarized zone to attack I Corp. and Dong Ha, the northernmost American outpost. From the west an NVA division of ten thousand soldiers with one hundred fifteen mechanized armor half-tracks moved out of Laos and into the Ashau and Quang Tri Valley to link up with two thousand enemy troops dug in at Khe Sanh.

The map coordinates, which King 18 had given me for the downed American fighter pilot, were three miles north of the long abandoned 5th Special Forces and 3rd Marine Amphibious Force fire support base of Khe Sanh.

The FSB was located in the northern end of the A Shau Valley which is a mile-wide flat-bottomed valley mostly covered with tall elephant grass and flanked by densely forested mountains ranging from three thousand to fifty-five hundred feet in height. This valley had long been a pathway and refuge for NVA moving equipment and armament along the nearby Ho Chi Minh trail just across the border in Laos.

The pilot's approximate location was eleven miles south of the DMZ and ten miles east of Laos in extremely rugged and treacherous terrain. (I still have the original special tactical map I used to look for the Air Force pilot and included a portion of it in this book.)

After crossing the mountain ridge northwest of Danang, I pulled maximum power, accelerated to 125 knots and dropped my altitude down to low level about two feet above the ground (Also known as "Nap of the Earth" – NOE). In our daily briefings, we had been told there were literally hundreds of NVA radar controlled 37mm anti-aircraft gun emplacements, 122mm rocket launchers and SA-2 Russian surface to air missile (SAMS) sites beginning fifteen miles north of our base.

The effect of "terrain masking" while flying NOE was critical for helicopters flying in enemy territory that contained radar-controlled weapons. Enemy gun radar avoidance was going to be a key factor if I was to survive and successfully find and pick up the downed pilot.

The map coordinate that King 18 had given me of XD 825475 was located in the center of the ten thousand NVA troop invasion that had come from Laos three weeks earlier. One hundred thirty-six years earlier, on March 6, 1836, one hundred eight-eight defenders of the Alamo in San Antonio, Texas, had been outnumbered thirty-two to one, and had been defeated and killed. I was now flying to a destination where my crew and I would be outnumbered twenty-five hundred to one! However, I believed if we flew in fast and low, surprise would be on our side. That advantage would be important for us to succeed.

On the intercom, I asked the crew chief and door gunner how much M-60 linked ammunition they each had. They both responded saying they had approximately six hundred rounds in three metal containers. I told them to open the containers and link all of the machine gun ammo together so they each had the capability of continuously firing all six hundred rounds if needed.

Their pintel-mounted machine guns, on each side of the helicopter, had a cyclic rate of fire of approximately six hundred rounds per minute. One minute of continuous shooting was all they each had. After they linked the ammo belts together I had them fire a short burst to make sure their machine guns were working properly. They were.

I briefly looked at Van saying, "How much ammo do you

have for your .38-caliber pistol?" He responded, "Six rounds is all." I locked the collective to briefly hold my low-level altitude, and from my shoulder holster, I handed him my Browning High Power 9mm semiautomatic pistol containing fourteen rounds, including the one in the chamber. "Here, take this in case we end up on the ground," I said. Van looked at me, grimaced, and paled visibly. "I doubt that it will come to that," I quickly told him, hoping that I had not prophetically sealed our fate.

Then I asked him to remove my Swedish K sub-machine gun from its soft-sided case between my seat and the center instrument console. (James Wesson with USAID let me keep it since his operation was being shut down and there were no records of the multitude of weapons contained in his arsenal.)

After Van inserted a full magazine in it, I took the little gun and wedged it in between my left shoulder and the side of the armor protected seat. The four extra magazines, each containing thirty-six rounds, were in a removable cloth bandolier, which I hung next to the gun. If we were shot down, and I survived the crash, at least I would be able to defend myself for a short time. Now we were as prepared as we could be for what I suspected was going to be a major gunfight.

The route that I had chosen to fly closely paralleled Highway #1 for approximately fifty miles. There were tens of thousands of fleeing South Vietnamese civilians and ARVN soldiers on the highway all heading south to Danang. Off in the distance, I could see huge plumes of black smoke and debris flying into the air from the outskirts of the old imperial city of Hue. The scene looked like something out of World War II and unlike anything I had ever witnessed in Vietnam.

Along the way, I began seeing numerous enemy rocket emplacements that looked like the SA-2 SAM sites I had seen in photographs at our TOC briefings. The missiles were sitting on forty-five-degree elevated launch pads and were approximately the length and diameter of a standard telephone pole.

The NVA obviously were prepared to fire the missiles at any opposing aircraft. At low level, I was not a viable target, but they probably wondered why a lone U.S. Army helicopter was flying north. Once past Hue, I turned further west to fly through the valleys created by the hills and mountains. There were several abandoned dirt airstrips and helipads at the southern end of the Ashau valley that I knew I would recognize when I got in that area.

While flying for the CIA, I had flown into Mai Loc, Dung Long, My Chan, and Da Ba, all rural helipads near the Khe Sanh AO, where I dropped off the American operators and Vietnamese intelligence officers. (See the enclosed map.) The temperature was in the high 90s and climbing rapidly. Low clouds were present and in some cases obscured the tops of the mountains, where I thought a lot of the radar-controlled gun emplacements were probably located.

After flying for approximately forty minutes, I saw one of the abandoned helipads at Dung Long in front of me. As I flew over it, dozens of NVA soldiers began firing their AK-47s at the helicopter. Unlike the Loach, which was relatively quiet as it flew with its four-bladed, fully-articulated rotor system, the Huey with its two large blades made a loud "wop, wop, wop" sound that was both distinctive and could be heard from far away. Apparently the NVA heard me coming and were prepared to shoot as I flew over. None of their bullets struck the aircraft, but I was now sure that we would be unable to have the element of surprise on our side. "Hold your fire until I tell you to shoot!" I yelled over the intercom at the two crewmembers.

I instructed Van to lower the clear Plexiglas lens on his helmet as I did the same with mine. At least the Plexiglas would protect our eyes and vision if an RPG blew out the front windshield. The enemy unit we flew over had several communication box trucks with tall antennas mounted on them flying the red and blue NVA flag.

I suspected they were alerting their "comrades" of my presence in the Ashau Valley as I continued to fly northwest to Khe Sanh. Now I was ten minutes away from downed pilot's coordinates and the epicenter of the North Vietnamese western invasion.

After crossing the Dung Long helipad, I turned west and flew alongside Highway QL #9 which led into Khe Sanh. On the highway there were thousands of soldiers walking with long convoys of mechanized armor, tanks, and half-tracks all headed east.

At first I thought they were South Vietnamese ARVN, but after I saw several NVA flags flying on the tank antennas, I realized they were the enemy! My heart sunk when I realized we were up against overwhelming odds and coming out of the rescue alive now was nearly impossible. But I was committed to the attempt and determined to try to save the American pilot, so I pressed on no matter the outcome!

When I reached the bend in the Song Thach River, I turned north, crossed over it and the highway, and immediately came under intense enemy small arms fire, from multiple locations, as I flew over the advancing NVA units. Bullets constantly impacted the bottom and sides of the helicopter and sounded like I was flying through a heavy hailstorm. "Start shooting now and don't stop; but keep some ammo!" I screamed at the crew chief and door gunner. I looked at the instrument panel and saw that most of the gauges had stopped working, so I knew it was only a matter of time before the engine quit or blew up!

I flew north over the Rau Quan River, three-quarters of a mile east of the abandoned Khe Sanh airstrip, which had hundreds of enemy vehicles parked on the sides lining it. "Van, turn the UHF radio to guard so that I can talk to the pilot," I yelled. He did as I asked and I said, "This is Coachman 22. Can you hear me on the ground, over?" There was no response so I called again. "This is Coachman 22. Can you hear me on the ground, over?" By now I was at the coordinates that King 18 had given to me, so I began circling the area while still flying at 125 knots. Very faintly I heard the pilot (Air Force Major Frank Welch) break squelch on the guard channel and whisper, "I can hear you, 22, please hurry. I'm completely surrounded by NVA who are closing in on my location. They are within fifty yards of where I'm hiding next to the river." I responded, "I'll be right there, buddy." Then I flew over his orange and white parachute which lay flat on the ground.

I came back around to the left, clipping the elephant grass with my blades. "Where are you in relation to your parachute?" I asked. He whispered softly, "About a hundred yards northwest next to the river. But it's too late; they are almost on top of me." I swiftly turned to the river to find the pilot and immediately started receiving continuous AK-47 fire from the assembled enemy troops below. Both crew members again started firing their machine guns, but the NVA were all around on the ground and their bullets were continuously hitting the underside of the helicopter.

Suddenly, the instrument panel and the center console containing all the radios exploded from a barrage of .51-caliber rounds. Futilely, I screamed on the guard frequency, "Mayday!

Mayday! Mayday! King 18 this is Coachman 22. We are going down!"

I leveled the aircraft, flew about a half mile away from the NVA troops and set it down in a small rice paddy just as the engine quit and began to smolder. "Everybody get out now and let's set up a defensive perimeter!" I shouted. Van and I quickly unbuckled our shoulder harnesses, took off our helmets and jumped out as the crew chief and door gunner pulled their machine guns from the pintel mounts and ran to a nearby shallow ravine. I grabbed my Swedish K and the bandolier containing its magazines and then Van and I ran to the crew. We jumped into the depression and I instructed the crew members to each set up their M-60's facing the direction from which we had just come. I realized I was still wearing my chicken plate vest with a survival radio tucked into its pocket in the middle. I pulled the little radio out and took off the armor plate.

The AN/PRC-90 survival radio was standard issue to military pilots and had the capability of transmitting and receiving voice communication on UHF guard frequency as well as transmitting a homing tone to be used as a locator beacon. Earlier that morning, as I did every time I flew, I checked to make sure it had fresh batteries and was working properly.

"Mayday! Mayday! Mayday! This is Coachman 22. We have been shot down and are on the ground. Can you hear me, King 18, over?" For a few seconds there was no response then suddenly he said, "Coachmen 22, I hear you Lima Charles, over!" (Meaning loud and clear.) "King 18, my crew and I are all okay and have set up a defensive perimeter on the ground near my helicopter, but there are several hundred NVA approaching us about four hundred yards away. They just killed the Air Force pilot because we heard sporadic shooting from his location a few minutes ago as we exited the helicopter. Is there any chance of getting somebody to come pick us up, over? I asked. "Coachman 22, Coachmen 6 is about eight minutes away from your location and will pick you and your crew up, over," he quickly answered.

I was stunned by his response and could not believe our good fortune! "Coachman 6" was my Battalion Commanding Officer, Lieutenant Colonel Harold Bixby, who was in charge of all the 62nd CAC aviation personnel and assets including the CH-47 Chinooks as well as the OV-10 and U-21 airplanes. Apparently, he had heard my first conversation with King 18 and was ten minutes behind me as I flew north to rescue the downed pilot. I was overwhelmingly relieved to know that I was not going to be killed by the approaching NVA and would shortly be picked up with my crew.

Within a few minutes, I began to hear the characteristic "wop, wop, wop" of an approaching Huey. I got on the survival radio and said, "Coachmen 6, this is Coachman 22. Can you hear me, over?" He said, "I can hear you five by five. Are you near the smoking helicopter?" I answered, "Yes, sir, we are about thirty yards away to its east in a shallow ravine." He said, "I'll land next to you and then let's get the hell out of this area." When his Huey came into view, I heard many AK-47s firing at it from the approaching NVA. Within a few seconds, he landed next to my crew and me and we jumped on board his helicopter, carrying our weapons.

As we took off, I leaned over to Van, slapped him on the back and said, "Man, we pulled that one out of our ass for sure!" (Sorry, everyone, that's a somewhat profane but widely-used pilot expression!) He was grinning widely and started to reply when suddenly a continuous barrage of .51-caliber machine gun bullets struck the bottom of the helicopter, shutting down the turbine engine! We fell from an altitude of approximately thirty feet, hit the ground extremely hard, spreading both skids. I was sitting on the metal floor of the cargo bay when we hit and instantly felt a horrendous pain in my lower spine that took my breath away.

When we slid to a stop, I could hear Lt. Col. Bixby moaning and saw him holding his right leg. I grabbed my sub-machine gun and hobbled to his front right door. (He was flying copilot with the aircraft commander, probably to log the flight time.) When I opened the door, I saw blood splattered all over the floor and his right foot dangling from a piece of his leather boot.

One of the .51-caliber rounds had come through the bottom floor board and severed his foot just above the ankle. When I reached in, unfastened his harness, and started to pull him out of the seat, he started screaming in pain and passed out. I managed to get him out of the helicopter and over my right shoulder in a "fireman's carry" to get him away from the helicopter which was beginning to burn.

As I turned to the front of the aircraft, I felt something hit me multiple times like a sledgehammer in my right side, hip, and leg. I turned around to run in the opposite direction and was hit again in my right buttocks. That knocked me off my feet and the CO and I fell to the ground. I realized that I had been repeatedly shot.

Lying on the ground, I looked up at the clouds and saw that the sky was beginning to clear above me. Although the multiple gunshot wounds were extraordinarily painful, the compression fracture of my lower spine was worse. I thought, *This is it. I can go no further and it's my turn to die.* Off in the distance I could hear numerous NVA soldiers' voices excitedly yelling and speaking in Vietnamese. They obviously were advancing to the second downed helicopter and all eight of us on the ground.

Rather than waiting for some dink in an NVA uniform to walk up and shoot me in the face with his AK-47, I decided to be the captain of my soul as William Earnest Henly wrote in his poem *Invictus* and take matters into my own hands. In my shirt pocket was a small pill bottle with twenty fifteen-milligram dextroamphetamine tablets in it. I had carried them with me since flying the missions for the CIA a few months earlier.

Late one night, several months earlier, I had taken one pill. Swallowing that one pill greatly increased my heart rate and blood pressure, and took away my fatigue, thus allowing me to continue flying on with the mission without resting or sleep. In the combat military pilot vernacular they were called "go pills."

With trembling, blood-covered hands, I removed the small cap and swallowed all twenty dextroamphetamine pills at one time softly saying to myself, *Please God, forgive me for what I'm doing.* As I had written in my poem earlier, while traveling to Vietnam on my first tour, I expected that my *beating heart…will soon stop forever.* I relaxed, looked up at the clouds and the blue sky, and lay still waiting for my heart to stop, death to overtake me, and put me to sleep.

Dextroamphetamine is a potent psychostimulant drug used widely by military air forces during prolonged, fatigue-inducing mission profiles. It increases physical strength, stamina, alertness, and endurance. Cardiovascular side effects include hypertension, increased heart rate, and vascular inhibition; *i.e.,* the vessels and arteries significantly constrict, allowing less blood flow. Generally, massive overdoses are not fatal.[6]

Unknowingly, I had just saved my life instead of ending it. Within a few seconds my face became flushed, and I felt a warm glow cascade from my neck down through my legs. The pain in my lower back and from the gunshot wounds subsided dramatically. Suddenly, I became acutely aware of my surroundings and began to feel much better. *Hallelujah!*

I rolled over on my right side and saw LTC. Bixby lying there passed out. My submachine gun, with the magazine bandolier, was next to me. I grabbed it and rose to my knees, carefully looking for the advancing NVA troops. Seeing them advancing a quarter of a mile away, I slowly and painfully stood up, grabbed my CO's shirt collar and in a crouch dragged him to where the six other crew members were gathered a short distance away. Falling down in their midst, I saw that they had set up a defensive perimeter, now with four M-60 machine guns. The CO's aircraft commander, with whom he had been flying, was a chief warrant officer. So of the group, I was the ranking officer, except for Lt. Col. Bixby who was totally incapacitated. More importantly, I had the only working survival radio.

None of the other crew members were seriously injured, so I asked them to look after Lt. Col. Bixby and to put a tourniquet above his severed foot to stop the bleeding. On the survival radio, I quietly called King 18 saying, "This is Coachman 22. Can you hear me, over?" Immediately, he answered saying, "This is King 18, I can hear you loud and clear. How many of you survived the second crash of the rescue helicopter, over? I answered "All eight of us; however, one is gravely injured with a severed foot, and I received several gunshot wounds, but am able to function for now, over." Then he told me great news. "Coachman 22, three Sandy A-1E's are in route to your location and are within five minutes of reaching you. They can provide close air support until you are rescued, over."

The Douglas A-1E "Skyraider" was an American single-seat attack aircraft that saw service between the late 1940s and early 1980s. It was a single engine, 2700 horsepower, piston-powered, four-bladed, propeller-driven airplane nicknamed the "Spad" after the French World War I fighter. Its cruising speed of 200 mph and range of fourteen hundred miles enabled it to stay on station for approximately seven hours which was much longer than any jet aircraft.

It carried four 20mm Vulcan cannons and eight thousand pounds of bombs on fourteen external hard points under the wings. With its empty weight of 11,968 pounds and maximum takeoff weight of twenty-five thousand pounds, the airplane could carry more than its own weight in armament! In Vietnam, because of its relatively slow speed, the A-1E was primarily used to protect search and rescue helicopters picking up downed pilots.

Within a few minutes of talking to King 18, I heard the approaching Sandys. When they roared over the advancing NVA troops, they begin to receive massive AK-47 and .51-caliber ground fire. They circled back one hundred eighty degrees overhead and began shooting at the enemy troops with their 20mm cannons. It was the most beautiful thing I had ever seen and heard and all the crew, except Lt. Col. Bixby, quietly cheered! Passing over the NVA, all three Sandys dropped their bomb loads. That stopped the enemy small arms fire for a while.

On my survival radio I heard, "Coachman 22, this is Sandy 6. How do you read me, over?" I responded, "I read you Lima Charles, Sandy 6. Welcome to the party and I'm really glad to see you guys, over." He laughed and said, "With all the NVA troops around here, it's more of a hornet's nest stirred up than a party."

I double clicked the transmitter button indicating that I had heard him. "Sandy 6, how long can you guys stay on station, over?" I asked. "All day, until you are picked up and rescued. We will rotate one aircraft at a time every few hours to refuel and rearm. But two of us will always be with you today," he responded. I was really relieved to hear that.

He and the two other Sandy's began to fly in a circular daisy chain pattern sporadically firing their 20mm cannons approximately fifty yards out, all around us. The sound was deafening because each .79-inch projectile contained a high explosive (HE) charge that detonated with the force of a small grenade upon impacting the ground. The cyclic fire of their cannons was six thousand rounds per minute, which was faster than the 7.62mm minigun I had fired while flying Loaches for the Warlords. The M61 Vulcan cannon was a hydraulically-driven six-barreled, air-cooled, electrically-fired Gatling gun-styled rotary cannon. It was the principal cannon armament of the United States military fixed-wing aircraft for fifty years.

After a few minutes of watching the A-1E's fire at the NVA soldiers, I checked my wounds and saw that they were not bleeding very much anymore. I had already lost a lot of blood and my Nomex flight shirt and pants were soaked in it, but I was alive and able to function.

After a few minutes I heard what sounded like a tank or mechanized armored vehicle coming to us from the opposite direction from where the NVA soldiers had been advancing. "Sandy 6, I think a tank is coming to us, over," I said. He replied, "I see him, it's a Chinese half-track with a .51-caliber machine gun mounted on the turret. We'll take him out!" He rolled in and fired two rockets, striking the vehicle and blowing it up. The Sandy's continued to fly and shoot around us as the day wore on.

It was now 1500 hours and we had been on the ground since about 0800. (Seven hours) The temperature was in the high 90s with 100% humidity and no one had any water. Being dehydrated helped stop my wounds from bleeding because my blood was thicker, but my mouth was exceedingly dry and I could barely swallow.

All of us were lying flat on our stomachs behind a short dry berm that had been part of a small rice paddy. Ten feet in front of us was a large stand of dense elephant grass. I saw part of the grass move and at first thought it was the wind blowing, but soon realized that only a small portion was moving.

I whispered to the other guys that the NVA might be moving closer to us through the tall grass. Very slowly, the edge of the grass nearest to me spread apart and three NVA soldiers peered out while still lying down. Immediately, I fired a three-second burst from my submachine gun into their upraised faces and saw a fine red mist explode from their faces as the bullets struck them and they collapsed in place. I replaced the spent magazine and waited for more enemy soldiers to rush us; however, nothing more happened.

I instructed one of the other crew members, that had set up his M-60 on the berm, to fire a 100-round burst into the elephant grass about a foot above the ground. He did as I ordered and we watched the grass move as the remaining NVA backed away or were killed in place. I was worried that they could easily throw hand grenades at us, since the elephant grass provided good cover and was so close to where we lay.

Soon the Sandys again started firing their 20mm cannons. I requested that they specifically concentrate on the nearby tall elephant grass. The precision of their firing, so close to us, was remarkable and deafening! Basically they shredded the remaining grass, denying the enemy troops any cover to sneak up on us.

Our defensive position was between a fifty-one-hundred-foot mountain to our immediate north and a thirty-one-hundred-foot mountain to the southeast. After about an hour, I heard three loud, unusual hollow sounds that went "thunk ... thunk ... thunk" in rapid succession. Within seconds, three explosions impacted seventy-five yards to east of where we lay. Then I understood that the sounds were coming from mortars being fired at us. "Sandy 6, we're under mortar attack and the tubes are somewhere to my west, over," I quietly said. "We'll try to find them, but they must be well-hidden because we haven't seen them yet." He replied.

Then I heard more "thunk ...thunk ... thunk" sounds and the mortars impacted thirty yards to the west of where we lay and I knew that we had been bracketed! "Sandy 6, more mortar rounds have exploded on the other side of us and they've got our range now. Please help, over!" He said, "Coachman 22, Roger that. But we still can't see them."

Then I heard "thunk ... thunk ... thunk" as three more rounds were fired at us. This time they impacted all around where we were lying and I was lifted off the ground slightly from the force of the concussion. At once I felt shrapnel hit me in the right arm, side, and wrist.

More mortar rounds began to impact around us and I heard several people cry out in pain. I picked up the survival radio, which had been knocked out of my hand and said, "Sandy 6, we are receiving mortar fire and cannot hold out long against this new attack, over." He said, "We saw where those rounds came from and we are rolling in now with rockets."

I watched as they dived and fired a short distance away to the west. As their rockets impacted the ground, two large secondary explosions occurred which meant that they had hit the tubes and a cache of unfired mortar rounds. Lying there with new shrapnel injuries and multiple gunshot wounds, I wondered how much longer I could last, but at least I had not yet exsanguinated!

(A term I recently learned from my VA cardiologist, Dr. Barton Campbell.)

Now the time was close to 1900 hours and we had been on the ground for twelve hours in the high heat and humidity, fending off the enemy's various attempts to capture and kill us. My throat was swollen from the lack of hydration and I could not swallow at all now. "Coachman 22, there is a Huey approximately ten minutes south of your location that will try to extract you, over," Sandy 6 said. "Roger that, we can't hold out much longer, over," I hoarsely replied.

A few minutes later, I faintly heard the distinctive sound of an approaching Huey. Although I could not see the helicopter, I began to hear the equally distinctive sound of many AK-47s shooting at it. Then to my dismay, I heard the characteristic "wop, wop, wop" sound fade, as it turned one hundred eight degrees and flew south away from my location. "Coachman 22, the co-pilot of the extraction helicopter just informed me that his aircraft commander (CW2 Henry Alvarez) and a passenger have been killed by the intense enemy ground fire and they have turned back to Danang; however, there is another Huey in route and will arrive at your coordinates within thirty minutes, hang in there!" Sandy 6 said. "Roger, sir. We are not going anywhere, over!" I raspingly answered. He keyed the mic and softly said, "I know, son, I'm watching you." His words carried much more meaning than either he or I knew at the time.

As the sun began to set behind the mountains to my west, and the shadows lengthened from the nearby tall trees and jungle, I wondered if we were going to be picked up before nightfall. I doubted that we could survive the night because the NVA were absolute masters at night attacks under the cover of darkness. The Sandy's A1-E's were not equipped to provide suppressive ground fire and close air support from their 20mm Vulcan cannons once it was dark.

My overpowering thirst, from the extreme dehydration and the loss of blood from my shrapnel and gunshot wounds, combined with the effects of having earlier swallowed twenty dextroamphetamine tablets, was severely weakening me. I was beginning to lose hope of ever being picked up and my will to live was quickly ebbing away.

While in advanced helicopter flight school in Savannah Georgia, a survival school training instructor once told us that "The will to live is crucial to your ultimate survival. Without it you will quickly die from either your current circumstances or by your own hand. You get to make the choice!"

He then went on to tell the story of a Canadian fighter pilot, who in 1964 was flying on a night training mission near the Arctic Circle. The jet engine flamed out as he was flying at thirty thousand feet. After many unsuccessful attempts to restart it, and several unanswered Mayday calls, he lowered the landing gear and set the fighter down on a large frozen lake. Immediately the airplane was covered with snow as it roughly rolled to a stop and came to rest.

Thinking the aircraft had broken through the ice and now was sitting under water on the lake bottom; the fighter pilot sat there for a moment. Then he took out his .38-caliber revolver, placed the barrel in his mouth, and blew his brains out the back of his head. Twenty minutes later, a rescue helicopter landed on the frozen lake next to him after having heard his Mayday call. The search and rescue crew dug through the deep snow, down to the cockpit, opened the canopy, and found the dead pilot. "Too late! Too late! Too late!" was all they could say.

In the dusk at 2000 hours, I wondered if it was "too late"

for us to be rescued. Then, in the far-off distance to the south, I once again heard the unforgettable "wop, wop, wop" sound of an inbound Huey. As it drew nearer, I also began to hear sporadic AK-47 ground fire, but not at the volume that it had been earlier. Sandy 6 and his two wingmen had been periodically flying over that area, trying to clear a corridor for a rescue helicopter to reach us, as they flew to and from Danang for refueling and rearming.

Everyone, except Lt. Col. Bixby, began to stir as the sound got louder from the approaching helicopter. "Sandy 6, please do everything you can to get the Huey safely in, so that we can be extracted, because I don't think we can survive the night, over," I whispered. My voice was completely gone now. "We will do everything we can to help, just have all your people ready to climb on board the second its skids touch down, over." Sandy 6 said.

Then he and the two wingmen began to strafe the area from our location back down the valley to where the Huey was approaching. They continuously fired their Vulcan cannons and rockets as the rescue helicopter neared our position. In a few minutes the Huey came into view. Turning to the small group, I whispered, "Listen up, everybody! Get in the middle of the rice paddy as close together as you can and be ready to jump into the helicopter bay area the instant its skids touchdown. I want two crewmembers with M-60s to sit on each side to help with suppressive fire as we lift off. Van, I need you and the Warrant Officer to carry Lt. Col. Bixby to the helicopter, because you guys only have pistols with you. I'll load last after everyone gets in." Everyone nodded their heads as the Huey slowed its speed and began to land.

The moment it touched down, twenty yards from us, Van and the other pilot picked up LTC. Bixby, and we all ran (I hobbled) to it, and crawled in through the open doors. As the aircraft took off, I saw my survival radio laying on the dirt berm, but it was too late to do anything about it. I regretted its loss because I had not thanked Sandy 6 for saving my crew and me.

We circled low level to the left and had only gone a quarter of a mile when all hell broke loose from the intensive NVA ground fire. The six M-60's began shooting simultaneously at the enemy troops from both sides of the helicopter. I was sitting in the left door with my feet dangling out and began firing my Swedish K at them too. I changed magazines as I emptied them, then I heard bullets striking the underbelly of the helicopter. Several came through the bare metal floorboard behind me and ricocheted off the armored back of the left pilots' seat. Metal fragments struck me on the right side of my face and eye. When I reached my right hand up, to cover my face, the little sub-machine gun slipped and fell out the open door. Now I was defenseless and unable to protect myself if we were shot down a third time. Frankly, I didn't care anymore because I was too dehydrated, exhausted, and weak from blood loss to fight anymore. The Vietnam War was over for me.

Suddenly we were not encountering any more ground fire and the six M-60's were silent having run completely out of ammunition. The only sound was the wind blowing in the open doors. I looked up at the rising moon to the east and murmured to myself ,*"Thank you dear God! Thank you!"* While lying in the muddy rice paddy, I realized that evil regimes, like the North Vietnamese communists, may come and go, but the indomitable nature of the human spirit does not. I was a living testament to that.

I remembered the night before, on April 28th, having written the following poem, which was my last, indicating a paradigm shift in my attitude about the war:

The Maimed Insane Sandpiper

The one-legged sandpiper hopped
awkwardly down the beach.
Always staying beyond the waters' grasping reach.
Searching and searching, always in vain,
Looking very foolish and not at all sane.
He searches and searches, both morning and night,
For that which is beautiful, truthful, and right.
Never does he realize his search is insane,
And will forever and always, be in vain.

Because of my serious physical condition, I don't remember much about the remaining flight back to Danang that night; however, it was uneventful and we were not fired upon anymore. We landed at the large concrete helipad outside the emergency entrance of the 95th Evacuation Hospital located on China Beach a few miles north of Marble Mountain.

Medical personnel ran out to the helicopter with two gurneys and loaded LTC. Bixby and me on them. We were taken inside the emergency room and someone, with angular scissors, removed my blood, dirt, and mud-covered boots and clothing. Lying there naked, I asked for a cup of water, but my voice was gone and my whispering was unintelligible.

An IV was inserted in my left arm and a female nurse with a pan of warm water and a large sponge began to wash the caked-on blood and grime off of my body, carefully avoiding the multiple gunshot and wounds to my torso and the shrapnel wounds to my face and right eye. "Please give me a drink of water," I mouthed the words to her. She looked at me, shook her head, and silently continued to clean me up. "Please, ma'am. I need a drink of water," I managed to pleadingly whisper.

She stopped and looked at me saying, "I can only give you a small sip now because you are heading into surgery." She took a metal pitcher and poured a small amount of ice cold water into a paper cup. She lifted my head and poured it into my parched and swollen mouth. I struggled to swallow the water and then the most incredible feeling I've ever experienced occurred. As the water passed down my throat, I could actually feel it spread out into my face, chest, arms, and legs. It was remarkably soothing to my dehydrated body and I craved more.

I thanked her and asked for more, but she shook her head saying, "After you get out of surgery." I nodded my head and whispered, "You guys need to know that I took twenty fifteen milligram Dextroamphetamine tablets this morning about nine o'clock." With a shocked look on her face, she said, "You did what?" I repeated what I had just said to her. She stood there a moment and then said "I'll be right back." She left and returned a few seconds later with a middle-aged gray-haired doctor in tow. I explained to him what I had just told her, and he said, "Don't worry, son, we can deal with that." He turned to the nurse and said "Go ahead and give him the injection." I nodded and closed my eyes as the nurse injected an anesthetic into my IV line.

I awoke early the next morning lying in a clean bed in the recovery ward surrounded by other soldiers who also had undergone surgery. There were bandages on my chest, hip, leg, and right buttocks. The right side of my face was also bandaged and a gauze patch covered my right eye. When a nurse walked by the foot of the bed, I tried to get her attention by raising my right arm, but realized it was wrapped in a bandage and tethered to a bed rail to limit its movement. Lying there I couldn't see any light from my right eye and worried that somehow my vision was gone.

A nurse saw me moving and came over to the left side of the bed saying, "Good morning, Captain Corvin. How do you feel?" I shifted on the bed and whispered, "A lot better than I did last night. May I have a glass of water?" She smiled and said, "Of course. I'll be back in just a moment with one." A few minutes later she returned carrying a half-filled glass with a straw in it. She leaned forward over the bed rail and gently placed the straw between my lips. I drank deeply, but didn't feel the amazing effect like the night before. I wasn't sure if what I had experienced, when I first drank the sip of water, was real or a hallucination. It didn't matter because I had plenty of water to drink now.

Later that morning two doctors came by and told me they had removed three bullets and several pieces of shrapnel from my torso, hip, buttocks, and arm and that I would heal okay. I also had a compression fracture of my lower spine at L4 and L5, which they said would heal by itself after two or three months. They were still concerned about tiny metal fragments in my right eye. The fragments could not be removed at the 95th Evacuation Hospital because of a lack of ophthalmologic surgeons.

They told me that I was going to be Medevac'd out of Danang and flown to Camp Zama, Japan, that night. "How is Lt. Col. Bixby?" I asked them. "He's resting well, but we had to remove his right foot above the ankle," one of the doctors said. I was sad to hear that because an injury of that magnitude was going to end his U.S. Army career. "Any more questions, Captain Corvin?" they asked. "What about the Huey aircraft commander and the passenger that were shot yesterday trying to rescue me?" I asked. They briefly looked at each other and said, "Both were killed instantly by gunfire. The passenger was Lieutenant Colonel

John Mott and he had only been in country thirteen days on his second tour." Hearing that saddened me even further.

I learned later that he was my dad's age with four teenage children. His oldest son, Joseph Anthony Mott, age twenty-one and a PFC in the U.S. Army, had been killed in Kontum, Vietnam, on June 7, 1969, after stepping on a mine. What an enormous tragedy it was for that family to experience two losses in three years from the same battlefield! The tragic circumstances of their deaths reminded me of a letter I once read written by President Abraham Lincoln. In it he eloquently expressed his condolences, on November 21, 1864, to a mother whose five sons were killed in the civil war:

Executive Mansion
Washington, Nov. 21, 1864

Dear Madam,

I have been told by the War Department that you are the mother of five sons who have died gloriously on the field of battle.

How weak and fruitless must be any word of mine which should attempt to beguile you from the grief of a loss so overwhelming. But I cannot refrain from tendering you the consolation that may be found in the thanks of the Republic they died to save.

I pray that our Heavenly Father may assuage the anguish of your bereavement and leave you only the cherished memory of the loved and loss and the solemn pride that must be yours to have laid so costly a sacrifice upon the altar of freedom.

Yours, very sincerely and respectfully,

– A. Lincoln[7]

Major Dodd, my commanding officer, came by that afternoon and told me that he would have all my things sent home. My parents were my emergency contact so everything was going to be sent to their house in Waco, TX. When I had arrived in Danang on my second tour, I signed a waiver of notification that prevented them from being contacted by the U.S. Army if I were wounded, but only if I was killed. Maj. Dodd said that once I reached Camp Zama, I could phone them and tell them what had happened. He also told me after my recovery I would be sent back to the United States for a thirty-day recovery period, after which I would be given a new stateside assignment.

When he left, I fell asleep exhausted from talking and learning about all the death and carnage that had taken place while others tried to save my crew and me. I didn't doubt that my attempt to save the downed Air Force fighter pilot was the right thing to do, even though the execution of the search and rescue had failed.

Later I was awakened by a nurse who handed me a clear plastic bag containing my wallet, dog tags, and my blood-covered watch.

That evening several other soldiers, who had been severely burned, and I were taken by ambulance to the Danang Air Force Base main medical departure terminal. There we were loaded on a specially-equipped hospital C-141 Starlifter jet transport and flown to Japan.

When I arrived at the hospital, I asked one of the nurses if I could call my parents back in Texas and let them know I was coming home in a few weeks. She told me that I could in a few days, after I was stronger. Four days later, I called my parents' home at 6:00 a.m. Japanese time, which was 9 p.m. Central Standard Time. The phone rang a couple of times and then my mother answered it. "Mom, it's me," I said as I struggled to keep from crying at hearing her voice. "Are you okay?" she asked frantically. "Yes, I'm in Japan at a military hospital recovering after having been slightly wounded in Vietnam, but I'm going to be okay, and the good news is I'm coming home soon!" (Tears are rolling down my cheeks now and my vision is blurred as I recall that conversation with her forty-five years ago. Some memories just *never* go away!) She handed the telephone to my dad and I heard her crying in the background. "Stan, Jr., are you okay?" he asked. "Yes, I am, Dad. But I'm in Japan at an Army Hospital in Honshu after I was slightly wounded a couple of weeks ago near the DMZ. I'll be home in a few weeks after everything heals. I had surgery on my right eye a few days ago and it's going to be okay too." I heard him breathe a deep sigh of relief and then he said, "Son, when you get home we'll go fishing at Lake Waco and drink some beer." I said, "I can't wait to get home and see y'all. I'll call as soon as I know when I will arrive in Dallas. Can you come pick me up?" He said, "Of course, just let us know when you'll get in." I said, "I'll call you once I know something. I love you and Mom. Goodbye." He said, "We love you too, son." Then I hung up the phone unable to talk any longer.

Six weeks later, after buying a new khaki uniform and shoes at the hospital PX annex, I boarded a Pan American World Airways 747 jumbo jet. I was walking with the aid of two crutches and had a large gauze patch on my right eye. The airplane had very few passengers, so the stewardesses took me to the back, next to the galley. Lifting the armrests on several connecting seats, they made a bed for me on which to lie. Exhausted from the exertion of walking so much, I slept most of the way back to Los Angeles LAX International Airport.

After thanking the crew and the stewardesses, I departed the airplane and began slowly walking down a long corridor leading to the main terminal and my connecting flight to Dallas. Halfway down the hallway, I saw three bald-headed, bearded Hare Krishna men, wearing long flowing orange robes, walking towards me. As they approached, one of them veered over to me and stopped in front of my path.

He looked at me a moment and then spat in my face! I stood there a second in amazement, then slowly leaned down and set my right crutch on the concrete floor. I tightly clenched my fist and as I quickly rose up, I hit him with all the force I could muster on the point of his chin, snapping his head back, knocking out several teeth and breaking his jaw! He fell backward onto the concrete floor and lay still. I glared at his *brethren*, who both raised their hands in submission as they rushed over to help him.

I took my handkerchief out of my pocket and wiped the spittle off my face and bandaged right eye. Reaching down, I picked up my crutch and looked at two nearby Los Angeles police officers who had watched everything unfold. They both smiled at me, and each gave me a "two thumbs up" sign, then turned and strolled back to the terminal.

Slowly walking on my crutches to my connecting flight home, I grimly thought, *This is what I fought and almost died for in Vietnam; the freedom to spit on me.*

Welcome to the USA. The land of the free, because of the brave!

EPILOGUE

After four weeks of recovery at my parents' home, I had been assigned to HHC, 3rd Brigade, 2nd Armored Division at Ft. Hood, Texas, as the legal officer. For all practical purposes, the Vietnam War was over and there were many returning helicopter pilots. I was told by the Department of Army that I would not be given another flying assignment soon because I had over five thousand hours of total flight time. Arriving at my office one morning, my brigade commander Colonel Anderson asked me to come to his office.

When I entered the room, there were several senior staff officers gathered together. At first I thought I might be in trouble; however, Colonel Anderson came over to me and I told me that I was being awarded two military decorations for my role in the Ashau Valley rescue on April 29, 1972. He ordered me to stand at attention and the Executive Officer proceeded to read the written citation for the Bronze Star with Valor device and a second Purple Heart, which then was pinned on my chest.

Afterward, I left and went upstairs to my office. My feelings were very ambivalent about receiving the awards because of the people who had been hurt and killed because of my decision to try to save the Air Force fighter pilot.

As the brigade legal officer, my staff and I were responsible for preparing all the trial documents for soldiers that were being court-martialed. The vast majority of the cases involved trying soldiers that were drug dealers and distributors of narcotics; a problem which was very prevalent on Fort Hood and the surrounding communities of Killeen and Copperas Cove. When they were found guilty, and they all were found guilty, I relished sending them to the military prison in Leavenworth, Kansas; many for 25 years at hard labor! My hatred for drug dealers was as intense as for the NVA and VC I killed in Vietnam.

One evening, later that summer, the phone rang in my Waco apartment and my dad said, "I'm meeting my best friend, Colonel Ed Skelton at the Randolph Air Force Base officer's club tomorrow evening. He's just back from flying in Vietnam and I would like you to go with me to meet him. Do you think you can go?" The next day was a Saturday so I said, "Sure Dad. It's been a long time since I last saw him as a young boy."

The next morning on our way down to Randolph Air Force Base, my dad told me about meeting Colonel Skelton on Iwo Jima in 1945, where they both served in the U.S. Army Air Corps as P-51D fighter pilots. They were in the same Army Air Corp unit and slept in the same tent, next to the flight line where their airplanes were parked.

They flew missions together over mainland Japan primarily escorting B-24 "Fortress" and B-29 "Stratofortress" bombers and strafing Japanese gun emplacements, troop convoys, and trains carrying military equipment. After WWII, they served together at various U.S. Air Force bases around the world.

Col. Eddie L. Skelton was born in Polk County, Arkansas, on September 17, 1922. After graduating from college, he joined the U. S. Army Air Corps as a fighter pilot. He became a highly decorated officer receiving the Silver Star, Bronze Star, and the

Distinguished Flying Cross for meritorious service above and beyond the call of duty.

After a thirty-year Air Force career, he and his wife Martha retired to New Braunfels, Texas. (He's now buried at the Ft. Sam Houston National Cemetery in San Antonio after dying on June 19, 2010, at the age of eighty-seven.)

Arriving at the Randolph Air Force Base officers' club, my dad and I walked into the white stucco, Spanish-style building. Dad had been stationed at the base thirteen years earlier, in 1959, and had been back frequently for various aviation conferences. We walked into the stag bar and waited at the entrance for our eyes to become adjusted to the dimly lit room. "Stan, come over here and join us," Col. Skelton yelled, waving his hand. We walked to his table and were greeted by him and four other pilots sitting there. Everyone stood up, shaking hands with my dad and me. Col. Skelton looked at me saying, "Stan, Jr., the last time I saw you, you were a skinny little kid." I laughed and said, "I'm all grown-up now, sir." Something about his voice was very familiar, but it had been at least fifteen years since I had talked to him, when I was twelve, so I didn't think about it anymore.

Dad and I sat down, and he ordered a round of beers for everybody at the table. After the waitress had delivered the ice-cold mugs, Col. Skelton turned to me and said "Stan tells me that you are an Army captain now and a helicopter pilot."

I said, "Yes, sir. I am—or at least was, because I'm now stationed at Fort Hood as a brigade legal officer. I returned from Vietnam this past June, where I flew Hueys out of Danang in I Corp." He smiled at me saying, "You Army helicopter pilots were crazy as hell over there! I know because my guys and I spent all one day keeping the NVA off eight of you that had been shot down in two helicopters in the Ashau Valley near Khe Sanh, during the Easter Invasion!"

Then I recognized his voice and the hairs stood up on my neck and arms as I asked. "Were you Sandy 6, flying an A-1E Spad on April 29th?" He looked at me in surprise saying, "Yes, but how in the world could you possibly know that?" I looked at him and huskily said, "Colonel Skelton, I was Coachman 22!" No one said a word for a few seconds. "You mean I was talking to you on the ground?" he asked incredulously. "Yes, sir! We talked all day on the guard frequency, as you and your guys kept the NVA from capturing and killing my crew and me, along with my commanding officer and his three crew members."

He sat there in stunned silence and then said, "Well, I'll be damned!" Then he rose and came over to me, we hugged and I whispered, "Thank you, sir. I wanted to say that to you when I was finally rescued, but I left my survival radio in the rice paddy after we got picked up." He leaned back still holding my arms, looked at me, and with tears in his eyes said, "Son, you are very welcome and I'm glad I was able to help you and the others."

I remembered then what he told me on the radio after I had learned the second rescue helicopter had turned back after their aircraft commander, CW2 Henry Alvarez, and Lt. Col. Mott, had been killed. "I know, son, I'm watching you," he had said. Indeed he and Someone else was too!

We both sat down and began to tell the story of how he and the other Sandy pilots saved my crew and me from certain death at the hands of the overwhelming number of NVA soldiers. As the story unfolded, pilots at the bar and other tables came over to listen and I can honestly say there was not a dry eye in the room that afternoon.

POSTLUDE

Some would say it was an amazing "coincidence" that my father's best friend saved my life that spring day. But you see, everyone, I do not at all believe in coincidences. Colonel Ed Skelton was there protecting me, of that I'm sure.

But now I am also certain that as I lay in the rice paddy, surrounded by the enemy and covered in dirt, mud and copious amounts of my own blood; I was also covered in the Blood of My Lord and Savior, Jesus Christ, who faithfully protected his warrior, "Captain Corvin the Avenger," at Khe Sanh in the Ashau Valley, Vietnam on April 29, 1972.

Selah! (Hebrew: "Pause and calmly think about that.")

CONVERSATIONS
WITH THE DEAD

The following people are all dead now; so the dialogs I had with them while writing this book, came from my recollection of the event being described and my imagination.

Everyone rest in peace and know that
you are not forgotten by your families or me!

NAME	RELATIONSHIP	DIED
Joy Corvin	My Mother	1976
Stan Corvin, Sr.	My Father	2002
Penny Corvin	My Sister	1988
Sgt. Maj. George Vidrine	5th SF Friend	2004
Major James C. Maher	Warlord CO	2003
Capt. John Barfield	Warlord XO	2005
Capt. Gordy Hines	Warlord Lead Pilot	2007
WO James Bateman	My Hooch-mate	1970
1st Lt. Arlen Richardson	Batman's Co-Pilot	1970
SFC James Gordon	Loaned Me Jacket	1970
Mr. James Wesson	USAID/CIA	1991
WO Bill Swofford	Pilot Friend (Frog Story)	1971
SP4 Don Broussard	Killed Crew Chief	1971
SP4 Charlie Robinson	Drowned Crew Chief	1969
Colonel Don Hobart	Air Force Friend	2008
2nd Lt. Craig Jeffers	Killed Commo Chief	1969
Capt. Van Cunningham*	My Co-Pilot	2003
Major Frank Welch	Downed Air Force Pilot	1972
CW2 Henry Alvarez	Killed Huey Rescue Pilot	1972
Lt. Col. Joseph Mott	Killed Huey Passenger	1972
Col. Ed Skelton	Sandy 6 Pilot	2010

FINAL THOUGHTS

I n his play, *Henry V*, circa 1598, William Shakespeare wrote the following:

> *"From this day to the ending of the world,*
> *we shall be remembered;*
> *we few, we band of brothers."*

> *"For he today, that sheds his blood with me,*
> *shall be my brother."*

NOTE

Captain Van Cunningham, who was my copilot when we were shot down twice trying to save the American fighter pilot, was diagnosed in late 2000 with a terminal case of Non-Hodgkin's Lymphoma due to his exposure to Agent Orange while flying in Vietnam. At the time of his diagnosis, Van was a senior Department of Army civilian in charge of personnel and manpower working at the Pentagon in Washington, D.C.

He was in Walter Reed Hospital undergoing chemotherapy on September 11, 2001, when at 9:47 a.m. American Airlines Flight 77, which was hijacked by five al-Qaeda-linked terrorists, crashed the airplane into the Pentagon. It hit 20 feet from his desk destroying his office and killing all of his staff. Sixty-four passengers were killed on the airplane, not including the terrorists. One hundred twenty-six people were killed in the Pentagon whose ages ranged from seventy-one years old down to three!

Van died from cancer in the hospital nine days later on September 20, 2001. I think from a broken heart!

ENDNOTES

[1] *This quote is from his address on Memorial Day 1894 to the graduating class of Harvard University.*

[2] *J.R.R. Tolkien, The Fellowship of the Ring: Lord of the Rings, part 1, (New York: Houghton Mifflin Company,1954), 68*

[3] *Aldous Huxley, Ape and Essence, (New York, NY, Harper and Brothers, 1948), 19*

[4] *William Sieghart, Winning Words: Inspiring Poems for Everyday Life, e-Book edition*

[5] *http://en.wikipedia.org/wiki/Easter_Offensive*

[6] *http://en.wikipedia.org/wiki/Dextroamphetamine*

[7] *Kione Longley, Buck Zaidel, Heroes for All Time: Connecticut Civil War Soldiers Tell Their Stories, (Middleton, CT: Wesleyan University Press, 2015), 230–231*

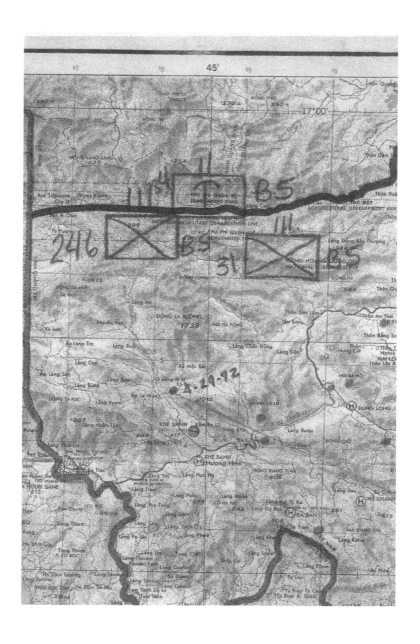

Colonel Ed Skelton ("Sandy 6") is the third pilot from the left standing in the front row.

President Reagan personally gave me this picture in 1986 for my help in raising funds for the three man statue located next to the Vietnam Veterans wall.

CPSIA information can be obtained
at www.ICGtesting.com
Printed in the USA
BVHW090247150921
616748BV00008B/631/J

9 780998 922256